ANTHROP
THE UNI   OF ARIZONA
NUMBER 64

Great House Communities Across the Chacoan Landscape

**John Kantner and Nancy M. Mahoney
Editors**

THE UNIVERSITY OF ARIZONA PRESS
TUCSON
2000

About the Editors

JOHN KANTNER received his Ph.D. from the University of California at Santa Barbara in 1999 and was appointed to the faculty of Georgia State University, where he is currently an assistant professor. His research on prehistoric Puebloan groups of the Southwest is focused on identifying the processes by which complex social and political institutions emerge in horticultural communities. Principles of human behavioral ecology and evolutionary theory provide the theoretical foundation for his investigations, and the analysis of prehistoric ceramics and regional spatial patterning provide the methodologies for interpreting the *archaeological* remains.

NANCY M. MAHONEY has a Master's degree in Anthropology from George Washington University and anticipates receiving her doctoral degree from Arizona State University in 2000. She has supervised surveys in New Mexico, Arizona, and Utah and is co-principal investigator of the Cottonwood Community Project in Utah. Her research focuses on identifying the relationships among social power, ritual authority, and economic advantage in ancient Puebloan communities, following the principles of structuration and practice theory.

Cover: Computer reconstruction of the Kin Klizhin great house positioned on the site in northwestern New Mexico. (Photograph and reconstruction by John Kantner.)

THE UNIVERSITY OF ARIZONA PRESS

Copyright © 2000

The Arizona Board of Regents
All Rights Reserved

This book was set in 10.7/12 CG Times

(∞) This book is printed on acid-free, archival-quality paper.
Manufactured in the United States of America.

08 07 06 05 04 03 7 6 5 4 3 2

Library of Congress Cataloging-in-Publication Data

Great house communities across the Chacoan landscape / John Kantner and Nancy M. Mahoney, editors
    p. cm. -- (Anthropological papers of the University of Arizona; no. 64)
Includes bibliographical references and index.
 ISBN 0-8165-2072-0 (pbk.)
    1. Pueblo Indians--Antiquities. 2. Chaco Canyon (N.M.)--Antiquities.
3. Pueblo architecture. 4. Pueblo Indians--Social life and customs.
5. Southwest, New--Antiquities. I. Kantner, John, 1967- II. Mahoney, Nancy M., 1968- III. Series.
E99.P9 G69 2000
978.9'82--dc21   00-008005

Contributors

Anderson, Rachel M.
    U.S. National Park Service, Chaco National Historical Park, New Mexico
Bower, Nathan
    Department of Chemistry, The Colorado College, Colorado Springs
Cameron, Catherine
    Department of Anthropology, University of Colorado, Boulder
Durand, Kathy Roler
    Department of Anthropology, Eastern New Mexico University, Portales
Durand, Stephen R.
    Department of Anthropology, Eastern New Mexico University, Portales
Ford, Cheryl A.
    U.S. National Park Service, Albuquerque, New Mexico
Gilpin, Dennis
    SWCA, Inc., Environmental Consultants, Flagstaff, Arizona
Greve, Darren
    Department of Chemistry, The Colorado College, Colorado Springs
Hata, Steve
    Department of Chemistry, The Colorado College, Colorado Springs
Hurst, Winston B.
    Consulting Archaeologist, Blanding, Utah
Jalbert, Joseph Peter
    Department of Anthropology, University of Colorado, Boulder
Johnson, Brian K.
    Professional Engineer, Santa Fe, New Mexico
Judge, W. James
    Fort Lewis College, Durango, Colorado
Kantner, John
    Department of Anthropology and Geography, Georgia State University, Atlanta
Kendrick, James W.
    Zuni Archaeological Program, Zuni, New Mexico
Ladwig, Jeffrey
    Department of Chemistry, The Colorado College, Colorado Springs
Lekson, Stephen
    University Museum, University of Colorado, Boulder
Mahoney, Nancy M.
    Department of Anthropology, Arizona State University, Tempe
Perlitz, Jacob
    Department of Chemistry, The Colorado College, Colorado Springs
Purcell, David E.
    SWCA, Inc., Environmental Consultants, Flagstaff, Arizona
Van Dyke, Ruth M.
    Department of Anthropology, California State University, Fullerton
Varien, Mark
    Crow Canyon Archaeological Center, Cortez, Colorado
Windes, Thomas C.
    U.S. National Park Service, Santa Fe, New Mexico

Contents

FIGURES

TABLES

Preface

John Kantner and Nancy M. Mahoney

The next time someone remarks that Chaco no longer needs to be a priority for archaeological research, show them a copy of ["Anasazi Regional Organization and the Chaco System."]

David E. Doyel 1992b: 12

A fellow archaeologist whose research is not in the American Southwest once asked why, after so many years of study, the Chaco "phenomenon" continued to be a focus of so much research. Surely, he surmised, all of the important questions about the Chacoans had been answered by now. It did not take long to demonstrate to him that despite remarkable advances in our knowledge, a number of critical questions regarding the origins and development of Chacoan patterns have yet to be answered. Studies of the Chacoan sociocultural tradition have remained a priority for archaeological research for two important reasons. The first is that we still cannot answer many of the most basic questions concerning how the Chaco "phenomenon" started, what it was, and why it ended. Perhaps even more importantly, the Chacoan archaeological record challenges long-held assumptions concerning the links among social hierarchies, political and economic centralization, ritual, and the demographic and geographic scales of ancient cultural systems.

During the past decade, several volumes have been published that synthesize empirical data from Chacoan sites and outline new directions for future research (for example, Crown and Judge 1991; Doyel 1992a). They provide key insights into chronology, exchange, agricultural production, resource procurement, social hierarchy, cultural landscapes, and the distribution of outlying great houses. These authors express diverse opinions regarding the existence and nature of a hypothesized Chaco "system." Some view the system as hierarchical and centralized (Sebastian 1991; Wilcox 1993), whereas others suggest that it was more of a communal-

ly based alliance (Judge 1989; Tainter and Gillio 1980; Toll 1985). Despite these divergent views, there is an overwhelming consensus that resolving these disagreements requires a focused investigation of communities located outside of Chaco Canyon (Doyel 1992a; Lekson 1991, 1996a; Sebastian 1992; Vivian 1996).

In recent years, several researchers have focused their investigations on outlying communities exhibiting Chacoan features. Because many of these projects were nearing completion and because many of the archaeologists were not in regular contact with one another, we decided to organize a symposium at the 1998 annual meeting of the Society for American Archaeology held in Seattle, Washington. The goal of this symposium was to bring together these researchers to share data and ideas about the prehistoric communities outside of Chaco Canyon. The symposium included both veteran scholars who had been working on Chacoan prehistory for some time as well as younger archaeologists who were investigating outlying communities as part of their dissertation research. The participants included both scholars working in the field of Cultural Resource Management and researchers from academic institutions. Stephen Lekson and Mark Varien served as discussants, and their different perspectives on Puebloan prehistory were a perfect complement to one another. All of the participants in the original symposium have contributed to the chapters in this book.

The chapters are organized into four parts according to their central themes. This organization is somewhat artificial, for certainly many of the contributors consider a wide variety of patterns according to the scope and scale of their investigations. But, in general, the division of the chapters into the following sections provides an effective way to consider important patterning identified by the authors' research.

Chapter 1 begins with a detailed exploration of the Chacoan sociocultural tradition with a special emphasis on a discussion of many of the unresolved issues that archaeologists are currently tackling. The authors consider why the study of communities outside of Chaco Canyon is important and propose several areas of research that should be pursued. The roles of the contributions to this volume are discussed in relation to these important avenues of investigation.

The chapters in Part I consider the basic question of how we define a great house community. Assumptions about the extent and permanency of great house communities provide the foundation for many models of the evolution of the Chacoan tradition. Part I challenges us to reconsider many of our ideas about the definition of great house communities. The contributors illustrate the variability in great house communities and provide an important foundation for developing a clear understanding of what exactly comprised a Chacoan community.

Part II assesses the critical question of the relationship between outlying great house communities and Chaco Canyon. The authors discuss investigations of outlying communities throughout the Chacoan world, from Red Mesa Valley, to the Rio Puerco in the east, up into southeastern Utah. They are virtually unanimous in their conclusion that outlying Chacoan communities possessed a considerable amount of autonomy, for architectural patterns and other material remains are distinct from patterns exhibited in Chaco Canyon. At the same time, however, there is obvious variability among the outlying communities, with some clearly involved in close relationships with Chaco Canyon and others appearing to have been almost completely independent.

Part III deals with economic and sociopolitical interactions both within and between outlying great house communities. These two chapters examine research areas outside of Chaco Canyon with the goal of reconstructing both relationships between households within Chacoan communities as well as between neighboring communities. Patterns of economic interaction in areas outside of Chaco Canyon were intense but also complex. Households and the communities containing them

were relatively autonomous, and they negotiated varied economic and sociopolitical relationships both internally and beyond community boundaries.

In the final section, two scholars with extensive experience in Southwestern archaeology consider the patterns identified in the first three parts. Unlike the majority of contributors to this volume, who focus on current empirical research within specific great house communities, these authors take a broad view not only of how current community research affects our understanding of the Chacoan sociocultural tradition, but especially of the role of these investigations within the larger purview of research on the prehistory of the American Southwest.

As a resource containing new empirical research regarding the definition of Chacoan communities, their connection to Chaco Canyon, and their internal organization and relationships with neighboring communities, this book discusses and evaluates both old and new ideas regarding the origins and development of the Chacoan sociocultural tradition. Overall, these studies demonstrate that on a local scale and a regional scale community studies can significantly advance our understanding of what the Chaco "phenomenon" was, from the outside looking in.

Acknowledgments

It has largely been the research of veteran Chaco archaeologists that has inspired the studies of great house communities included in this volume. We are much in debt to the major advances in knowledge of the Chaco tradition that these scholars have provided. The work discussed herein would not have been possible without their important contributions to our knowledge of the prehistory of the American Southwest.

The editors thank the staff of the University of Arizona Press and especially Carol Gifford (Department of Anthropology) for their patience and efforts in preparing this volume for publication. Christiann Kantner contributed her expertise toward editing and standardizing many of the illustrations in this book. María Nieves Zedeño kindly furnished the Spanish translation of the Abstract. Finally, a special debt of gratitude is extended to Gwinn Vivian, whose guidance and support have made this volume possible.

Great House Communities Across the Chacoan Landscape

CHAPTER ONE

Chacoan Archaeology and Great House Communities

Nancy M. Mahoney and John Kantner

After some eight centuries, the monumental masonry structures in Chaco Canyon still stand several stories tall almost in defiance of our ability to explain why they were constructed and the activities that occurred within them. In the centuries between A.D. 850 and 1150 (Fig. 1.1), at least 18 puebloan-style buildings known as "great houses" were constructed in and around Chaco Canyon, a relatively barren wash located in the arid San Juan Basin of northwestern New Mexico (Fig. 1.2). These structures remain some of the most massive and beautiful architectural features ever constructed in the ancient Southwest.

Even less well understood are the numerous great house communities located outside of Chaco Canyon. Many were situated at the edge of the San Juan Basin, which is roughly bounded by the uplands north of the San Juan River on the north, the Jemez uplift on the east, the Mount Taylor and Dutton plateaus on the south, and the Carrizo-Lukachukai-Chuska highlands on the west. Additional contemporaneous communities existed in areas of the northern Southwest that are surprisingly distant from Chaco Canyon. In many ways, these outlying communities were miniature versions of the complex architectural landscape of Chaco Canyon, complete with their own great houses, great kivas, road segments, and other material culture mirroring that found in the central canyon. Although these "great house communities" have been the subject of occasional study throughout the past century, only in the past two decades has their relationship with Chaco Canyon been investigated. The result of this research has been the exponential increase in our knowledge of the number of great house communities with Chacoan features, from perhaps 50 in the early 1980s to more than 200 today.

To provide a conceptual landscape in which to place the chapters in this volume, the following review of Chacoan archaeology includes an outline for a new focus on Chacoan communities. After a brief description of Chaco Canyon and outlying great house communities, we discuss the concept of a regional system and

outline many of the unresolved issues of Chacoan archaeology, including chronology, sociopolitical hierarchy, economic interaction, roads, and scale and system definitions. We propose that community studies will be fundamental to resolving many of these issues, but we also recognize that the state of knowledge on outlying Chacoan communities is still in its infancy. The chapters presented in this volume therefore represent an

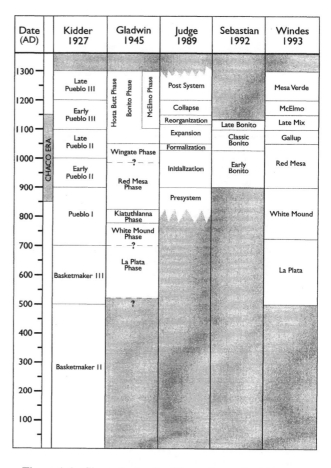

Figure 1.1. Chronologies for Chaco Anasazi prehistory. In this volume, most of the authors use the traditional classification established at the 1927 Pecos Conference.

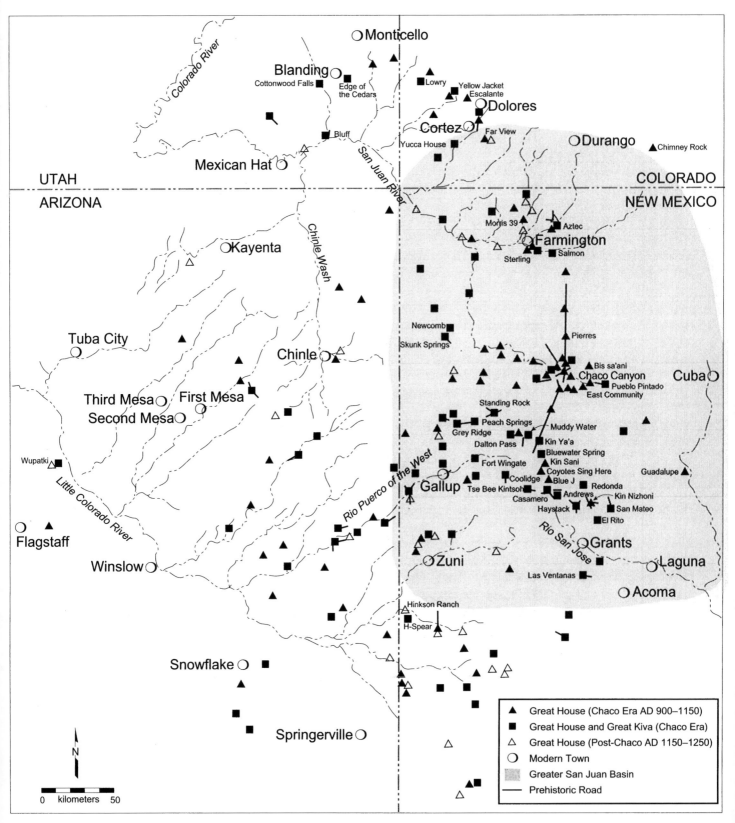

Figure 1.2. Distribution of great house communities in the northern Southwest. Named communities are discussed in this volume.

Figure 1.3. Pueblo Bonito in Chaco Canyon. (Photograph by John Kantner.)

evaluation of community-centered research conducted thus far, focusing in particular on what we regard as the three fundamental questions that will allow us to address the unresolved issues of Chacoan archaeology: first, how do we actually define a Chacoan community?; second, what is the relationship between outlying communities and Chaco Canyon?; and third, how did these outlying communities interact with one another? Only when we have the answers to these questions will we really be able to identify the extent of the Chaco system and determine its origins and function.

ARCHAEOLOGY IN CHACO CANYON

The largest great houses in Chaco Canyon once stood four or five stories and contained more than 650 rooms (Fig. 1.3). The roofs of these immense structures required so many timbers that trees were harvested from forests up to 80 km (50 miles) away (Judd 1964). Chaco Canyon great houses were planned structures with geometric layouts that displayed distinctive architectural characteristics not present in most puebloan architecture. These features included core-veneer and banded masonry, multiple stories, blocked-in kivas, large and tall rooms, and enclosed plazas (Lekson 1984). In addition, most of the canyon great houses appear to have been oriented toward the cardinal directions and may have incorporated features marking solstice events (Sofaer 1997). Clearly the effort expended on the design and construction of these buildings surpassed that of any previous structures in the prehistory of the northern Southwest and greatly exceeded utilitarian necessity.

A century of archaeological investigations of Chaco Canyon great houses has not provided straightforward answers to how they were used. Excavations at Pueblo Bonito and Pueblo Alto reveal that domestic activities took place in a surprisingly small portion of the rooms, indicating that these structures were not entirely residential. These investigations have also uncovered hundreds of empty and featureless rooms whose purpose remains obscure (Windes 1987). In contrast, clear evidence from other great house features (kivas, plaza areas, and trash mounds) indicates that communal activities revolving around ceremonial events likely occurred at many of these structures.

Exotic items recovered from several great houses tell us that those who used the structures had access to ex-

Figure 1.4. A residential structure located across from Pueblo
Bonito in Chaco Canyon. (Photograph by John Kantner.)

tensive trade networks. Copper bells, macaws, and marine shell were acquired from as far away as Mexico,
and turquoise and obsidian were imported from other
regions in the northern Southwest. Thousands of pottery
vessels and raw lithic materials were also imported for
use in both domestic and ritual activities within the canyon. This evidence leaves us wondering who lived in
these structures and who participated in the activities
that took place there; it is possible that these were not
always the same people.

Great houses stood in marked contrast to typical residences, or "unit pueblos," that were the primary habitations during the Chaco era (Fig. 1.4). These residences
usually contained fewer than 20 rooms and probably
housed nuclear or extended families. They lacked the
multistory construction, elaborate masonry, planned
symmetry, and other hallmarks of great house architecture (Truell 1986). The small houses were relatively
dispersed throughout the canyon, but tended to occur in
settlement clusters associated with individual great
houses (Windes and others, this volume). The relationship between residents of unit pueblos and the great
houses remains unclear. Did small house residents have

access to these structures? Did they labor to construct
the great houses? If so, was this accomplished through
coercion or as a communal effort? This great house-
small house dichotomy has fueled persistent debate over
whether the distinctive architectural style of the Chacoan great houses represents elite residences, communal
ritual facilities, or ethnically distinct villages (see
Vivian 1990, 1996).

In addition to great houses and small residences,
Chaco Canyon contained numerous great kivas (Fig.
1.5), shrines, rock art panels, water control features,
and ancient roads. Stein and Lekson (1992: 87) contend
that many of these features linked the physical (natural)
and cognitive (built) landscapes into a broader "sacred
geography." For example, these scholars suggest that
most roads both within and outside of Chaco Canyon
either ran between great houses or led to shrines that
had visual links to both natural and cultural features
(see also Windes 1991).

Chacoan great kivas were massive circular subterranean structures that were used for large-scale ceremonies. These structures clearly had their architectural
roots in earlier Basketmaker great kivas and contained

Figure 1.5. The great kiva located in the plaza area of the Chetro Ketl great house in Chaco Canyon. (Photograph by John Kantner.)

floor features similar to those found in Pueblo I "over-sized" pit structures (Wilshusen 1988). Across the Chacoan world, great kivas were built both as separate structures and as features incorporated into great house architecture. As with great houses, isolated great kivas tended to be associated with contemporary settlement clusters.

OUTLYING CHACOAN COMMUNITIES

Since the early part of the 20th century we have known that several Chaco-style buildings existed outside of the canyon (Martin 1936; Morris 1919; Roberts 1932), but it was not until the 1970s that archaeologists first began to systematically document the extent of Chacoan sites in the northern Southwest (Marshall and others 1979; Powers and others 1983). Research during the past two decades has revealed that Chaco-style buildings were spread across an area encompassing more than 100,000 square kilometers (38,600 square miles) centered on the Four Corners region (Lekson and others 1988). Originally called "outliers," these great houses contained many of the same architectural attributes as their counterparts in Chaco Canyon, although they varied more in size and configuration.

A critical debate concerns whether the presence of Chacoan traits was the result of local emulation or direct influence from Chaco Canyon (for example, Van Dyke 1999b; Wilcox 1993). Each position has distinct implications for the existence and nature of the hypothesized Chacoan regional system (Hurst, this volume; Van

Dyke, this volume). Because this debate is far from resolved, the authors herein have carefully avoided use of the term outliers, for it suggests that great houses located outside of Chaco Canyon were in some way subordinate to or under the control of Chaco Canyon residents. There has also been some confusion as to whether the term outlier refers to outlying great houses or to the communities in which they were situated. Therefore, in general the authors have opted to use the more benign term "Chacoan great house" to refer to any architecture that shares a substantial number of traits with the archetype great houses located in Chaco Canyon. Similarly, the term "outlying great house" refers to great house architecture located outside the central canyon.

Perhaps the key unifying feature of outlying great houses is that they can be readily distinguished from contemporary residential structures by their size and relatively elaborate masonry (Lekson 1991). As in the canyon, dispersed small houses formed loose settlement clusters around most outlying great houses (although a few isolated great houses have been identified; Powers and others 1983: 183). These clusters are typically referred to as "Chacoan communities" or "great house communities" (Doyel and others 1984). The term Chacoan communities is more inclusive, because many outlying communities precede and succeed the occupation of their associated great houses. Still other communities within the Chaco region appear to have lacked great houses altogether. Knowing the size, organization, and longevity of these outlying communities is crucial to understanding the local sociopolitical context in which Chacoan structures were or were not established.

Chaco-era great kivas in outlying areas are typically located in close association with great houses, but they exhibit a substantially higher degree of uniformity than do great houses (Lekson 1984: 51–52; Vivian and Reiter 1960), at least as they have been traditionally defined (see Lekson 1999: 75). This uniformity may indicate that organizational structures existed at different scales during the Chaco era. For example, ritual activities associated with great kivas may have been highly structured or shared at a regional level, whereas particular local sociopolitical contexts may have structured the layout and use of great houses.

THE REGIONAL SYSTEM CONCEPT

Wilcox (1979, 1980) was the first to employ the term "regional system" to describe the architectural and settlement patterning in the Hohokam area. However, it was Marshall and Doyel (1981) who first used the term regional system to describe the distribution of great houses, great kivas, and road segments throughout the Colorado Plateau (Vivian 1996: 45). The application of the term regional system to the Chaco tradition has sometimes been criticized because it implies political and economic integration regardless of the empirical evidence for the existence of these processes. Lekson (1991: 48) argues to the contrary, asserting that the Chacoan roads are in and of themselves the "least ambiguous evidence of a regional system in the Anasazi Southwest." It is likely that the presence of an architecturally dense "center" in Chaco Canyon also heavily contributes to the adoption of this concept. In either case, demonstrating the relationship between outlying great house communities and the central canyon may be the most important means to determining the principal social, political, ritual, or economic interactions that structured the Chacoan world.

Since the early 1980s, the term regional system has served as an umbrella for widely divergent models that pose varying degrees of centralization and integration. Chaco has alternately been characterized as a tribute-gathering state (Wilcox 1993), a redistributive system (Judge 1979, 1993; Lekson 1999: 45; Schelberg 1984), a ritually based pilgrimage center (Judge 1989; Toll 1984, 1985), a network of entrepreneurial elites (Sebastian 1991, 1992), a peer-polity system (Van Dyke, this volume), and a cooperative agrarian enterprise (Vivian 1989). The basic tenets of these models have been described in detail in several books and edited volumes (Crown and Judge 1991; Doyel 1992a; Judge and Schelberg 1984; Sebastian 1992; Vivian 1990), each of which posits different functions for great houses and distinct relationships between Chaco Canyon and outlying communities.

Several researchers believe that the hypothesized Chaco system is actually a manifestation of a cultural tradition (Doyel and Lekson 1992; Durand and Durand, this volume; Lekson 1991, 1996a), shared world view (Fowler and Stein 1992), or "common ideational bond among what may have been ethnically, linguistically, or culturally diverse populations" (Stein and Lekson 1992: 87; see also Vivian 1989). Although there is little to disagree with in these statements, they are problematic in that they would serve equally well as explanations for the homogeneity of, for example, Basketmaker III cultural traits. But Chaco is not Basketmaker III. It was during the Chaco era that people began marking the landscape with labor-intensive and visually impressive structures. These structures permanently altered the built environment and fixed the location of ritual or communal gatherings for several generations and sometimes for centuries (Bradley 1996). For more than 200 years, Chaco Canyon was the locus of the most elaborate manifestation of these structures, suggesting that Chaco was the first relatively long-lived political and demographic center in the prehistory of the northern Southwest.

The existence of a common ideational bond or shared world view during the Chaco era appears fundamental and undeniable. Yet statements relegating the Chaco "phenomenon" to a pan-Anasazi cultural trend do not explain how and why these monuments were built nor identify the sociopolitical contexts in which this construction occurred. They also allow us to avoid describing the principal social, political, ritual, or economic interactions that structured the relationships between Chaco Canyon, outlying great house communities, and community residential settlements.

UNRESOLVED ISSUES IN CHACOAN ARCHAEOLOGY

Many of the models mentioned above still figure prominently in the literature (Crown and Judge 1991; Doyel 1992a; Lekson 1999; Vivian 1996). However, several studies during the last decade have provided empirical information that exposes inadequacies in our understanding of Chacoan patterns and challenges some widely held beliefs regarding the Chacoan sociocultural tradition. Although most of these studies have been published, their cumulative implications for our understanding of Chaco Canyon, the outlying communities, and the regional system concept as a whole have not been comprehensively outlined. In this section, we attempt to identify and discuss some of the critical issues in Chacoan archaeology that remain unresolved.

Chronology

Recent dating of canyon and outlying great houses has challenged conventional wisdom regarding the emergence of the Chaco phenomenon. Tree-ring dates from Pueblo Bonito (Windes and Ford 1992: 79; 1996) demonstrate that construction began in the late A.D. 800s. The pueblo began as a substantial hamlet, part of which was a large arc-shaped room block. Similarly shaped room suites were typical of room blocks dating to the 800s excavated by the Dolores Archaeological Project in southwest Colorado (Breternitz 1988). However, Pueblo Bonito was distinct from these large Pueblo I

villages in four important respects: (1) the presence of big-room suites five to ten times the size of small house suites, (2) a lack of internal features in surface rooms, (3) the presence of full-height masonry walls and possibly multistory construction, and (4) the longevity of occupation exhibited by remodeling events (although some small houses in the canyon were also occupied for long intervals; Truell 1986). Similar big-room suites dating to the late 800s are probably present at Una Vida, Peñasco Blanco, and perhaps Kin Bineola (Windes and Ford 1996), and may form the cores of many other late 9th- and early 10th-century great houses.

Windes and Ford (1992) identify early dates at several great houses south of Chaco Canyon, on the Chuska valley slope, and in the Red Mesa Valley, suggesting that the emergence of this architectural form was not unique to the canyon during the late 9th and early 10th centuries. For example, big-room suites at the Peach Springs and Skunk Springs great houses likely date to the late A.D. 800s, and construction dates in the 900s are postulated for great houses at Guadalupe, Sterling, and Ft. Wingate (Van Dyke, this volume; Windes and Ford 1992). This dating may indicate that several important and possibly competing centers were established outside of Chaco Canyon before it became crowded with great houses during the middle to late 11th century.

What do these early big-room suites tell us about the origins of the hypothesized Chaco system? Windes and Ford (1996) interpret the suites as storage facilities based on their lack of internal features. This function is indeed a possibility, but it seems that the size of the rooms in these suites (many are larger than 50 square meters per room) would have exceeded the needs of the 10 to 75 people residing in Pueblo Bonito during its early occupation phase (Bernardini 1999). If these rooms were used for storage, then they were intended for more massive quantities than any previous or contemporary building. It is possible that multiple communities used these structures for storage or that these suites are early examples of the "over-engineering" typically associated with Chacoan structures.

Early construction dates are not reported for great houses in the Mesa Verde and Zuni regions, encouraging us to follow Neitzel's (1994) lead and rethink how the boundaries of great house distribution changed between A.D. 900 and 1050 and again during the 1100s. Perhaps these shifting boundaries can be linked to Toll's (1991: 97–98; Toll and McKenna 1997: 132–138) research demonstrating that the origin of pottery imported into the canyon shifted from the south during the 900s, to the west during the 1000s, and finally to the north during the 1100s. More secure dates from outlying great houses are necessary to investigate this relationship and to avoid reifying the Chaco distribution maps as synchronic systems.

Two additional aspects of Chaco Canyon chronology deserve our attention. One is that Roberts (1991 [1927]) excavated an early trash mound under Pueblo Bonito's western plaza that had stratigraphy mirroring that found in the Pueblo Alto mound. The stratigraphy consisted of layers of ash and debris separated by charcoal that were so distinct that Roberts (1991) stated it was easier to excavate in natural rather than arbitrary layers. This description is remarkably similar to descriptions of the distinct trash layers found in the Pueblo Alto mound (Windes 1987: 588–607), which Toll (1985) has interpreted as evidence of periodic feasting events. However, the early Bonito midden contained neckbanded gray wares and Red Mesa white wares from bottom to top, indicating their 10th-century deposition (Windes 1987: 627–628). Apparently the activities that produced the later trash mounds at Pueblo Alto and Peñasco Blanco may have already been occurring during the A.D. 900s.

Another important aspect of canyon chronology is that no indisputable evidence that Chacoan great kivas were constructed prior to A.D. 1040 has been identified (Windes and Ford 1996: 308), although the great kiva at Kin Nahasbas might possibly date to the late 900s (Mathien and Windes 1989). The physical and symbolic links between great houses and great kivas were not established until almost 200 years after construction of the first great houses began; apparently two centuries passed before the long tradition associated with earlier great kivas became enmeshed in the Chacoan architectural pattern. Comparing the distribution of 10th- and early 11th-century great kivas and great houses might provide a picture of competing types of community organization.

Hierarchy

In her study of the sociopolitical organization of Chaco Canyon, Sebastian (1991, 1992) challenges us to look for evidence of institutionalized leadership in the material record rather than trying to identify the leaders themselves. She offers several examples of construction and planning that presumably could not have been accomplished without full-time leaders and several more traditional indicators of sociopolitical hierarchy. Sebastian cites labor investment in architecture; the presence of settlement hierarchies; the differential distribution of prestige items; differences in mortuary treatment; and the construction, maintenance and operation of water

control facilities as evidence that institutionalized leadership existed within Chaco Canyon.

The difficulty with these indicators of leadership is that, at least in theory, each has alternative interpretations. For example, the construction of great houses and water control facilities undoubtedly required planning and organization, but labor estimates do not indisputably demonstrate that they required full-time leaders or large labor forces to complete (see Lekson 1984). Earle (1978) and Netting (1990) caution that large-scale agricultural projects can be the protracted collection of smaller *ad hoc* projects that were organized at the family or festive level and that often operated better without centralized control. More cross-cultural research on how labor is organized for constructing comparable facilities is necessary before we can use labor estimates to make inferences regarding political organization. Reconstructing labor estimates and construction events for great houses outside of Chaco Canyon will also help to determine leadership requirements for these architectural features.

Perhaps the most convincing evidence for leadership is the presence of a small number of elaborate burials in Pueblo Bonito, the largest great house inside or outside the canyon. Unfortunately, because their excavation occurred without the benefit of modern data-recovery techniques (Judd 1964; Pepper 1976), the context of these burials is difficult to determine. The burials were recovered from the oldest portion of the great house and based on associated artifacts, such as Red Mesa Black-on-white ceramics, the two richest burials may date to the late A.D. 900s, and others may have been interred in the 1000s (Akins 1986; Pepper 1976). Some interpret these burials as evidence that an economically privileged class resided in great houses (Akins and Schelberg 1984; Nelson and others 1994; Wilcox 1993). Others point out that these interments may reflect the ritual status of the deceased rather than wealth accumulation associated with social stratification (Pepper 1976). The distinction here is subtle, yet critical, for determining how the proposed Chaco system may have operated. Wealth accumulation would indicate that power in the Chacoan world was obtained through control over material resources, whereas ritual status might indicate power was achieved through control over nonmaterial resources such as ceremonial or astronomical knowledge. This would set Chaco apart as a relatively complex society with a sociopolitical hierarchy that emerged despite a lack of economic centralization.

Akins' (1986) study of mortuary remains from Chaco Canyon revealed that individuals buried in Pueblo Bonito were, on average, taller and in better health than individuals buried in small houses. Her interpretation that the Pueblo Bonito individuals had access to better nutrition supports the view that great houses were the residences of economically privileged elites, although Akins also notes that the great house skeletal materials still exhibited some nutritional deficiencies (see also Palkovich 1984). Access to relatively better nutrition may turn out to be an important status marker in past puebloan societies. However, restrictions on the analysis of human remains means that we will not be able to easily investigate this possibility in the near future and will make resolving the issue of Chacoan hierarchy more difficult by removing an important source of data.

Economic and Material Distribution

Recent research on material distributions and exchange has effectively ruled out classic redistribution as the *raison d'être* of the hypothesized Chaco system and seriously challenges models asserting that such a system would have been sustained through control over trade and exchange (for example, Judge 1979; Neitzel 1989; Schelberg 1984). Toll (1985, 1991) and Mathien (1985, 1997b) have demonstrated that both utilitarian and exotic items were imported into the canyon but there is no evidence that they were then redistributed back to great house communities. Work in outlying great house communities indicates that low quantities of pottery were imported from distant areas of the Chaco world (Eddy 1977; Gilpin and Purcell, this volume; Kantner and others, this volume; Pippin 1987; Van Dyke 1997a; Windes and others, this volume), and even fewer imports are reported in small communities without Chacoan architecture (Reed 1998).

Relatively rare items imported from distant sources (such as shell, turquoise, copper bells, and macaws) have been found in several canyon great houses (see Mathien 1986, 1993). The scarcity of these items, the distance across which they traveled, and the contexts in which they have been recovered indicate that they were highly valued and that their distribution was restricted (Lekson 1999, this volume). However, the fact that turquoise and shell are also recorded in appreciable numbers at canyon small houses and in outlying communities may indicate one of two possibilities: small house residents either maintained autonomous long-distance trade relations that included the exchange of valuables, or they received these items as gifts or in exchange for labor or goods (possibly staples) from great house residents who controlled access to these valuables.

Toll (1991) effectively demonstrates that the quantity of exotic material in canyon great houses is minor when compared to the large numbers of imported utilitarian items. With an accumulation spanning two centuries, the limited quantity of exotic materials in Chaco Canyon undermines the notion that a Chaco system emerged through centralized control over the production or exchange of prestige goods (Toll 1991: 101). Such is not the case for utilitarian goods, as thousands of pots, lithics, and animals were imported into Chaco Canyon. Further data from outlying communities are required before we can determine if these utilitarian items were specifically produced for export to Chaco Canyon. A lack of evidence for specialized production would challenge long-held assumptions regarding the link between regional settlement hierarchies and economic centralization.

If all these items were imported into Chaco Canyon, what was going out? Although the sample of excavated outlying great houses is small, it does not appear that copper bells, turquoise, or other valuable items were exported to great house communities in substantial quantities. Toll (1985, 1991) has suggested that nothing was going out; rather, people periodically made pilgrimages to the canyon and their belongings were deposited during their participation in ceremonial events. Others propose that something nonmaterial, such as ritual knowledge, may have been exported as a controlled commodity (Judge 1991; Kantner 1999).

It seems unusual that such a vast regional system could exist without distinctive status markers or symbols of political office. Yet, it appears there were no nonarchitectural symbols or commodities that were distinctively "Chacoan," meaning that their distribution was restricted exclusively to canyon and outlying great houses. Archaeologists have considered cylinder vessels as possibly Chacoan status items, although for the most part these vessels have been found only in Chaco Canyon (Neitzel and Bishop 1990; Toll 1990). Currently the known distribution of this pottery form is too restricted to think it might have been used as a systemwide symbol. Furthermore, Toll and others (1992) also propose that Dogoszhi-style hatching on white wares was not a "Chacoan" elite design style but rather a variant of a broader category representing a temporal stage in puebloan pottery design.

It is possible that we are not recognizing status items or that perishable materials such as macaw feathers were distributed as status markers (Lekson 1999). On the other hand, the lack of status markers may indicate that no group was capable of controlling the manufacture or exchange of durable material goods during the Chaco era.

Roads

Depending on how the evidence is interpreted, the Chacoan road system consisted of between 209 km and 2,414 km (130 to 1,500 miles) of road segments that averaged about 9 m in width (Vivian 1997a: 23–24). These roads are often cited as evidence of centralization and integration on a regional scale (Lekson 1991; Lekson and others 1988; Powers 1984). Originally, the road system was presumed to have had an economic function by reducing transportation costs for the movement of either people or goods between great house communities and Chaco Canyon (Ebert and Hitchcock 1980; Judge 1984; Obenauf 1980; Powers and others 1983; Wilcox 1993). It was assumed that these roads were interconnected, linking outlying communities to the canyon center like spokes on a hub (Tainter and Gillio 1980: 102).

We now know that not all roads lead to Chaco. Ground-truthing of many hypothesized roads demonstrated that only a few road segments clearly linked outlying great houses to each other or to Chaco Canyon (Roney 1992). And unlike the Inkan road system, Roney (1992) and Kantner (1997) have convincingly demonstrated that Chacoan roads were not engineered to facilitate transportation of people or goods across difficult terrain. Vivian (1997b: 47) reaches a similar conclusion in his recent reevaluation of the economic function of roads, concluding that Chacoan roads were over-engineered for a society with no pack animals or wheeled vehicles.

These observations do not belittle the importance of roads as physical and symbolic links between communities throughout the Chaco region. Vivian (1997a: 29) has revealed that roads within the San Juan Basin exhibit a relatively standard morphology and are repeatedly associated with shrines, great houses, and great kivas. He argues that there was a shared concept of road construction and context of use. Those shared conceptions may also have operated within great house communities located beyond the San Juan Basin. Roney (1992: 130) emphasizes how the shorter road segments within communities probably served to integrate public architecture within dispersed residential settlements. Similarly, through a GIS-based analysis of Chacoan roads, Kantner (1997) concludes that local integration

best explains the road patterning in several great house communities in the southern San Juan Basin, because road efficiency tended to be focused on connecting great houses to other community buildings or to nearby hamlets.

Fowler and Stein (1992: 118) propose that in addition to integrating contemporary settlements, roads created historical links by connecting Chaco-era great houses with post-Chacoan community structures. It is unclear if such roads were constructed during or after the Chaco era, but either way, their research highlights the fact that Chaco-style roads remained important symbols within local communities well after A.D. 1150.

Scale and System Definition

Doyel (1992b: 6) notes that a key variable in understanding the Chacoan patterns is scale. Proposed demographic and geographic scales of the Chaco region present vexing problems for modeling the social, political, ritual, and economic interactions that may have structured internal relationships. Part of the problem is that not everyone agrees on how to measure scale. Do we include all areas that exhibit architecture that appears to be Chacoan? Do we just include those areas from which materials flowed into Chaco Canyon? And what does the geographical scale indicate about the number of people interacting either with the canyon or with one another? Based primarily on architectural features, the Chaco phenomenon is often perceived as a multi-tier settlement hierarchy with a distinct center (for example, Neitzel 1994, Powers and others 1983). Add in the road system, and what emerges is a settlement pattern that is usually presumed to be the manifestation of a centralized political system or a tributary economy (Johnson 1980; Judge 1993; Lekson 1999; Neitzel 1989; Powers 1984; Schelberg 1984; Steponaitis 1981; Wilcox 1993; Wright 1994).

Was Chaco a system? In general, the rationale for proposing the existence of a regional system is grounded almost exclusively in architectural patterning. As Vivian points out, it is assumed that the relatively standardized architectural form of great houses attests to the existence of an organized system of regional scale, and yet it is far from clear what "level of standardization implies political organization, economic interdependence, or shared world view" (Vivian 1996: 51). We do need a better understanding of architectural variability and standardization among outlying great houses in order to sort out local, regional, and system-wide patterning, but without more substantial investigations of artifact assemblages from entire communities, we will not be able to identify social differentiation or the intensity of interaction within and among Chacoan communities.

A critical problem with many popular scenarios is that the density and nucleation of Chaco-era settlements is probably far below what is necessary to maintain a well-integrated system, especially for an oral and pedestrian society (Roscoe 1993). Consistently small village size and considerable variability in the distribution of great houses do not support models that posit the Chaco people as belonging to a centralized polity. Much of the Chaco-era population likely resided in dispersed communities composed of generationally mobile households (see Varien 1997: 246). In most parts of the Chacoan world, centralization and associated economic demands would have been difficult to maintain, because most people could have simply walked away from an overtaxing political situation (Kantner 1996a). Only after A.D. 1150 did the investment in domestic architecture and agricultural facilities appear substantial enough to deter relocation as a viable alternative to exploitation (Kendrick and Judge, this volume).

At this stage, it should not appear radical to state that we cannot know if Chaco was a system, or what sort of system it was, without understanding the nature and organization of great house communities. Consistently small village sizes and an irregularly dispersed settlement system are inconsistent with cross-cultural models of centralized polities. It is these settlements that would have sustained a regional system, and we know very little about their economic, social, or political relationships with one another, with Chaco Canyon, or with other non-Chacoan groups. Fortunately, archaeologists are increasingly turning their attention to the study of outlying communities and our knowledge of them is growing rapidly. Although a focus exclusively on Chacoan communities will never be able to definitively resolve all of the issues presented in this section, research outside of Chaco Canyon is providing data that are necessary if we want to develop a comprehensive picture of the Chacoan phenomenon, its origins, and its role in the evolution of puebloan groups of the northern Southwest.

A NEW FOCUS ON GREAT HOUSE COMMUNITIES

How will a focus on great house communities advance our understanding of Chacoan society? The community is arguably the smallest social unit in which political, economic, and social institutions are created

and reproduced through several generations. In 1949, Murdock asserted that "the community and the nuclear family are the only social groups that are genuinely universal" (from Kolb and Snead 1997). Since then, others have pointed out that communities are fundamental to social and economic integration in formative agricultural societies (Johnson and Earle 1987: 131) and are typically the highest decision-making body above that based on kinship (Adler 1996a: 97; Adler and Varien 1994). Community-level integration is critical for defense, risk aversion, trade, and capital investment in technology (Johnson and Earle 1987). Communities are also important social units for resolving disputes, negotiating land tenure, and providing a potential pool of mates (Adler 1996a).

Lipe (1970: 86) has emphasized that communities are the minimum territorially based aggregates that are capable of maintaining themselves through time and that include mechanisms for transmitting the principal content of their culture from one generation to the next. As such, the community would have been the fundamental social unit in which Chacoan political, economic, and ritual behaviors were sustained and reproduced at the local level, regardless of the existence of a regional political authority. Developing a better understanding of great house communities is an important step in building regional-scale models of Chacoan society.

Fortunately for archaeologists, communities are geographic locations as well as social units (Varien 1999: 21). In comparison to its demographic constituency, the geographic location of the community's territory remains relatively constant through time. Communities experience emigration, immigration, births, deaths, and other demographic processes that constantly alter the constituency of the social group, whereas occupation of the territorial unit may span several generations or even centuries. According to Varien (1999), communities in the Mesa Verde region consisted of the persistent occupation of territories through several decades or centuries, even though the geographic and demographic scale of these communities varied across space and through time. This stability facilitates the use of community-based analyses for examining cultural change.

Defining Great House Communities

Kolb and Snead (1997) have recently called for a definition of community that has clear archaeological correlates. They draw heavily from Lipe's definition (1970: 86) and emphasize that social reproduction, subsistence production, and the social recognition of members are all crucial components of any viable community. They suggest that minimum demographic units, the identification of productive resources, and mechanisms of boundary maintenance (both physical and symbolic) are reasonable archaeological correlates related to each of these components.

Communities also have temporal, geographic, and demographic dimensions (Varien 1999: 22). The temporal and geographic dimensions are defined by the fact that members must reside within a small enough territory frequently enough to permit regular face-to-face interaction (Murdock and Wilson 1972). The demographic dimension refers to the upper and lower limits of community population size; the community must be larger than the individual household or kin group and below the apparent limits for community size in nonstratified societies (Kosse 1993; Varien 1999). Each of these dimensions must be considered in order to identify Chacoan communities with archaeological data.

Archaeological approaches to identifying communities in the American Southwest have relied on the spatial distribution of recognizable residential sites; communities are defined as relatively dense clusters of habitations surrounded by zones containing few or no sites. Breternitz and Doyel (1987: 184) suggest that a community is identified by contemporaneity among the sites in these clusters and that it will often include a hierarchy of site types. Similarly, Adler and Varien (Adler 1990, 1996a; Adler and Varien 1994; Varien 1999: 145) identify communities and boundaries by spatial clustering of residential sites and the presence of public architecture. These approaches have become the basis for the archaeological identification of Chacoan communities (Kantner 1996a; Lekson 1991; Powers and others 1983; Wills and Leonard 1994: xiv).

Unfortunately, the dispersed communities identified in much of the Chacoan world are not as easily recognized as later aggregated communities. Furthermore, identification of Chacoan communities has typically been limited to full-coverage survey in a 1–km to 2–km (0.6 to 1.2–mile) radius around a known great house (Marshall and others 1979; Powers and others 1983; Warburton and Graves 1992; Windes 1993a); only a few surveys have extended beyond this range (Eddy 1977; Hayes and others 1981; Irwin-Williams and Baker 1991). Many of the contributions to this volume suggest that great house communities often integrated habitations located some distance away from the great houses themselves. For example, Gilpin and Purcell (this volume) have identified habitations as distant as

3 km away from the Peach Springs great house, beyond which are specialized sites that define the boundaries between communities. They suggest that although Chacoan communities would have centered on a stable core of habitations where the great house was located, other nearby clusters of habitations also would have been considered part of the great house community. Certainly, our understanding of the Chaco phenomenon will require serious reconsideration if a substantial number of structures in great house communities were used only seasonally, as Windes and others (this volume) propose for the East Community.

An important avenue of research is to determine if residential structures in Chacoan communities were used for substantially less time than great houses. Varien's (1999) research demonstrates that, until A.D. 1150, residential settlements in the Mesa Verde region were constructed of a combination of earth and masonry architecture and were probably not occupied for longer than a single generation. In contrast, great houses were solid masonry structures that appear to have remained in use for up to a century. Accordingly, Varien proposes that great houses operated as long-term centers marking the territory of residentially mobile households (see also Kendrick and Judge, this volume). If true, we need to consider why households were willing to invest their labor in high-visibility architecture (great houses, great kivas, roads) rather than in major agricultural features that might benefit the entire community. As suggested by Kendrick and Judge (this volume), perhaps labor was seen as the primary factor limiting production, at least in the Montezuma Valley, and Chacoan great houses were constructed as a way to attract laborers and encourage residential stability.

A discussion of the geographic and temporal scales of great house communities is incomplete without a consideration of their demographic structure. Mahoney (this volume) demonstrates that when we take structure use-life into account, the momentary population of many Chacoan communities is well below 200 people within a 2–km (1.2–mile) radius around a great house. This number is far below the population necessary to provide enough mates to sustain a reproductively viable community (Wobst 1974). Not until after A.D. 1150 were single communities large enough to meet the minimum population threshold required for a viable mating network (Varien 1999: 213). This means that individuals in communities probably needed to interact regularly with members of neighboring communities. Mate exchange would have increased the frequency of interaction and the potential for alliances between communities, ultimately reducing the autonomy of any single community. Additional investigations of demographic patterns in Chacoan communities and the mechanisms that were employed to sustain them are needed. For example, more cross-cultural research will be necessary to determine whether the low population densities characteristic of the Chacoan world were substantial enough to sustain nonproducing local or regional elites.

Great House Communities and Chaco Canyon

An understanding of the scale and nature of the proposed Chaco system will not be possible until the relationship between great house communities and Chaco Canyon is determined. Despite the increasing number of community studies (Eddy 1977; Fletcher 1994; Irwin-Williams and Baker 1991; Marshall and others 1979; Mobley-Tanaka 1993; Powers and others 1983; Warburton and Graves 1992), there is considerable disagreement as to what the archaeological patterns indicate about community interaction with the central canyon. For example, several scholars (Kane 1993; Wilcox 1993) suggest that outlying great house communities were developed by Chaco Canyon as outposts for obtaining needed resources, either by "capturing" existing communities or by establishing new settlements. In contrast, others (for example, Durand and Durand, this volume; Kantner 1996a; Kendrick and Judge, this volume; Van Dyke 1999a) contend that outlying communities were for the most part independent, forming relationships with Chaco Canyon only within the context of local sociopolitical negotiations.

Much of our understanding of the relationship between Chaco Canyon and distant great house communities has been influenced by the seminal study of Bis sa'ani (Breternitz and others 1982). Survey and excavations revealed that this community, located not far from the central canyon, had been established all at once around A.D. 1100. Accordingly, the researchers labeled Bis sa'ani a "scion" community, which was contrasted with "ancestral" communities that had existed for some time before being drawn under Chaco Canyon's influence. The research at Bis sa'ani suggested that great house communities were commonly established by a centralized authority in Chaco Canyon. This idea of the "scion" community has contributed to the view that outlying communities were actively established and perhaps forcefully integrated into the Chaco system by active Chacoan leaders (for example, Wilcox 1993, 1996). At the very least, the conventional wisdom has been that

the vast majority if not all of great house communities were closely integrated with the central canyon, which heavily influenced local social, political, and economic organization (Judge 1991; Lekson 1999; Neitzel 1994; Schelberg 1992). From this perspective, great houses are argued to have been established at the behest of the canyon as physical representations of this relationship.

As an increasing amount of research has focused in areas outside of Chaco Canyon, very little evidence for other "scion" communities has been identified. In fact, Bis sa'ani is the only community that was indisputably established as a new settlement during the Chaco era; other candidates exist, but none have yet been adequately investigated. Other community-based research is beginning to erode the belief that great houses were actively established under the guidance of a centralized authority into an integrated regional system. Durand and Durand (this volume) emphasize that a more parsimonious explanation would be that Chacoan patterns outside of Chaco Canyon are better understood as representations of a regional style and shared social patterning rather than evidence of an integrated system. Certainly the data that new studies are generating are consistent with their suggestion.

Architectural evidence indicates that outlying great houses, which are often thought to be clear representations of a community's interaction with Chaco Canyon, exhibit considerably more variability than previously thought. Van Dyke's research (this volume; see also 1998, 1999b) demonstrates that many great houses outside of Chaco Canyon were locally constructed by builders who were either unaware of the architectural details characterizing canyon great houses or who chose not to include them. Van Dyke (this volume) proposes that outlying communities constructed superficially Chacoan great houses only in the context of competitive emulation; similar architectural styles did not necessarily represent integration into a Chaco-centered system. Hurst's discussion (this volume) of one of the few excavated great houses indicates that communities outside of Chaco Canyon had varying motivations and access to information on how to construct Chacoan architecture such as that found at Edge of the Cedars. A similar conclusion is reached by Jalbert and Cameron (this volume) in their comparison of architecture in the northern great house communities of Bluff, Far View, and Chimney Rock. They support the contention that great houses were architecturally quite variable, with some primarily reflecting local architectural precepts and others, such as Chimney Rock, more closely mimicking the great houses of Chaco Canyon.

Evidence from other artifact classes supports the contention that Chaco Canyon and outlying communities did not regularly engage in mutual economic exchange. Kantner and others (this volume) write that ceramic exchange suggestive of frequent interaction was common between nearby outlying communities but that few vessels were imported from outside these local areas. This conclusion is supported by Van Dyke's (1997a) study of trachyte-tempered pottery, which concludes that the famous Chuska pottery that was imported to Chaco Canyon in great quantities (for example, Toll and McKenna 1997) was rarely exported from the canyon to other parts of the Chacoan world. The independence of outlying communities is further supported by Gilpin and Purcell's (this volume) examination of ceramics from Peach Springs, which shows that local communities and even households within communities negotiated their own exchange relationships. Even the East Community reveals artifact patterning that differs substantially from its neighbors farther down Chaco Canyon (Windes and others, this volume). Overall, the ceramic and lithic evidence indicates that outlying communities were perhaps more independent from Chaco Canyon than models of system hegemony often imply. However, the distribution of valuables among great house communities does indicate that a prestige-goods economy centered on the canyon was a factor shaping sociopolitical relationships that should not be lightly dismissed (Durand and Durand, this volume; Hurst, this volume; Lekson, this volume).

Relationships Within and Among Great House Communities

To what degree were great house communities independent or autonomous from one another? Kolb and Snead (1997: 617) suggest that the strength of a physical or symbolic boundary is an important strategy in maintaining community-level autonomy and identity. These boundaries can take many forms, including shrines, enclosing walls, or a distinctive ceramic style. Although we are not aware of any indisputable examples of boundary maintenance in the Chacoan world, archaeologists have yet to make a concerted effort to look for them. A lack of strong boundary maintenance may indicate that political entities through most of the Chaco era were relatively permeable. In this regard, the suggestion by Kantner (1997) that small, isolated great houses appearing late in the Chaco era may represent boundary markers between large outlying communities is intriguing.

Community autonomy can be investigated by examining exchange relationships among Chacoan communities. Research by Kantner and others (this volume) on pottery exchange indicates a significant number of vessels were being traded to nearby communities. However, the amount of interaction (as measured by pottery exchange) exhibited by communities varied considerably, shaped both by geological barriers and sociocultural relationships. Some communities interacted more intensively with their neighbors and may be viewed as having been less autonomous than those communities that seemingly avoided reciprocal economic interaction with their neighbors. Kantner and his colleagues interpret the latter as more centralized and externally competitive communities that may have established ties to more distant areas, perhaps as they sought external alliances to aid in local sociopolitical competition.

Gilpin and Purcell (this volume) examine household autonomy in the Peach Springs great house community. Through analysis of pottery exchange, they conclude that some households appear to have had independent trade relations with distant parts of the Southwest that were independent from their relationships with Chaco Canyon. A similar pattern can be seen in the samples of imported materials recovered from households in the East Community (Windes and others, this volume) as well as in the household economies of the Montezuma Valley (Kendrick and Judge, this volume).

As Varien (this volume) points out, the degree of political and economic household autonomy within great house communities is significant because it affects the underlying mechanisms that would have supported a regional system. During the Pueblo II period, there tended to be a close association of residential settlements with the most productive soils. This tendency, coupled with frequent household mobility, leads Varien (1999) to argue that land tenure systems in Chacoan communities were probably based on usufruct, the right to freely use unoccupied property, rather than exclusionary property rights. Where productive land was relatively abundant, such as in the Montezuma Valley, usufruct rights probably enhanced household autonomy with regard to subsistence; good farm land was available for the taking and labor may have been the limiting factor. In their study of the Lowry community, Kendrick and Judge (this volume) propose that early in the Chaco era, households did indeed enjoy a high degree of autonomy. However, competition both for productive lands and especially the labor to work them became manifested in great house architecture, which provided an arena for assembling larger lineage groups and establishing intercommunity relationships. Kendrick and Judge see this process as resulting in a great deal of intracommunity competition and variable intercommunity interaction as local households and lineages attempted to build larger alliances and pool labor in the face of rapidly growing populations, a process that would have eroded household autonomy.

The Montezuma Valley, however, is one of the better areas of the Chaco world for successful horticulture. In areas where productive land was scarce, usufruct rights may have created a situation that required considerable sharing and maintenance of egalitarian standards for survival (for example, Kantner 1999). Egalitarian principles could have prevented households from taking more land than their share and restricted where they could move. Such egalitarian political and economic principles would have reduced the autonomy of individual households and likely mitigated against great house elaboration and competition both within and between great house communities in the Chacoan world.

FUTURE DIRECTIONS

The research needed to develop a richer and more systemic understanding of the Chacoan world requires careful examination of both the great houses and residential structures that comprise Chacoan communities. With the exception of the Guadalupe and Bis sa'ani communities, excavation of small sites has not been in-

tegral to archaeological research at outlying great house communities. The chapters in this volume demonstrate what can be learned from these communities based on focused investigations of great house and habitation sites and provide a solid foundation for further research on outlying Chacoan communities. Particularly important for answering many of the remaining questions on the origins and development of the Chaco sociocultural tradition will be collaborative efforts that explore similarities and differences in the development of communities in various parts of the Chacoan world. The goal of this research should be a temporally sensitive reconstruction of the Chacoan landscape that will provide us with a unique perspective on relationships not only among neighboring communities, but also between these outlying communities and Chaco Canyon.

Acknowledgments

The authors gratefully acknowledge the guidance and comments of the following people: Donna Glowacki, Michelle Hegmon, Keith Kintigh, Joan Mathien, Gregson Schachner, Kim Sonderregger, Ruth Van Dyke, Mark Varien, Gwinn Vivian, David Wilcox, Tom Windes, and an anonymous reviewer. Their assistance has greatly improved the quality of this chapter. However, they are in no way responsible for any errors in fact or logic.

Part 1

Defining the Chacoan
Great House Community

Figure Part 1. Computer reconstruction of the Chimney Rock
great house positioned on the site in southwestern Colorado.
(Photograph by Frank W. Eddy; reconstruction by John Kantner)

CHAPTER TWO

Redefining the Scale of Chacoan Communities

Nancy M. Mahoney

What constitutes a Chacoan community? Understanding the scale and organization of Chacoan communities is essential for determining if Chaco operated as a system and for identifying the interactions that structured the relationships between outlying communities and Chaco Canyon. However, our knowledge of the political, economic, and social organization of Chacoan communities remains largely in the realm of speculation. Lekson (1991: 42) has pointed out that a primary reason we know little about the structure and variability of Chacoan communities is that surveys are typically limited to the immediate vicinity of great houses and that those sites may represent only a portion of the entire community. Lekson also notes that unresolved issues of contemporaneity make it difficult to determine the areal extent and population size of these communities. Some of these issues may be resolved by examining the spatial and demographic scale of great house communities and by considering the implications of scale for models of the Chacoan world.

In this chapter I review the geographic and demographic scales of Chacoan communities using full-coverage survey data from areas surrounding four great houses in different sections of the Chaco region. The spatial location of residential sites relative to great houses is examined for each of the surveyed areas. Next, use-life parameters for Pueblo II period residences are used to estimate the momentary population of each community. Based on these analyses, it appears that great houses were not always situated within the largest local community and that Chacoan "communities," as they are traditionally defined, were probably too small to have constituted demographically viable social entities. Instead, the boundaries of social interaction for many Chacoan communities need to be extended to 80 square kilometers (30 square miles) or more in order to encompass a population large enough to ensure continued social reproduction. These observa-

tions have implications for developing social and political models of Chacoan communities, including the potential for surplus production, the scale of integration, the spacing between outlying great houses, and interaction with communities without great houses.

DEFINING COMMUNITY

Before examining the demographic and geographic scales of great house communities, we should first consider how archaeologists define "community." Varien (1999: 21) points out that communities are "both people and place." Communities represent the *social units* in which individuals negotiate land tenure, mobilize labor, resolve disputes, and acquire mates (Adler 1996a: 98). But these social units are territorially based, and therefore communities also represent geographic units with spatial limits. As such, archaeologists have increasingly made the community the primary unit of analysis (Kolb and Snead 1997).

In their recent review of archaeological community studies, Kolb and Snead (1997: 610) cogently discussed the need for a definition of community that is both "conceptually meaningful and archaeologically visible." Currently, the definition proposed by Murdock and Wilson is the one most widely used by Southwestern archaeologists. They define communities as "the number of people who normally reside in face-to-face association" (Murdock and Wilson 1972: 255). This definition is intuitively satisfying and corresponds well with archaeologically identifiable settlement clusters. In the northern Southwest, archaeologists typically identify non-nucleated communities by locating relatively dense clusters of contemporaneous habitations surrounded by zones with few or no settlements (Breternitz and Doyel 1987: 184). This definition corresponds well with conventional descriptions of a Chacoan community, which has been typically identified as a settlement cluster within a 1-km to 2-km (0.6- to 1.2-mile) radius of a great house (Doyel and others 1984; Marshall and others 1979; Powers and others 1983).

In contrast to Murdock and Wilson, Kolb and Snead (1997: 611) define community as the smallest territorial unit necessary for successful social and subsistence reproduction. Based on this definition, archaeologists should consider the minimum number of people and smallest geographic area that would be required to maintain a reproductively viable social unit. In many cases, Kolb and Snead's definition would need to include more people than just those residing in frequent face-to-face association, that is, local settlement clusters.

Rather than choose between alternate definitions of community, we can distinguish between two scales of interaction and make a distinction between *residential* and *sustainable* communities. Residential communities correspond to spatially distinct clusters of residences, where face-to-face interaction would have occurred on a daily basis. In contrast, sustainable communities correspond to the spatial and demographic scale of the social "network" required to maintain these residential communities. These larger networks may be overlapping and less bounded than residential communities. In most cases, each sustainable community would have been comprised of multiple residential communities and may or may not have been a socially recognized entity. Great house communities, as they have traditionally been defined, represent only a portion of the sustainable community necessary for their continued existence.

GEOGRAPHIC AND DEMOGRAPHIC SCALES OF SUSTAINABLE COMMUNITIES

For agricultural societies, the geographic scale of individual communities is restricted by the maximum distance people will regularly travel on foot to tend fields or collect resources (Varien 1999: 153–154). In summarizing cross-cultural studies, Arnold (1985: 34) reports that subsistence agriculturalists regularly travel a maximum of about 7 km to 8 km (4.3–5 miles) from their residences to cultivate fields. If we consider this distance to be the maximum radius of the total area in which daily face-to-face interaction could occur, then we obtain a geographic area of between 154 and 200 square kilometers (59 to 77 square miles) for ancient farming communities. Similar distances were identified for obtaining resources necessary for the production of pottery; people will travel maximum distances of 7 km for raw clay and 10 km (6.2 miles) for glaze, slip, or

other paint resources (Arnold 1985: 51–56). Bradfield (1971: 21) estimated that the Hopi traveled a maximum distance of 7 km to tend fields prior to the introduction of burros.

Research by Stone (1991a: 347) on the movement of Kofyar farmers revealed that under conditions of more *intensive* cultivation, farmers would not travel beyond 2 km (1.2 miles) to participate in agricultural work groups. Under intensive farming conditions, then, regular interaction among community members primarily occurs within only a 2-km radius of primary residences (Varien 1999: 154). This radius would effectively limit the spatial scale of such communities to 13 square kilometers (5 square miles), an area that seems consistent with the size of settlement clusters or *residential* communities during the Chaco era. However, archaeological evidence for agricultural technologies indicates that in many areas farming strategies during the Pueblo II period were *extensive* rather than intensive (Varien 1999: 214–216). Therefore, it is possible that some territories associated with Chacoan communities encompassed the *maximum* area of 150 to 200 square kilometers.

Ancient communities also have demographic parameters. Several cross-cultural studies report that the upper limit of community size for middle-range societies is between 1,500 and 2,000 people (Adler 1990, 1994; Kosse 1993; Lekson 1990). Minimum estimates are more difficult to establish. Although as few as 75 people can constitute local settlements (Adler 1989: 37, Table 1), the social networks required to sustain such groups extend beyond village boundaries. Through a computer simulation, Wobst (1974) demonstrated that under most conditions, a minimum of 475 people is necessary to provide enough potential mates to constitute a demographically stable social unit. Applied to Chacoan communities, Wobst's simulation means that their persistence depended, in part, on participation by individuals in social networks that included almost 500 people. This exercise should not be viewed as an attempt to redefine communities as mate-exchange networks, but these target numbers may be used to identify the *minimum demographic and spatial scales* of social interaction required to maintain a small residential community (Hantman 1983). Although it is clear that not all communities persisted beyond a few generations, at least half of all great house communities continued to be occupied throughout the succeeding post-Chaco period (A.D. 1150–1250). It is likely that these long-lived communities persisted, in part, because they were able to maintain social interactions with enough people to establish successful mate-exchange networks.

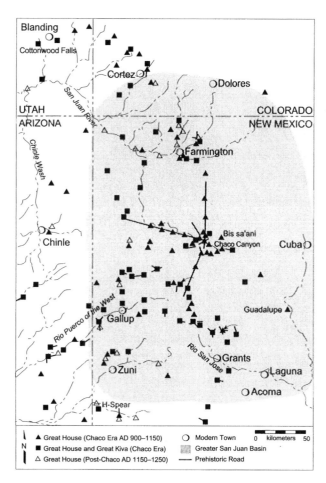

Figure 2.1. Location of Bis sa'ani, Cottonwood Falls, H-Spear, and Guadalupe great house communities.

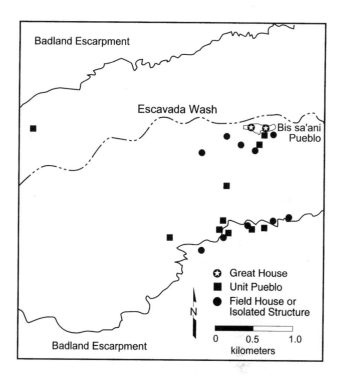

Figure 2.2. The Bis sa'ani community (adapted from Breternitz and others 1982: 454, Fig. 93).

SUSTAINABLE CHACOAN COMMUNITIES

With the estimate of 475 people in mind, I examined the demographic scale of four Chacoan communities: Bis sa'ani, Cottonwood Falls, H-Spear, and Guadalupe (Fig. 2.1) These communities were selected because each has settlement data from full-coverage pedestrian survey and because each is located in a different district in the Chaco region. Comparisons across these distant districts may reveal common organizational features fundamental to the social and political structure of Chacoan communities.

Bis sa'ani

Bis sa'ani is a 37-room great house located 15 km (9.3 miles) north of Chaco Canyon. The great house is located on a mesa top overlooking the floodplain of the Escavada Wash. Full-coverage survey of 10 square kilometers (3.9 square miles) surrounding the great house revealed 10 small pueblos and 10 isolated structures or limited use areas, all of which were contemporaneous with the great house (Fig. 2.2). Tree-ring dates, archaeomagnetic dates, and ceramic assemblages recovered from excavations at the great house and surrounding community structures indicate an occupation between A.D. 1100 and 1150 (Breternitz and others 1982: 56, 69).

Cottonwood Falls

Located in southeast Utah, Cottonwood Falls has a great house with more than 50 rooms, a detached great kiva, and two prehistoric roads. During the summers of 1996 and 1997, Arizona State University conducted full-coverage survey across approximately 14 square kilometers (5.4 square miles) within two separate block areas around the great house (Mahoney 1998a, 1998b). Surface collections of ceramics from the great house suggest it was primarily used between A.D. 1050 and 1175, but occupation probably continued into the early 1200s. Preliminary analysis of ceramic assemblages from

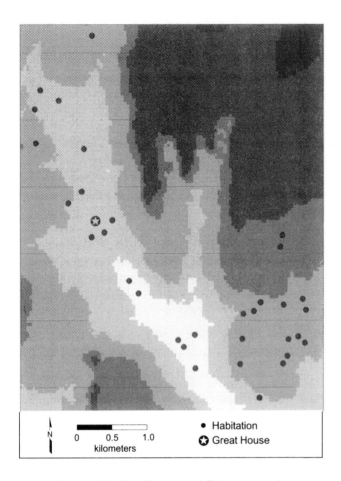

Figure 2.3. The Cottonwood Falls community.

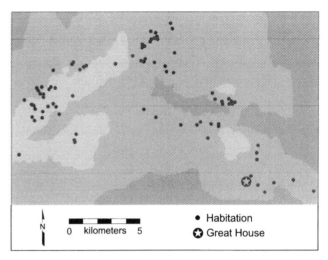

Figure 2.4. The H-Spear great house and community sites in the Ojo Bonito Project area.

the surrounding sites indicate that 33 residential structures were contemporaneous with the Cottonwood Falls
great house (Fig. 2.3).

H-Spear (OBAP)

H-Spear is a relatively small great house located near
the intersection of the Zuni River and the Arizona–New
Mexico state line. The site was identified during the last
season of survey in the southern portion of the Ojo
Bonito Archaeological Project (OBAP) research area
(Mahoney and others 1995). H-Spear consists of a 3-m-
high rubble mound and a great kiva 14 m in diameter,
both of which are surrounded by an earthen berm. The
great house is estimated to have been a high-roofed
single-story structure containing 12 to 14 rooms. Ceramic assemblages from test pits placed in the berm
indicate use of the great house and kiva between A.D.
1050 and 1125–1150 (Mahoney and others 1995). Full-
coverage survey of 55 square kilometers (21 square
miles) around H-Spear revealed that approximately 86

residential structures or field houses were contemporaneous with the great house (Fig. 2.4).

Guadalupe (RPVP)

Guadalupe Ruin is a single-story, 50-room great house
located on top of a narrow mesa in the middle of the
Rio Puerco Valley, about 40 miles northwest of Albuquerque (Baker 1991a: 16; Pippin 1987: xv). Tree-ring
dates record initial construction during the late A.D.
900s and a use-life until at least the mid-1200s. Excavations at Guadalupe (Pippin 1987) indicate that only 25
of the 50 rooms were in use between 960 and 1130.

The community surrounding Guadalupe was investigated as part of the Rio Puerco Valley Project (RPVP;
Irwin-Williams and Baker 1991). Between 1970 and
1981, full-coverage survey was conducted across approximately 105 square kilometers (40 square miles)
and more than 1,700 sites were recorded (Baker 1991a:
13, 27). Detailed seriation of ceramic assemblages by
Durand and Hurst (1991) indicate that a maximum of
110 habitations were occupied during any 15-year interval during the Chaco era (Fig. 2.5).

Examination of the community maps shows that if
we restrict investigation of great house communities to
residential structures within a 2–km (1.2–mile) radius
around a great house, we will miss a significant portion of the Chaco-era population (Figs. 2.2–2.5). The
surveyed area around each great house varies from 10
to 105 square kilometers. Despite this significant difference in coverage, there are some consistent patterns in
the distribution of habitation sites. All of the study areas

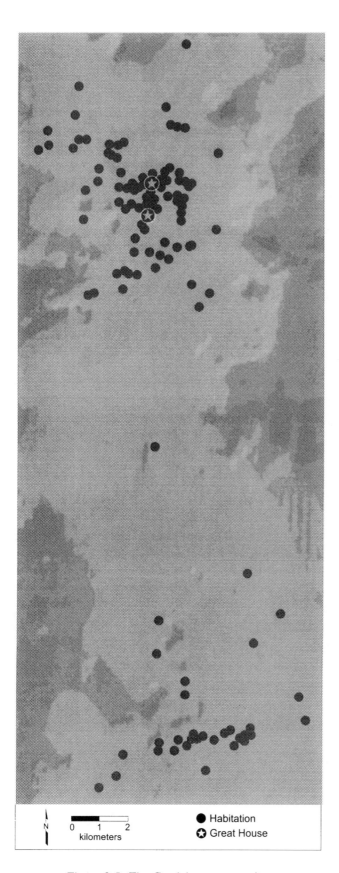

Figure 2.5. The Guadalupe community.

larger than 10 square kilometers contain significant clusters of habitations located at some distance from the great houses (Figs. 2.3–2.5). It is likely that if the study area around the Bis sa'ani great house were extended, it also would include additional settlement clusters. In some cases, these distant clusters match or exceed the density of the clusters in the immediate vicinity of each great house. This settlement pattern suggests that Chacoan influence was not equally pervasive on the Puebloan landscape; however, with current data we can do little more than speculate about the relationships between these clusters and nearby great house communities.

DEMOGRAPHIC SCALE OF SUSTAINABLE CHACOAN COMMUNITIES

For each community, I calculated total population from surface architecture at habitations judged to be contemporaneous with each great house. The primary method used to establish contemporaneity was the tabulation of temporally diagnostic ceramics from great houses and residential sites. Depending on the available data, either rubble area or room counts were converted into population estimates for each site. Following Schlanger (1987: 569–599), I assumed that 10 square meters of rubble were equivalent to one room and that one room was equivalent to one person.

For Cottonwood Falls, I calculated rubble area for every site dating between A.D. 1050 and 1175. Population estimates for Guadalupe and H-Spear were estimated from previously established room counts (Table 2.1A), which were derived from total rubble areas and the average size of excavated rooms in their respective areas. I obtained the total room count for the Bis sa'ani community from the published excavation report (Dykeman 1982: 840).

Total population estimates for the study areas range well above and below Wobst's estimate of a mating network size of 475 people (Table 2.1A). This wide range is primarily a function of the total area surveyed around each great house. Before controlling for area, the total population estimates for each community must be adjusted. Total population is not an accurate representation of the actual *momentary population*. For example, it cannot be assumed that all sites assigned to the Late Pueblo II period were occupied at the same time (Powell 1988). Recent research on structure use-life by Varien (1999: 107) demonstrates that many residential structures were occupied for only a decade of a century-long archaeological phase. To get more accurate population estimates for each Chacoan community, I used

Table 2.1. Characteristics of Population Estimates for Study Areas

	Cottonwood Falls A.D. 1050–1175	H-Spear A.D. 1050–1150	Guadalupe A.D. 1056–1091	Bis sa'ani A.D. 1100–1150
A. Derivation of total population estimates based on 10 square meters of rubble = 1 surface room = 1 person				
Number of sites	33	86	110 maximum	21
Total rubble area (m^2)	3060	6550	(not reported)	
Estimated room count	306	655	971[1]	62[2]
Total population	306	655	971	62

1. Baker 1991b: 308.
2. The room counts were reported in Dykeman (1982: 840). The total room count for the Bis sa'ani community included the rooms in the great house (but did not include kivas), which effectively doubled the total room count and population for this small community. Room counts for great houses were excluded from each of the other study areas because these structures often contained larger rooms and may not have been used primarily as residences. Therefore, the relationship between rubble area, room size, room count and population is unlikely to be the same as for unit pueblos. Adding great house room counts would not have had as dramatic an effect on total population estimates for any of the other study areas.

	Cottonwood Falls	H-Spear	Guadalupe	Bis sa'ani
B. Momentary population parameters for surveyed areas surrounding each great house, using 16-year, 42-year, and 80-year estimates for settlement use-life				
Period length in years	125	100	70*	50
Total population	306	655	971	62
Minimum momentary population, 16 years	39	105	222	20
Average momentary population, 42 years	103	275	606	52
Maximum momentary population, 80 years	196	524	971	62

* This time interval for Guadalupe incorporates the definition in Durand and Hurst (1991) that sites assigned to this period were also assigned to three 10-year to 30-year long periods.

	Cottonwood Falls	H-Spear	Guadalupe	Bis sa'ani
C. Minimum size of territories needed to reach 475 people for each great house, using average momentary population estimates				
Total survey area (km^2)	14	55	105	10
Average momentary population	103	275	606	52
Population density	7.4	5.0	5.8	5.2
Network area (km^2)	64*	95	82	91

* The population density for the Cottonwood Falls area is probably inflated because the survey was designed to cover areas where the highest density of residential architecture was expected to occur. As a result, the minimum territory required for a sustainable social network is probably larger than this estimate.

Varien's average, minimum, and maximum use-life estimates of Pueblo II and Pueblo III period residential sites to convert total population estimates into momentary population parameters. The upper and lower momentary population estimates identify what portion of the total population could have been contemporaneous, considering the estimates of settlement use-life and the total duration of the archaeological period.

Varien's research shows that Mesa Verde Pueblo II and Pueblo III period unit pueblos were occupied for between 16 and 80 years, and usually for less than 42 years (Varien 1999: 107, Table 5.4). He reports that the two Pueblo II period site components have estimated occupation spans of 16 and 26 years, suggesting that Pueblo II sites may have been occupied for considerably shorter periods than the average Pueblo III period site.

This is not surprising, considering that in many parts of the Southwest the transition to full height masonry walls did not occur until after A.D. 1100 (Varien 1999). Nevertheless, I used Varien's minimum, average, and maximum use-life estimates to generate momentary population parameters by dividing the total length of the Late Pueblo II period for each area by 16, 42, and 80 years and then dividing the total population estimate by those results.

Momentary population estimates for each area are presented in Table 2.1B. Except for Guadalupe, which encompasses an area of more than 100 square kilometers (38.6 square miles), the *average* momentary population estimate for each community is far below the 475 people required for a demographically stable social network. It is most instructive to look at the momentary population figures for Cottonwood and Bis sa'ani because they represent study areas equivalent to the maximum territory (10–14 square kilometers, 3.8–5.4 square miles) archaeologists typically survey to define Chacoan communities. According to the average estimates, there were fewer than 105 people living around Cottonwood Falls and fewer than 60 people around Bis sa'ani at any one time. Assuming constant population densities, a territory of more than 90 square kilometers (34.7 square miles) around most great houses would have been required to reach momentary populations of 475 individuals. Average use-life may actually be lower, reducing these population estimates further, and population densities for the Cottonwood and Bis sa'ani communities are inflated because survey areas were designed to target zones of dense residential occupation and did not include the resource areas associated with these communities.

EVALUATING THE SCALE OF SUSTAINABLE COMMUNITIES

Before moving to the implications of these demographic and spatial parameters for models of Chacoan communities, it is necessary to consider the viability of periodic social interaction across areas of 100 to 150 square kilometers (38.6–57.9 square miles). There are several reasons to think that regular interaction could have occurred at this scale. First, the size of these areas corresponds well with the ethnographically derived estimates of the size of territories exploited by communities with extensive farming practices (that is, a territory with a 7-km to 8-km radius; Arnold 1985). Second, research by Hantman (1983: 246–249, Tables 22 and 23) demonstrates that prior to A.D. 1150, the minimum ex-

tent of demographically viable social networks in the Black Mesa and Apache–Sitgreaves areas was more than 100 square kilometers. Hantman (1983) found that his hypothetical mating network areas corresponded to boundaries that occurred every 14 km (8.7 miles) in the Apache–Sitgreaves area (see F. Plog 1983). He reports that although these network areas did not correspond to measurable variability in black-on-white ceramic design style, network boundaries could be identified through variability in corrugated pottery style (Brunson 1979), in the distribution of ceramic technology (McAlister 1978), and in lithic raw material use (LaPere 1979; F. Plog 1983: 306–307). The correlation between plain wares, technological style, lithic materials, and network boundaries suggests that social interaction across areas of 100 square kilometers or more was probably frequent and informal. The relatively consistent geographic scale of these social networks was undoubtedly a product of the widespread, dispersed-settlement pattern that characterized the Pueblo II period, even in regions lacking great houses.

Prior to A.D. 1150 in most of the Plateau Southwest, the geographic scale required to achieve populations of 475 people was consistently larger than 40 square kilometers (15.4 square miles; Table 2.1C). Even in the core Mesa Verde area, one of the most densely populated regions during the Chaco era, momentary population estimates for both Sand Canyon and Goodman Point communities are fewer than 260 people within 25.5 square kilometers (Adler 1990: 232, 1992: 13). For comparability, Adler's estimates were recalculated to make them more consistent with my estimates for population in the other study areas. I assumed one person–one room (instead of 1.5 persons) and a 20-year-use-life, yielding a momentary population estimate of 252 people. Even if a constant population density of 10.2 people per square kilometer is assumed, a minimum area of 46 square kilometers is required to reach a population of 475 people. An exception may be the Peach Springs community (Gilpin and Purcell, this volume; Powers and others 1983). Using the same methods, I calculated an average momentary population of 263 people in the 1.4 square kilometers around the Peach Springs great house. Although population density drops off beyond a 3-km radius from the great house (Gilpin and Purcell, this volume), this estimate is considerably higher than all the other communities examined here. The large residential community around the Peach Springs great house (A.D. 975–1050) requires us to examine what social and environmental factors contributed to differences in scale among Chacoan communities.

Social interaction across areas large enough to encompass hypothesized mating networks remains unexamined for most outlying great house communities, primarily because we lack large block surveys for areas approaching 50 square kilometers (19 square miles). Interaction on this scale would have included multiple residential clusters in any part of the Chaco world. If we are to truly understand the social, political, and economic organization of Chacoan communities, and the larger Chaco "system," then it is essential that we investigate interaction at the proper scales.

Identifying social networks, or sustainable communities, with archaeological data is not as straightforward as drawing a 7-km radius around each great house. As demonstrated for H-Spear and Guadalupe, we cannot assume that great houses were the geographic centers for surrounding populations. Nevertheless, if great houses were related to social networks, then we should expect to see evidence of frequent social interaction within a 50 to 150 square kilometer area that includes a Chacoan structure. Stephen Plog (1989, 1990; Braun and Plog 1982) has argued that social networks similar to those proposed here can produce spatial discontinuities in absolute or relative frequencies of materials or stylistic symbols. Studies such as Hantman's (1983) demonstrate that this is not an unreasonable expectation.

IMPLICATIONS FOR THE ORGANIZATION OF CHACOAN COMMUNITIES

The scale of residential and sustainable communities during the Pueblo II period encourages us to reconsider several aspects of Chacoan communities. Many models of the Chacoan system posit that great house communities produced surplus staples either for tribute to local or regional leaders (Schelberg 1984; Wilcox 1993), for competitive feasts hosted by aspiring leaders (Kantner 1996a), or for communal storage (Judge 1993; Toll 1985). Although some surplus production may have been possible, the demographic and geographic scales of most great house communities show that sustained overproduction would have been difficult to achieve and maintain. In the cases examined here, residential communities surrounding great houses contained fairly small populations residing in dispersed household units. The surpluses generated by households in great house communities situated in marginal environments were probably neither large nor predictable (Hegmon 1991; Robertson 1997). Although sustainable communities contained larger populations, the concomitant increase in geographic scale reduces the likelihood that surpluses

could have been controlled by local or regional leaders. Roscoe (1993) points out that dispersed populations are more resistant to coercive political power, especially in societies where potential leaders did not have pack animals, standing armies, or a written language. In addition, in the case of Chacoan communities that were neither geographically nor socially circumscribed, residents could simply have moved to a new location to avoid the pressure of aspiring leaders (Betzig 1988: 59; Carniero 1981; Roscoe 1993: 115–116).

Postulating that surplus production for communal storage was a main function of great house communities also seems unwise. The organization of these residential groups was clearly not structured to facilitate cooperative agricultural production. Far more communal or corporate labor was invested in the nonutilitarian architecture of great houses, great kivas, and roads than in features that would have enhanced agricultural productivity for the community (but see Wilshusen and others 1997). In addition, the fact that Pueblo II period residences were dispersed and often located on or near arable land probably means that households typically farmed fields in their immediate vicinity, independent of other households in the same community. In short, any food surplus most likely would have been generated by individual households *for their own use* (as a risk-buffering strategy). Periodic communal events may indeed have been financed by individual household production, but it seems unlikely that more than a few individuals, much less an army or an elite class, could have been continuously supported. To clarify this issue we need to develop testable models of great house communities that are based on reasonable estimates of population, agricultural productivity, and human responses to political pressure.

Another aspect of communities that needs to be reconsidered is *integration*. An important aspect of social integration, especially when it involves ritual, is that it reinforces social ties among dispersed populations (Durkheim 1965). Anthropologists recognize that social integration is an important way for communities to promote many types of cooperation, such as food sharing in times of scarcity (Ford 1972). It has been suggested that great houses were locations of activities that served to integrate social groups (Adler 1996a: 98). If this was the case during the Chaco era, then integration was most likely targeted at sustainable rather than residential communities. Farmers in the same residential community would have been subject to the same environmental perturbations, so sharing within residential communities would not have been an ideal solution to offset food shortages. In addition, residential communities typically numbered fewer than 100 people (or 25 families) and probably involved daily face-to-face interaction. It is unlikely that these individuals would have required elaborate integrative facilities to maintain social ties. Furthermore, great houses probably did not operate primarily as integrative facilities. Unlike great kivas, great houses were not designed to provide unrestricted access to large groups of people (Cooper 1995).

Stephen Plog has argued that "as groups in the Southwest became less mobile and more restricted to particular areas, patterns of widespread resource-sharing evolved toward more restricted networks of obligations." He proposed that these localized networks did not have boundaries or formal divisions but were often "defined by areas where information and material exchange was much more frequent than similar exchanges with other surrounding groups" (Plog 1989: 144–145). Although this type of network cannot explain the construction of great houses, it might help explain their distribution during the Chaco era. The spacing between great houses may have been related to the size of the social network necessary to maintain those communities. In most regions, neighboring great houses were separated by distances of 7 km (4.3 miles) or more, which means that the size of sustainable communities would have reached 40 square kilometers (15.4 square miles) before they began to overlap and compete for members. If so, the smallest territory in which the population would have reached 475 people would have included multiple residential communities.

Remaining are interesting questions regarding households in the residential clusters that lacked great houses. Were they strongly affiliated with a distant great house or social network? Or were they independent and resistant to Chacoan sociopolitical organization? Kantner (1995: 18) surmised that these settlements or "hamlets" most likely formed through fissioning as some community members chose to resist aspiring Chacoan leaders. He contends that this option existed only where there was expansive and available tracts of arable soil (Kantner 1995: 18). This may be true for many hamlets, but it seems unlikely that fissioning alone could have produced the multitude of settlements without great houses

that were occupied during the Pueblo II period. Nevertheless, if fissioning did occur, what sort of interaction would we expect between great house communities and nearby hamlets? Clarification requires more information from unit pueblos in communities without great houses.

In future studies of Chacoan communities, it is critical that we continue to measure social interaction at multiple demographic and geographic scales. The distinction made here between residential and sustainable communities demonstrates how geography and demography are fundamental to any community study, especially when dealing with issues concerning hierarchy, integration, and centralization. The organization of great house communities and the Chacoan world will be better understood as we continue to evaluate social, political, and economic interaction within both residential and sustainable communities.

Acknowledgments

The Bureau of Land Management granted permission for archaeological investigations around the Cottonwood Falls great house and the survey was funded in part by a Graduate Research Support grant from Arizona State University. Many people were involved in recording the community sites in and around Cottonwood Wash, including Danielle Arnet, Cynthia Bates, Deborah Berner, Vanessa Bonet, Daniel Chong, Michelle Cotty, Eric Cox, Jeremy Davis, Andrew Duff, Sarah Heltne, Brian Kranzler, Paulette Leach, Katie Lyons, Christopher Messina, Sarah Paciorek, Gregson Schachner, Kim Sonderreger, Elizabeth Tierney, and Brian Villmoare. Information on settlements from the Guadalupe community was generously provided by Steve Durand. Keith Kintigh contributed data from the Ojo Bonito Archaeological Project. Inspiration for this study came from many discussions with Mark Varien on communities and demographics in the Mesa Verde region. I extend thanks to John Kantner, Michelle Hegmon, Wesley Bernardini, Mark Varien and two anonymous reviewers, all of whom provided valuable comments on this chapter. Any errors in logic or fact are my sole responsibility.

CHAPTER THREE

Peach Springs Revisited: Surface Recording and Excavation on the South Chaco Slope, New Mexico

Dennis Gilpin and David E. Purcell

In 1976, Robert Powers, William Gillespie, and Stephen Lekson of the Chaco Center inventoried the Chacoan "outliers," as the sites were then called, and conducted detailed studies of three communities: Bis sa'ani, Pierre's Site, and Peach Springs (Powers and others 1983). The Peach Springs community is located between Crownpoint and Tohatchi on the South Chaco Slope along the Coyote Canyon Road, a prehistoric roadway that has been projected to run from Standing Rock to Peach Springs to Grey Ridge (see Fig. 1.2; Nials and others 1987). In the Peach Springs community, Powers, Gillespie, and Lekson recorded 54 sites in an area of 3.5 square kilometers (1.4 square miles), including the great house, the great kiva, 37 small houses, and a number of other sites with miscellaneous functions. The community as a whole dated from A.D 500 to 1300. Data recorded by Powers, Gillespie, and Lekson suggest that residences in the community began to be established between about 500 and 900 and that the community had the greatest population density from around 975 to 1050, remained relatively stable from 1050 to 1175, and was depopulated quite rapidly from about 1175 to 1300.

Since 1996, SWCA, Inc., Environmental Consultants, has been conducting archaeological survey and excavation along Navajo Route 9, which runs through the Peach Springs community, passing approximately 500 m south of the great house (Fig. 3.1). These archaeological investigations had two major goals: to reconstruct the growth and development of the community and to investigate trade and redistribution of goods within the community. The primary reason for wanting to know about the growth and development of the community was to understand how the presence of a Chacoan great house affected community organization. Did a community exist at Peach Springs before the Chacoan great house was built? Did the construction of the great

house change the organization and function of the community? Hypothesized functions of great houses range from elite residences to communal buildings and include storage units and redistribution centers for the wealth, surplus, or necessities of a community. One way to investigate the function of a great house in a community is to examine how imported goods are distributed (1) among small houses within the community, (2) between the great house and small houses, and (3) among different communities. The SWCA team attempted to reconstruct the growth and development of the community by dating sites as accurately as possible using ceramics and then plotting which sites were occupied during different intervals in the history of the community. We investigated trade and redistribution by documenting the distribution of imported ceramics and flaked stone materials at different sites and in different time periods. Unexpectedly, ethnobotanical studies also provided evidence of trade when agave pollen was recovered from one site.

SWCA surveyed nine miles of Navajo Route 9 in the late winter of 1996 and identified 12 sites, 7 within the Peach Springs Chaco Culture Archaeological Protection Site (established in 1980 under Public Law 96–550, Title 5). All 12 sites were tested in the fall of 1996, and 8 of them were further investigated in the summer of 1997, 4 within and 4 outside of the Chacoan Protection Site. Out of the three tested and four excavated sites within the Chacoan Protection Site, only one (NM-Q-13-55) had extensive cultural deposits extending into the right-of-way, and these deposits were mostly midden material. In contrast, excavations at two sites located 2.4 km and 3.2 km (1.5 and 2.0 miles) east of the Chacoan Protection Site exposed multiple pit houses that provided information on the economy and interaction within the extended community. To place the results of SWCA's excavations in a broader but comparable context, Dennis Gilpin conducted in-field analyses of ce-

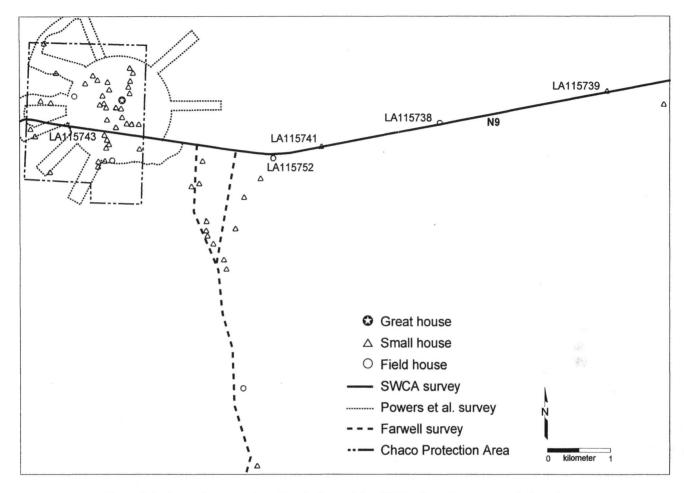

Figure 3.1. Area of survey along Navajo Route 9 by SWCA, Inc., Environmental Consultants.

ramics in transects through the middens of structures outside of the highway right-of-way, including the great house, 11 small houses, and one ancillary structure.

The recognition that the Peach Springs community was substantially larger than the core area studied by Powers, Gillespie, and Lekson led SWCA researchers to draw on a third study in the vicinity, Farwell's (1980) survey of New Mexico State Road 566. Data recorded by Farwell on sites east and south of the core community augmented the N9 survey material on the area east of the core community so that the SWCA team was able to more precisely define the scale and boundaries of the Peach Springs community as a functioning whole. On the other hand, studying the community at this scale required the use of data from three projects, each with different goals, methodologies, and even different types of site numbers. Powers, Gillespie, and Lekson used only field numbers with the PS prefix; Farwell filled out Museum of New Mexico Laboratory of Anthropology forms and received LA numbers; the

Table 3.1. Site Numbers Used for Survey and Excavation in the Peach Springs Community Area

Laboratory of Anthropology	Navajo Nation	Powers, Gillespie, and Lekson (1983)
LA 115738	NM–Q–12–69	
LA 115739	NM–Q–12–70	
LA 115741	NM–Q–12–72	
LA 115743	NM–Q–13–55	PS–37
LA 115752	NM–Q–13–58	

SWCA group filled out both Navajo Nation and LA site forms and assigned both numbers to each site (Table 3.1). Because of the limited areal coverage of the two linear surveys (N9 and State Road 566), documentation concerning the borders of and settlement within the Peach Springs community is still incomplete. However, by presenting information from these three projects in a consistent format, we hope to aid others investigating this area.

THE COMMUNITY CORE

Archaeologists calculate minimum-use dates from the earliest ending date to the latest beginning date for the date ranges of all decorated ceramics represented at a site. Based on survey, excavation, and in-field ceramic analyses at selected sites, Gilpin determined minimum-use dates for 20 sites, including the great house, 18 small houses, and an ancillary structure. He calculated mean ceramic dates (Christenson 1994; South 1972) for 15 sites, including the great house, 13 small houses, and the ancillary structure (Hasbargen and others 1998). The minimum-use dates show that the community core was occupied from A.D. 700 to 1200, with limited use between 1250 and 1300. Mean ceramic dates range from 1007 to 1091. The great house has a minimum-use date of 950 to 1075 and a mean ceramic date of 1052, which places its use coincident with the peak occupation of the entire community.

One of SWCA's goals was to reconstruct the growth of the community by calculating more precise dates for the occupation of individual structures. Our investigations largely confirmed the long occupation spans estimated by Powers and others (1983, Tables 8, 9); the average minimum-use interval was 195 years. This figure does not mean that the average house was actually occupied that long, although the deep middens associated with many of the sites may reflect long occupations, but that decade-by-decade reconstruction of community growth and development on the basis of surface materials may not be possible. Still, plotting which habitations were occupied during any particular 50-year interval according to the minimum-use dates does reveal general trends. The earliest occupation of the community, before about A.D. 900, was at five structures (PS–1 through PS–5, Fig. 3.2) along the north-south ridge west of Berry Canyon Wash. From 900 to 950, the community expanded extremely rapidly, so that by about 950, 16 of the 20 structures represented in Gilpin's sample were occupied. The community reached its greatest size in terms of number of habitations occupied from about 1000 to nearly 1100, when 17 of the 20 sites (including the great house) were occupied, and small houses were established to the west of the ridge above Berry Canyon Wash. Sometime between about 1050 and 1100, the community began to decline relatively slowly, with 13 small houses occupied around 1100, 9 inhabited around 1150, and only isolated evidence of occupation after about A.D. 1200.

A similar reconstruction of population growth based on the evidence recorded by Powers and others (1983)

largely corresponds with the reconstruction of settlement growth. Powers and others (1983: Tables 8, 9) estimated the length of occupation and number of rooms at each site in their survey area, for a total of 511 rooms. Since each Puebloan family typically used a suite of rooms, including a living room, milling rooms (sometimes), and several storage rooms, the population of a habitation was roughly equivalent to the number of rooms there. In estimating the total population of a community, though, one must take into account that not all structures were occupied at the same time and that people typically established a residence, added on to it, and abandoned it during a period of time. Plog (1974) devised a method for estimating changing population at a settlement and in a region. He argued that even at peak population, only 78 percent of the rooms in a residence or region were occupied. He further estimated that in periods preceding and following the peak period of occupation, people were occupying only half as many rooms as they were occupying during the peak period. Applying Plog's formulas to the statistics on site size and site date in Powers and others (1983: Tables 8, 9), the population of the Peach Springs survey area can be estimated as 32 people from A.D. 500 to 900, 184 from 900 to 975, 368 from 975 to 1050, 258 from 1050 to 1175, and 55 from 1175 to 1300.

Ceramics in the community core were overwhelmingly Cibolan. Utility wares were about 87 percent Cibolan and 13 percent Chuskan. Only four sites had higher than average percentages of Chuska Gray Ware: PS–21 (53.7% of utility ware was Chuskan), PS–23 (32.8%), PS–26 (17.6%), and PS–20 (17.6%). All of these sites except PS–26 are in the same neighborhood (the ridge west of the great house), suggesting that different parts of the Peach Springs community had different trading partners and that trade was not controlled by the occupants of the great house. The occupation spans of the houses with the most Chuska Gray Ware extended from A.D. 950 to 1100, and mean ceramic dates ranged from the 1050s to 1080s, so localized concentration of imported ceramics does not merely reflect a group of habitations dating to a specific time period. The importation of Chuska Gray Ware appears to have declined generally after the 1050s, but the range of variability in the amount of Chuska Gray Ware at contemporaneous residences is as great as the change in the amount of Chuska Gray Ware through time.

White ware was overwhelmingly Cibolan (92.8%), with 6.2 percent Chuskan; also represented were Tusayan White Ware (five sites), and Mesa Verde White Ware (three sites). The sites with the most Chuska White Ware

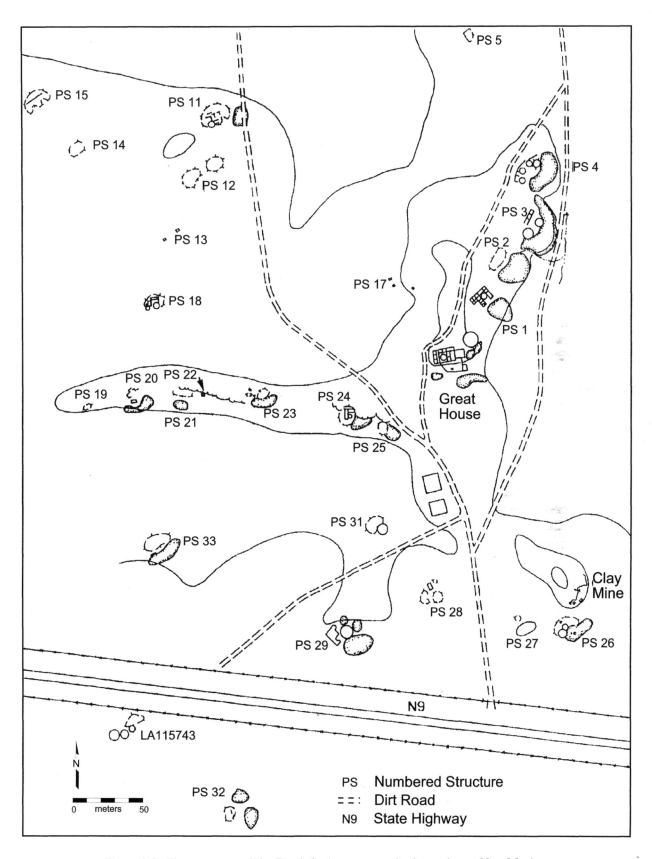

Figure 3.2. The core area of the Peach Springs community in northwest New Mexico.

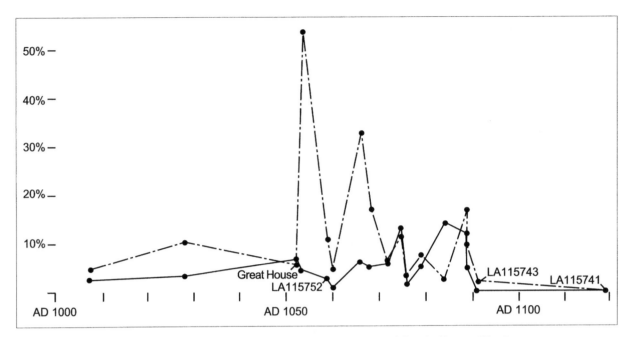

Figure 3.3. Distribution of Chuskan ceramics. Dotted line indicates Chuska
Gray Ware as a percentage of gray ware at individual sites; solid line indicates
Chuska White Ware as a percentage of white ware at individual sites.

(PS–3, where Chuska White Ware constituted 13.5% of white ware; PS–5, 12.2%; and PS–32, 14.3%) are not the same sites where Chuska Gray Ware was most common. The amount of Chuska White Ware appears to have increased slightly from the A.D. 1050s to the 1080s, but, as was true for Chuska Gray Ware, the range of variability in the amount of Chuska White Ware at contemporaneous residences is as great as the change in the amount of Chuska White Ware through time (Fig. 3.3). Red ware constituted 8.1 percent of the decorated sherds in the sites and increased through time (Fig. 3.4). Most of the red ware (81.6% on average at each site) was White Mountain Red Ware, with Show-low Red Ware present at only two sites in the community core, and Sanostee Orange Ware, San Juan Red Ware, and Tsegi Orange Ware present at only one site each.

Flaked stone material appeared to have been procured primarily from local sources. The most common imported lithic raw material was Zuni Mountain chert, which occurred at 12 of 15 sites and on average constituted 17.8 percent of the flaked stone assemblages. Chert from Washington Pass (now called Narbona Pass) was recorded at only 5 of 15 sites and on average constituted only 2.1 percent of the flaked stone assemblages. Two of the three Washington Pass chert flakes were observed at PS–21 and PS–23, which also had the

greatest amount of Chuska Gray Ware of any sites in the community. Two flakes of Cerro Pedernal chert were recorded at one site.

SWCA tested seven sites and conducted excavations at four sites in the Chacoan Protection Site, which extends beyond the core community. These sites were all habitations ranging in date from the Basketmaker III to early Pueblo III period (A.D. 500–1175), but six of the seven sites had only artifacts, isolated features, or both extending into the right-of-way. The most extensively investigated site in the core community (NM-Q-13-55) was a Pueblo II period habitation consisting of a room block outside the right-of-way and an artifact scatter. Middenlike deposits extending into the right-of-way were excavated, resulting in the recovery of 2,769 ceramic sherds, 172 flaked stone artifacts, and 37 ground stone artifacts. Hasbargen and others (1998) calculated the minimum-use date as A.D. 950 to 1175, with a mean ceramic date of 1091, the latest mean ceramic date for any site in the community core. This artifact assemblage was consistent with the assemblages from sites that were subjected to in-field analyses. Utility ware ceramics were 96.4 percent Cibolan and 3.2 percent Chuskan. White ware ceramics were 98.6 percent Cibolan and 1.2 percent Chuskan. Red wares constituted only 6.5 percent of decorated ceramics, a fairly low percentage for a site this late, and were overwhelmingly White

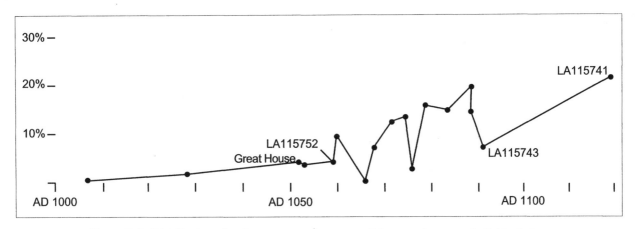

Figure 3.4. Distribution of red ware as a percentage of decorated ware at individual sites.

Mountain Red Ware (92.5%) with 7.5 percent Showlow Red Ware (Hasbargen and others 1998). Flaked stone material was mostly of local derivation (Greenwald 1998), with 19.9 percent Zuni Mountain chert (compared to a 17.8% average for the entire community) and 4.1 percent Washington Pass chert (compared to an average of 2.1% for the entire community).

COMMUNITY CORE AND PERIPHERY

Chacoan communities are usually defined as clusters of habitations a short distance, no more than 2 km (a mile) or so, from a great house. In her chapter on Chacoan communities, however, Nancy Mahoney points out that, anthropologically, communities are usually defined as populations in which people have face-to-face interaction, resource sharing, and shared ideologies. To be reproductively sustainable, large enough to provide each individual with a marriageable partner, a community needs a population of about 475 people (Mahoney, this volume). In order to evaluate whether site clusters such as those identified as Chacoan communities were actually reproductively sustainable communities, it is necessary to know how many people lived in them. In her study of Bis sa'ani, Guadalupe, Cottonwood Falls, and H-Spear, Mahoney determined that reproductively stable Chacoan communities were likely made up of multiple house clusters, including the primary cluster around a great house but also consisting of other house clusters lacking great houses. At the four sites she examines in her chapter, Mahoney concludes that reproductively stable communities covered areas of 150 to 200 square kilometers (58 to 77 square miles). As noted above, even during its peak occupation, the Peach Springs

community as defined by the survey area of Powers, Gillespie, and Lekson would not have had the 475 people needed for a reproductively stable community. What, then, were the limits of the reproductively sustainable community?

In a survey adjacent to but unrelated to the studies along the N9 right-of-way, Farwell (1980) found 20 sites extending 5.5 km (3.4 miles) south of N9, followed by a paucity of prehistoric sites until she reached the Church Rock area of the upper Puerco River drainage. The sites recorded by Farwell ranged in date from the Kiatuthlanna phase (A.D. 800–1000) to the Hosta Butte phase (A.D. 1030–1125) and included 13 habitations and several sites with miscellaneous features. The six pre-Hosta Butte phase sites were located within 3 km (1.9 miles) of the Peach Springs great house and ranged in size from one to ten rooms. The nine Hosta Butte phase sites, which would have been contemporaneous with the peak population of the cluster surrounding the Peach Springs great house, were all habitations. They ranged in size from 1 to 5 room blocks, each with 5 to 60 rooms for a total of approximately 150 to 215 rooms. Eight of these sites were in the same area where the pre-Hosta Butte phase sites were located.

Approximately 2 km south of the southernmost Hosta Butte phase site, 5 km (3 miles) south of the Peach Springs great house, Farwell encountered a cluster of three undated prehistoric sites that included a field house and two upright-slab features. These sites could have been associated with a Hosta Butte phase site located 1 km even farther to the south. Similarly, SWCA recorded and tested a habitation site (NM–Q–12–70) 8 km (5 miles) east of the Peach Springs great house and partially excavated a field house (NM–Q–12–69) 5 km east of the great house.

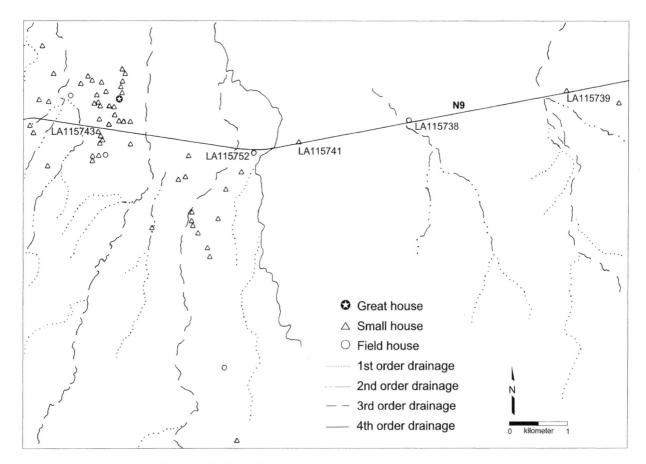

Figure 3.5. Peach Springs community core and peripheral sites.

Altogether, then, the investigations of Power and others (1983), Farwell (1980), and SWCA (Gilpin 1998; Phillips and others 1997; Skinner and Gilpin 1997) support a definition of a site cluster that is most dense at its center around the great house and less dense at its periphery, 3 km (about 2 miles) from the great house. Approximately 5 km from the great house, we begin to see specialized sites associated with other clusters. These other site clusters included habitations and apparently lacked great houses, although they have not been well documented. In general, the overall organization of the Peach Springs community seems to conform to the pattern proposed by Mahoney, consisting of multiple small house clusters, only one of which contained a great house (Fig. 3.5).

EXCAVATIONS OUTSIDE THE CORE COMMUNITY

The SWCA crew tested five sites and excavated four sites outside the Peach Springs Chacoan Protection Site. Two excavated sites outside the community core (NM-Q-13-58 and NM-Q-12-72), however, had the most extensive architectural remains encountered during the project, and one of them (12-72) dated to the early A.D. 1100s, when the community core was in decline.

Site NM-Q-13-58

Visible during the survey as only 52 sherds and a stone chopper within the right-of-way, site NM-Q-13-58 revealed when excavated a masonry-lined pit house with an attached masonry granary (Feature 20), a small shallow pit structure, possibly two occupation surfaces, various formal hearths and firepits, and two middens (Fig. 3.6). Material recovered included 447 ceramic sherds, 55 flaked stone artifacts, and 31 pieces of ground stone. Pottery indicates a minimum-use date of around A.D. 1050 to 1100. The mean ceramic date is 1059, the fifth earliest of the sites dated using this method.

The architecture of the site was between what would be expected at a field house or seasonal habitation (a relatively simple pit house) and what would be expected at a permanent residence (a masonry room block

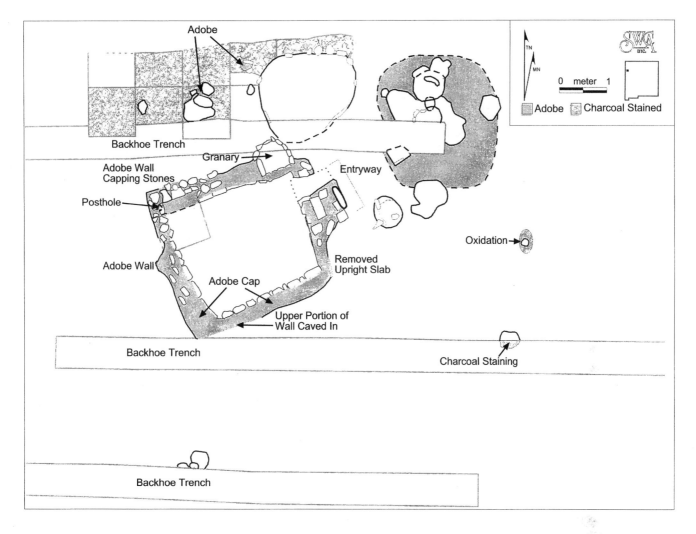

Figure 3.6. Plan of site NM–Q–13–58.

and kiva). The rectangular, masonry-lined pit structure had 3 floors and 21 floor features: a hearth, 2 firepits, a clay-lined pit, 6 postholes, and 2 pits in the lowest floor; 2 hearths, 2 firepits, an ash pit or side hearth, 2 postholes, and a pit in the middle floor; and a firepit in the uppermost floor. Radiocarbon dates indicate that the pit structure was originally built with earthen walls sometime between about A.D. 1000 and 1035. The masonry lining of the pit structure was associated with the uppermost floor and was composed of coursed sandstone blocks laid in clay mortar chinked with small tabular sandstone spalls and sherds in a style similar to Pueblo Bonito Type II (A.D. 1020–1060; Cordell 1984, Fig. 8.7A; Judd 1964, Plate 10; Lekson 1984, Fig. 2.4, Table 2.1; Vivian 1990, Fig. 8.18). Two stones just above floor-level in the north wall and one stone in the east wall of the structure had holes drilled into them (Greenwald 1998: 324); these may have served as loom anchors.

The style of the masonry veneer, the types of sherds used in the veneer, and radiocarbon dates suggest that the masonry veneer was added between about A.D. 1050 and 1060. When the veneer was added, Feature 20, a cylindrical granary with a capacity of 0.85 cubic meters, or approximately 30.0 cubic feet, was added to the outside of the pit structure. Bradfield (1995: 8) states that the Hopi require 20 to 24 bushels of maize per person per year for food, barter, seeds, and as a hedge against crop failure. A bushel of shelled maize occupies a volume of about 1.24 cubic feet. Feature 20, the only identified permanent storage feature on the site, may have held as much as 24 bushels, enough food for one person for a year or more or for a family of four for approximately two to three months. This small storage capacity reinforces the suggestion that it was not a year-round habitation but instead a seasonal field house.

The numerous hearths, firepits, and charred squash seeds, maize cobs, and kernels all reveal that more cooking and consumption of cultigens was occurring here than at any other excavated house in the project area. According to Cummings and her colleagues, maize was recovered from 12 of 14 flotation samples from the site, and 35 maize cobs came from the excavated deposits. One specimen recovered from the midden deposits may possibly be a cotton capsule base. Agave pollen was identified on an unclassified Cibolan black-on-white sherd associated with a firepit and pot rest (Cummings and others 1998). Curious is the near absence of faunal remains (only 20 bones, all from small mammals) and projectile points, showing that faunal resources must not have been as important here as at site NM–Q–12–72.

Site NM–Q–13–58 was the only site SWCA investigated where decorated ceramics were more common than utility wares (by a ratio of 62.0% decorated to 38.0% utility), but among the decorated sherds, jars were more common than bowls. In other respects, though, the artifact assemblage was typical of the assemblages at sites in the core community. Utility wares were overwhelmingly Cibolan (92.5%), as were white ware ceramics (98.4%); all other sherds were Chuskan. Red wares constituted only 4.1 percent of decorated sherds, which is typical of sites this early, but the red ware assemblage was unusual in that all sherds were Showlow Red Ware as opposed to the White Mountain Red Ware that dominated collections from other structures (Hasbargen and others 1998). Virtually all the flaked stone (92.7%) came from local sources (Greenwald 1998); Zuni Mountain chert was the only imported material and constituted 7.3 percent of the flaked stone artifacts, less than half of what was typical at sites within the community core.

The final interpretation of the function and significance of site NM–Q–13–58 is still problematic. The small amount of storage space, the ubiquity of maize, the large number of extramural hearths and firepits, and the limited evidence for exploitation of faunal resources all point to an interpretation of this site as a field house. On the other hand, the masonry veneer in the rectangular pit structure demonstrates a greater investment in and permanence to the structure than is typical at field houses. Masonry-lined pit structures are usually interpreted as ritual, but the structure at site 13–58 is rectangular whereas kivas are typically round or D-shaped. (Rectangular kivas with loom holes in the floor slabs and with loom blocks on the floor date after A.D. 1250; for example, see Hargrave 1931.)

Our assessment is that site NM–Q–13–58 should be interpreted as a field house with an unusual amount of labor investment because of its location on a major drainage. Using the concept of stream ranking (Strahler 1952) to classify drainages in the N9 project area, Gilpin (1998: 19–21) determined that the Peach Springs community core was on a third-order stream; site 13–58 was on a fourth-order stream, the highest ranking in the area (Fig. 3.5). It is noteworthy that such labor investment occurred at the height of the Chacoan occupation of the Peach Springs community, when year-round habitations within the core community were unit pueblos, blocks of 10 to 15 rooms with a kiva in front. Chacoan masonry and architecture have been interpreted in a number of ways, for example as elite or communal construction. Site NM–Q–13–58 could be interpreted as marking a field belonging either to elites or to the community.

Site NM–Q–12–72

Recorded during survey as a scatter of 89 sherds and a ground stone fragment, site NM–Q–12–72 consisted of one surface structure (probably of jacal or adobe), three pit houses, two slab-lined hearths, two pits, a midden, and one infant burial (Fig. 3.7). Materials recovered included 1,657 ceramic sherds, 91 flaked stone artifacts, and 46 pieces of ground stone. Ceramics indicated a minimum-use date of A.D. 950 to 1125 and a mean ceramic date of 1119, the latest mean ceramic date of any site SWCA investigated. Radiocarbon dates show reuse of the settlement about 1275 to 1325. Stratigraphy, mean ceramic dates, and sherds cross-mended from different features revealed that the three dwellings were occupied sequentially in the early 1100s, with Feature 9 constructed first, Feature 5 next, and Feature 8 built in the fill of Feature 9. Feature 4, an adobe or jacal surface structure with an interior hearth, was the last structure to have been used in the 1100s, and it was reused from about 1275 to 1325, when Features 6 and 7 (slab-lined hearths) were constructed.

Most of the faunal material recovered, including deer or antelope, jackrabbit, cottontail, woodrat, turkey, and red-tailed hawk bones, indicates a greater reliance on faunal resources than at any other site in the project area (Potter 1998). More projectile points (five) came from here than from any other site (Greenwald 1998). Maize appeared in only half of the eight flotation samples, and maize cobs were not nearly as common as at site NM–Q–13–58 (Cummings and others 1998). Although ground stone was more plentiful than from any

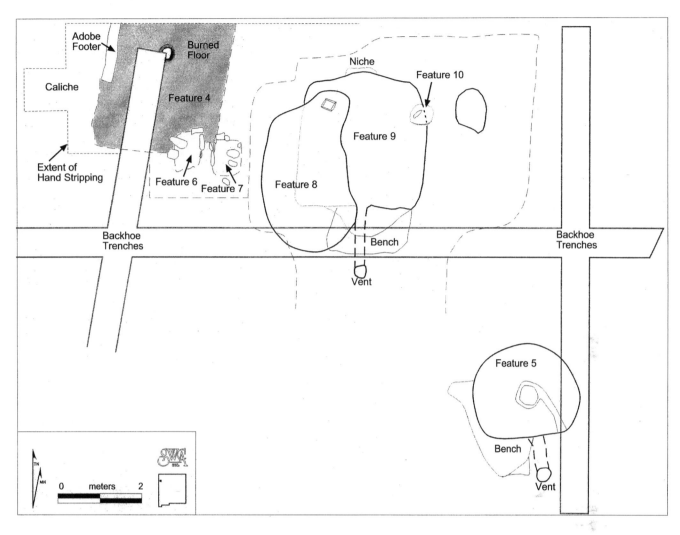

Figure 3.7. Plan of site NM–Q–12–72.

other site, the ratio of ground stone to ceramics was much lower than at site NM–Q–13–58.

Utility wares were overwhelmingly Cibolan (96.7%). Chuska Gray Ware was more poorly represented (0.8%) at NM–Q–12–72 than at any other site SWCA investigated; it had been replaced by Mogollon Brown Ware, the second most common utility ware (2.6%). White ware ceramics were 99 percent Cibolan and these were predominantly Chaco-McElmo Black-on-white. Little Colorado White Ware was as common as Chuska White Ware. Red wares constituted 21.7 percent of decorated sherds, the highest of all the sites, and included White Mountain Red Ware (83.0%) and Showlow Red Ware (17.0%; Hasbargen and others 1998).

Most flaked stone (94.5%) was derived from local sources; Zuni Mountain chert constituted 4.4 percent of flaked stone artifacts (about one-fourth as much Zuni

Mountain chert as occurred at sites within the community core), and the remaining 1.1 percent was obsidian (Greenwald 1998).

Based on the material evidence, site NM–Q–12–72 represented seasonal use of the Peach Springs community based less on agriculture and more on hunting. Trade networks were broader and more focused on areas to the south compared with the earlier settlements in the community. Although based on a sample of only two, the contrast between two excavated seasonal sites outside the community core, one (NM–Q–13–58) dating to the A.D. 1000s and the other (NM–Q–12–72) to the 1100s, is striking. Site 13–58 had an agricultural function and contained a masonry-lined pit house with an appended storage facility. Site 12–72 was more focused on hunting and consisted of sequentially occupied, earthen-walled pit houses that lacked storage facilities.

COMMUNITY DEVELOPMENT

Ceramic minimum-use dates of sites within the Peach Springs community suggest that the community was used for about 300 years. It grew extremely rapidly from A.D. 900 to 950, coincident with the original use of the great house location. The community was relatively stable from 950 to 1050 or the late 1000s, but slowly declined during the next 100 to 150 years, with only isolated evidence of occupation after about 1200.

Artifact assemblages indicated heavy dependence on locally produced ceramics and on local sources for flaked stone material. Chuskan ceramics, the most commonly imported pottery in the community core, constituted less than 10 percent of most ceramic assemblages, but the amount of Chuskan pottery on individual sites was highly variable, suggesting household-level rather than community-level ties to ceramic production areas in the Chuska Valley. On the other hand, Washington Pass chert was relatively uncommon, even though it was most frequently recovered from the sites that contained the most Chuska Gray Ware. Overall, Zuni Mountain chert was the most commonly imported lithic material in the community, constituting on average 17.8 percent of the flaked stone.

By the early A.D. 1100s, when the community core was midway through its 150-year decline, subsistence and settlement patterns began to change. Whereas habitations in the 1000s consisted of unit pueblos with substantial amounts of storage, and even a field house that apparently warranted considerable labor investment (site NM–Q–13–58), by the 1100s at least some residents of the greater community area were relying less on agriculture and more on hunting and were occupying the area only seasonally, residing in pit houses with no storage facilities. Exchange networks had also changed considerably by the early 1100s. At the latest site investigated (12–72), red ware constituted 21.7 percent of decorated sherds and included White Mountain Red Ware (83%) and Showlow Red Ware (17%). This site was also the only one with Mogollon Brown Ware and Little Colorado White Ware. These imports indicate increased trading with areas to the southwest, particularly the Puerco River Valley of northeastern Arizona. By this time Zuni Mountain chert from the south had dropped to only 4.4 percent of the flaked stone assemblage.

This comparison of community developmental history and patterns of exchange shows that these two variables are relatively independent of one another. Thus, although the community architectural plan and organization were established rapidly and persisted for about a century, individual households within the community developed their own external trade networks, linking them not so much to Chaco Canyon but to other communities within the Chacoan "system." As early as the A.D. 1050s, some exchange with communities to the southwest, outside the San Juan Basin, was taking place. In the declining years of the community, at least one household was occupied on a seasonal basis and it traded more extensively with communities to the southwest than had any of its predecessors.

Acknowledgments

The work by SWCA at Peach Springs was performed under the administration of the Navajo Nation Historic Preservation Department, Roads Planning Program, and for the Bureau of Indian Affairs, Navajo Area Office, Branch of Roads.

CHAPTER FOUR

Sunrise, Sunset: Sedentism and Mobility in the Chaco East Community

Thomas C. Windes, Rachel M. Anderson, Brian K. Johnson, and Cheryl A. Ford

Chaco Canyon has long been known for its massive buildings and perceived dense occupation along its 35-km length (21 miles), with a center located around Pueblo Bonito (Hayes and others 1981; Lekson 1984). This perception, however, is skewed by the lack of in-depth studies of communities in and around Chaco Canyon (except see Doyel and others 1984; Windes 1993a). The premise of a population void around Chaco Canyon proper (Lekson 1989: 80) is misleading, because occupations existed immediately to the north, west, and south. Furthermore, numerous communities occurred elsewhere in the San Juan Basin with occupation densities that surpassed those in Chaco Canyon, such as at Newcomb and Skunk Springs in the eastern Chuskan foothills. At Newcomb, two avenues were so tightly packed with settlement that there was no break in the cultural deposition for 3 km (nearly 2 miles). Nearby Skunk Springs exhibits remains of more than 100 houses along an area little more than a kilometer in length and aligned along what may be multiple avenues (Lekson 1997: 33; Marshall and others 1979). The term "avenues" is accurate, for there were two parallel rows of houses situated back-to-back along suspected walkways that are not unlike residential streets in an American city.

Chaco Canyon contained five dense communities, each with a Chacoan great house and 40 to 60 small houses that were first settled in the late A.D. 800s or early 900s (Fig. 4.1: Padilla Well, South Gap, Fajada Gap, Chaco East, and Pueblo Pintado). Common denominators for these five communities included an early great house, a cluster of small houses with substantial quantities of refuse, widespread evidence in the form of ceramics and construction materials that indicated an initial A.D. 900s occupation, an absence of great kivas, community spacing of from 9 km to 13 km (6 to 8 miles; Loose 1979: 359), settlement in the prominent

gaps that had eroded through Chacra Mesa that provided multiple storm runoffs useful for farming (Judge and others 1981), ubiquitous evidence for corn processing, and widespread turquoise craft activities. Notably, all of the communities were visually interlinked by a system of communication shrines (Hayes and Windes 1975), and all were probably connected by a road system running the length of Chaco Canyon.

Unfortunately, prehistoric habitation at and around Pueblo Bonito continues to attract intense study, such that other centers are virtually ignored (Windes and Ford 1992). The longevity of the Pueblo Bonito community and the multiple phase components represented in the 40 houses there make it the most difficult group of sites to understand, a situation mirrored at the westernmost community of Padilla Well. As one moves east to communities farther up Chaco Canyon, however, the archaeology becomes progressively easier to decipher because of the relative lack of sequential multi-component occupations. The community around Fajada Butte, 8 km (5 miles) east of Pueblo Bonito, consisted of 54 small houses of the Late Pueblo I through Pueblo III periods in an area of approximately 966 hectares (2,386 acres; Windes 1993a: 359). Two closely associated great houses, Una Vida and Kin Nahasbas (not on map), were part of this community (Mathien and Windes 1989). Another community existed around the Pueblo Pintado great house at the very east end of Chaco Canyon, which marked the eastern boundary of Chacoan settlement in this region. It contained two separate areas of about 30 hectares (74 acres) with 25 Pueblo II period houses and 96 hectares (237 acres) with 20 late Pueblo II–early Pueblo III period houses. Another 12 Pueblo II period houses were clustered 2 km (1 mile) to the west. Aside from a few small sites on Chacra Mesa to the east, Chacoan settlement ceases,

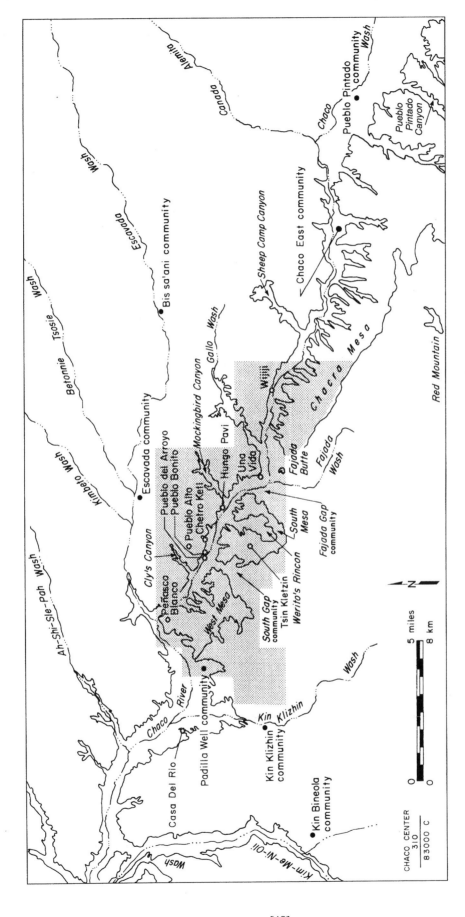

Figure 4.1. Important great houses and communities in the Chaco Canyon region. The shaded area is Chaco Culture National Historical Park.

[40]

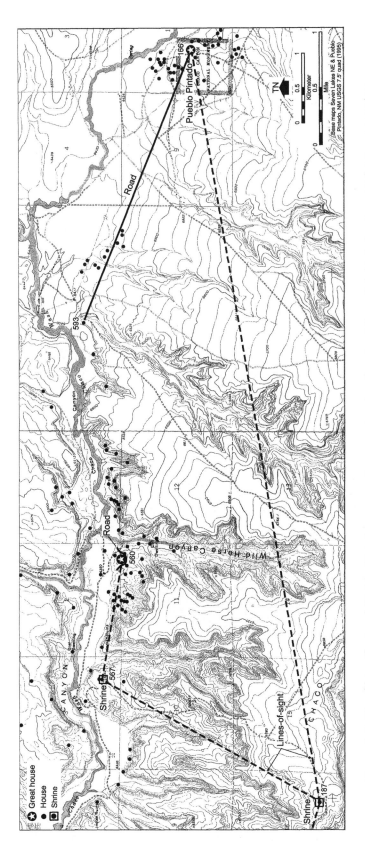

Figure 4.2. The Chaco East and Pueblo Pintado community areas showing the visual line-of-sight shrine-to-great house connections (dashed lines) and the visible prehistoric roads (solid lines). Stars mark the great houses and dots indicate the small-house sites.

although a sizable later settlement spanning the McElmo and Mesa Verde phases (A.D. 1175–1300) did exist on Chacra Mesa (Roney 1996) east of Pueblo Pintado Canyon. Chacoan occupation is unknown farther to the east, northeast, and north except for the nearby Bis sa'ani community on Escavada Wash (Doyel and others 1984).

In 1988, a third community was discovered in the 21.5-km (13.4-mile) stretch between Pueblo Pintado and Fajada Butte, located about 14 km (8.7 miles) east of Fajada Butte and 7.5 km (4.6 miles) west of Pueblo Pintado (Fig. 4.1). The setting of this East Community within the narrow confines of the canyon provides a good test case for appraisal of occupational permanency, an important aspect of community studies (Mills 1994; Nelson 1994). It also offers the potential for examining similarities and differences in occupation between two possibly different cultural groups: Chacoan and Mesa Verdean.

THE CHACO EAST COMMUNITY

Despite intense reconnaissance for Chacoan communities and great houses in the 1970s and 1980s, the East Community long avoided detection, although Homer Hastings, a former park superintendent, told Windes in 1989 that its location was once known by the Chaco park staff in the early 1950s. The greater community area, roughly 1,143 hectares (2,823 acres or 11.5 square kilometers), was inventoried over a period of seven years. In the past, this community would have been considered an "outlier," along with nearby Pueblo Pintado (Marshall and others 1979; Powers and others 1983), despite its location within Chaco Canyon (Fig. 4.2). It might also have been considered a "scion" community that lacked previous occupation, perhaps forming as a result of expansion from the lower canyon (Vivian 1990). This community may have also functioned as part of the "Chaco Halo," which some scholars believe supplied economic (agricultural) benefits to the lower canyon (Doyel and others 1984).

The Setting

At the East Community, Chaco Canyon is narrow, less than 560 m across at the bottom and 1 km (about a half mile) between cliffs, with an elevation difference of 550 m between the mesa tops and canyon bottom (Fig. 4.2). Unlike the canyon within the park, ridges suitable for occupation exist along both sides of the canyon. The main canyon floor is too alkaline for horticulture (Judd 1964: 230–231) and is dominated by greasewood and saltbrush, but a number of side drainages mark the potential arable lands for the area. In total, these side drainages provide approximately 138 hectares (341 acres) for run-off (*ak-chin*) farming along a 5-km (3–mile) stretch of Chaco Canyon. In the surrounding canyon walls, two prominent breaks that extend north and south directly from the heart of the community provide the greatest agricultural potential (83 hectares). Considering the amount of arable land and the necessary hectares per year per person needed (Adler 1994: 91; Cully and others 1982: 159), a maximum of about 100 to 150 people could have subsisted here.

It is these two side canyons that probably attracted the initial settlement. The one to the north leads out of Chaco Canyon to the plain and rolling hill country and a broad drainage basin; it has a potential farming area of about 25 hectares. To the south, Wild Horse Canyon extends 3 km (2 miles) back into Chacra Mesa with a potential area for run-off agriculture of 58 hectares, roughly half of the farming area for the entire community. It is 160 m wide at its mouth but, due to a gentle gradient, it is the only side canyon along Chaco Canyon that has not become incised. This canyon, we speculate, was literally the bread-basket for local farming activities. Runoff is slow along this side canyon, the soils are best for crops, and grasses within it are always lush in wet years. Even so, the limited lands would have provided sustainable food production for the community perhaps, but not enough for surplus exchange.

The pattern of observed rainfall at the East Community and Pueblo Pintado is similar to that in lower Chaco Canyon. However, Chacra Mesa offers the first sharp deflection for spring and summer storms crossing the San Juan Basin from the southwest. The pass (Pueblo Pintado Canyon) near Pueblo Pintado often draws summer storms in, keeping them localized for extended periods. The resultant updrafts affect the thermal dynamics, producing increased precipitation and cooler temperatures over Pueblo Pintado and the East Community. Isolated pockets of large conifers grow along the south side of the canyon near the East Community and,

as one continues to the east, centuries-old ponderosa pine, Douglas fir, and mountain juniper are visible in small stands that still thrive on Chacra Mesa. A unique stand of aspen is located in a side canyon in the community area, and broad-leaf yucca appears at its western extent.

Seven years (1992–1998) of rain gauge monitoring at the head and mouth of Wild Horse Canyon reveal that annual precipitation there is consistently higher (at 250 mm; nearly 10 inches) than the 218 mm (8.6 inches) of precipitation that falls in lower Chaco Canyon. During the growing season (May through September), rainfall is also comparatively more plentiful. However, the elevation there, which at 1,936 m is 75 m higher than Una Vida and Pueblo Bonito, generally means a shorter, riskier growing season, which is already risky enough in lower Chaco Canyon. We believe that the same marginal conditions impacted the Pueblo Pintado community, because being an additional 50 m higher (at 1,987 m), it received slightly more rainfall (264 mm) but was also colder. Accordingly, it is likely that the absence of house occupation even farther to the east was environmentally determined primarily by a growing season that was too short, although sociopolitical factors such as a cultural boundary separating early Gallina peoples to the east and northeast may have also played a role in limiting occupation. In either case, during all periods, small groups apparently used the area only ephemerally (Chapman and Biella 1980). Although there was dense habitation in the canyon at the East Community (and at nearby Pueblo Pintado), including Mesa Verdean, Chacoan occupation was practically absent on adjacent Chacra Mesa. At nearby Pueblo Pintado Canyon, which cuts through Chacra Mesa, however, an almost exclusively Mesa Verdean settlement existed on top of Chacra Mesa to the east, but no habitations have been found in the broad adjacent valley and Chaco drainage basin to the north.

Communication Links

Two tangible communication links tied the East Community to settlements up and down Chaco Canyon and beyond (Fig. 4.2). A prehistoric road ascended the canyon, looped around the East Community great house (29Mc 560) on the ridge and then descended back to the canyon bottom, a route that was also evident at other great houses (Fowler and Stein 1992; Stein and Lekson 1992). This road likely connected to another that extended west from nearby Pueblo Pintado and then dropped into the head of Chaco Canyon via a series of cut steps (29Mc 593). Twelve Red Mesa-era houses bordered the road just before it dropped into the canyon, affirming an initial 10th-century road use. An *herradura* (Nials and others 1987: 11–14), or road-side shrine, marked the descent into the canyon. This prehistoric road most likely followed the bottom of the canyon past the East Community all the way to Peñasco Blanco at the west end of Chaco Canyon, although no evidence for it now exists in the sediment-filled bottomlands.

A second set of features also demonstrates the linkage of the East Community with other Chacoan communities. In the 1970s, Hayes and Windes (1975) demonstrated that a visual network existed that tied odd, amorphous features located on high elevations to Chacoan great houses throughout the San Juan Basin and beyond. Location, shape, the lack of cultural material except for turquoise, and the presence of a covered stone bowl filled with turquoise at one site marked these as special-use shrines. Shrine 29Mc 187 was discovered in 1975 on top of Chacra Mesa near the East Community. It visually tied Pueblo Pintado to shrines near Fajada Butte (Fig. 4.2), a distance of 22 km (13.7 miles), and from there on to all the lower canyon's great houses. Located in 1994 on a bluff overlooking the East Community, 29Mc 567 visually connected with the East Community great house 1.7 km (a mile) distant. Subsequent fieldwork demonstrated that it and the Chacra Mesa shrine were visually connected across a maze of 3.7 km (2.3 miles) of irregular mesa topography; clearly the shrines were not randomly placed. Shrine wall-masonry style indicates an 11th- or 12th-century construction, although few cultural materials exist to properly date the shrines.

Dating the Community Sites

Because no excavations have been conducted, temporal placement of the East Community sites relies on architectural remains and ceramics. Architecture provides useful clues to the period of house construction and use, but mostly distinguishes the early sites from the later ones. Houses containing predominantly Red Mesa Black-on-white ceramic assemblages, representing the earliest periods of occupation, were built primarily of mud and spalls, a technique that contrasts sharply with later constructions of tabular and block-stone masonry.

Ceramics provide the primary temporal control for site use, and nearly 21,000 ceramics were field-tallied from a sampling area of 37,172 square meters for the 82 inventoried sites. We identified these ceramics (Table 4.1) using standard Chaco Center nomenclature (Toll and McKenna 1997; Windes and McKenna 1989). A slight majority of the material came from Red Mesa Black-on-white assemblages, dating between A.D. 875–900 and 1050. For finer control, this period was subdivided into 50-year intervals based on the relative frequency of sherds with wide neckbanding (900–950), narrow neckbanding (950–1000), and neck- and overall-indented corrugation (1000–1050). At some early sites, Red Mesa and wide neckbanded (and plain gray) pottery dominated, a combination probably dating to the late 800s and one that is not found at sites in lower Chaco Canyon. This early ceramic assemblage also appeared first in the Pueblo Pintado community.

Gallup Black-on-white, the ceramic hallmark for the Classic Bonito phase (A.D. 1050–1100), was widespread. On a few sites it numerically overwhelmed other painted types, a situation, again, practically nonexistent for small house sites in lower Chaco Canyon. However, many habitations were first occupied in the A.D. 900s and showed only minor occupation in the late 1000s, as indicated by their low frequencies of Gallup Black-on-white.

Surprisingly, ceramic evidence for habitation use into the early A.D. 1100s, marked by Chaco-McElmo Black-on-white and White Mountain Red Ware, was rare. If house and room counts are any indication, this period represented the smallest population density overall in the East Community. In contrast, occupation in lower Chaco Canyon during this period was common and may represent one of its most intensive periods of use (Windes 1987: 402–404), particularly around Pueblo Bonito. Early 1100s houses were also common at nearby Pueblo Pintado.

Finally, there was again a widespread occupation in the area in the late A.D. 1100s and 1200s in the form of reoccupied houses and new houses. The majority of these settlements appeared early in this interval, dominated by classic northern McElmo Black-on-white ceramics attributed to a late 1100s production. This intense late occupation is evident east of the East Community, shifting to the top of Chacra Mesa east of Pueblo Pintado Canyon (Roney 1996). Overall, classic Mesa Verde Black-on-white, marking occupation by 1250 or later, was rare.

Shifting House Locations Through Time

The small Basketmaker occupation in the East Community consisted of probably no more than a couple of pit houses, adjacent to shrine 29Mc 567. Subsequent

Table 4.1: Ceramics Tabulated from the Chaco East Community Sites

Ceramics	Temper: Sand (Cibola)	Trachyte (Chuska)	Sherd-andesite (Cibola–Mesa Verde)	No. of sherds	%
CULINARY POTTERY					
Lino Gray (rims, necks)	26	0	0	26	T
plain gray	2,658	89	45	2,792	13
wide neckbanded	363	3	9	375	2
narrow neckbanded	992	118	31	1,141	5
neck indented corrugated	233	38	20	291	1
indented corrugated	3,628	749	1,196	5,573	27
Pueblo II rims	58	14	133	205	1
Pueblo II–III rims	37	9	14	60	T
Pueblo III rims	42	4	39	85	T
Mummy Lake Gray*	37	0	6	43	T
unclassified rim fillets	257	45	44	346	2
Subtotals	*8,331*	*1,069*	*1,537*	*10,937*	*51*
PAINTED POTTERY	Bowls	Jars	Ladles		
Cibola White Ware:					
BM III/P I mineral or carbon	33	2	4	59	T
Red Mesa Black-on-white	893	946	91	1,930	9
Escavada/Puerco Black-on-white	171	209	8	388	2
Gallup Black-on-white	399	777	15	1,191	6
Chaco Black-on-white	17	71	0	88	T
Chaco–McElmo Black-on-white	111	48	1	160	1
Southern Cibola types	5	2	0	7	T
unclassified P II and P III mineral	489	854	30	1,373	7
unclassified white ware	647	1,884	23	2,554	12
Chuska White Ware:					
Tunicha/Newcomb/Burnham Black-on-white	10	16	0	26	T
Chuska/Toadlena Black-on-white	17	7	2	26	T
Nava Black-on-white	1	0	0	1	T
unclassified mineral or carbon	18	24	0	42	T
Tusayan/Little Colorado White Wares	38	10	0	48	T
Mesa Verde White Ware:					
Mancos Black-on-white	59	33	5	97	T
McElmo Black-on-white	168	53	6	227	1
McElmo/Mesa Verde Black-on-white	464	103	13	580	3
Mesa Verde Black-on-white	190	22	4	216	1
unclassified white ware	303	244	9	556	3
Smudged	22	1	0	23	T
White Mountain Red Ware:					
Puerco/Wingate Black-on-red	99	5	0	104	1
St. Johns Black-on-red and polychromes	19	0	1	20	T
other unclassified	92	7	0	99	1
San Juan Red Ware	28	5	1	34	T
Tsegi Orange Ware	34	16	1	51	T
Navajo/Historic	21	133	0	154	1
Subtotal	*4,348*	*5,494*	*212*	*10,054*	*48*
Total				20,991	99

NOTE: T = trace (less than 0.5%).
* Mummy Lake Gray is a Pueblo III Mesa Verde gray ware.

early Puebloan occupation of the area (Pueblo I period) appears to be nearly absent from the Pintado area down canyon to Shabik'eshchee Village (the type site for Basketmaker III; Roberts 1929), a distance of 16.5 km (10 miles). The first small houses (A.D. 875–900 to 950) in the East Community (n = 12; Fig. 4.3 *top*) mostly clustered in two groups on the south side of the canyon adjacent to the great house. The majority were built at the base of the talus or in the north-facing ledges, with all but two situated on the south side of the canyon. In contrast, the great house was constructed out in the open.

In the second period (A.D. 950–1000), 19 houses were concentrated in the same two areas and often directly on top of earlier habitations (Fig. 4.3 *bottom*). The two houses on the north side were also still used. By the end of the third period (A.D. 1000–1050; represented by Red Mesa ceramics), there were 28 houses in the same two areas (Fig. 4.4, *top*), but now none remained on the north side of the canyon. Twelve of these structures were close to the great house and seven more were clustered in an area just east of the great house. Both groups flanked the mouth of Wild Horse Canyon, the principal area for horticulture.

During the fourth period, which corresponds with the Classic Bonito phase (A.D. 1050–1100), 30 houses show some ceramic evidence of occupation or use (Fig. 4.4, *bottom*), with three built on the north side. Most of them were new structures built near the great house. During the early A.D. 1100s, 13 houses were occupied (Fig. 4.5, *top*). For the first time, there was significant building on the north side, mirroring the north-side construction occurring at this time in the Pueblo Bonito community of the lower canyon. Seven of the 13 houses of this period were on the north side of the canyon, with 4 houses on top of the mesas, representing the first mesa-top occupations. Nevertheless, there was a dramatic reduction in the number of houses from the previous period. Small house occupation in the immediate vicinity of the great house also disappeared.

During the last puebloan use of the area (A.D. 1175–1300), the 39 houses were more widely scattered than in any previous period except perhaps in the early A.D. 1100s (Fig. 4.5 *bottom*). Eleven of them were on the north side of the canyon, some representing the first use of south-facing cliff ledges for occupation. It is during this long period that the majority of houses revealed occupation or use, especially during the very late 1100s or early 1200s. There were also a number of cliff shelters built for storage, a strategy not utilized in earlier times.

Esoteric Features and Community Structures

Aside from the great house, the East Community does not reveal other esoteric features that might be construed as community structures. Tower kivas and great kivas are absent. In fact, there seems to be a conspicuous absence of formal great kivas in Chaco until about A.D. 1050. Interestingly, stone circles, esoteric structures that were always placed to be visibly linked with great kivas (Windes 1978), are unknown in the East Community area despite exhaustive searches for them.

From ceramic dating we know that the East Community great house (29Mc 560, Fig. 4.6) was used throughout the puebloan occupation, although architecture and middens reflect two dominant periods of use. The early, single-story architecture clearly marks the house as an A.D. 900s construction with about 25 rooms and a back wall 40 m long. The prominent midden accumulated in the late 1000s, similar to middens at most of the other canyon great houses (Windes 1987: 561–667), and probably reflects seasonal deposition like that noted for Pueblo Alto and Pueblo Bonito (Toll 1985; Windes 1987). Except for the plaza-enclosing wall built in the 1000s, there is no evidence of the later construction that was common at great houses in the lower canyon. Conversely, nearby Pueblo Pintado (29Mc 166) shows architectural and ceramic debris for construction in the 900s to early 1000s, but the towering structure remaining today appears to have been built only in the middle to late 1000s, as if it had become the new focal point for the area. Pueblo Pintado also yielded massive, late 1000s midden deposits.

Community Integration

Aside from ties to the outside world, two factors seem to have drawn the small houses and great house together: visibility and distance from the small houses to the great house. Most habitations within the main community area were built with line-of-sight visibility to the great house. The visual connection within 2 km (1.2 miles) of the great house was particularly strong during the Chacoan occupation before A.D. 1000 (93% of 14 houses) but then declined, reaching its lowest frequency after 1175 (77% of 30 houses), when there was a concerted expansion to the north side of the canyon. Considering the irregular and broken topography along the south side of the canyon where the majority of houses were located, it is likely that the intervisibility

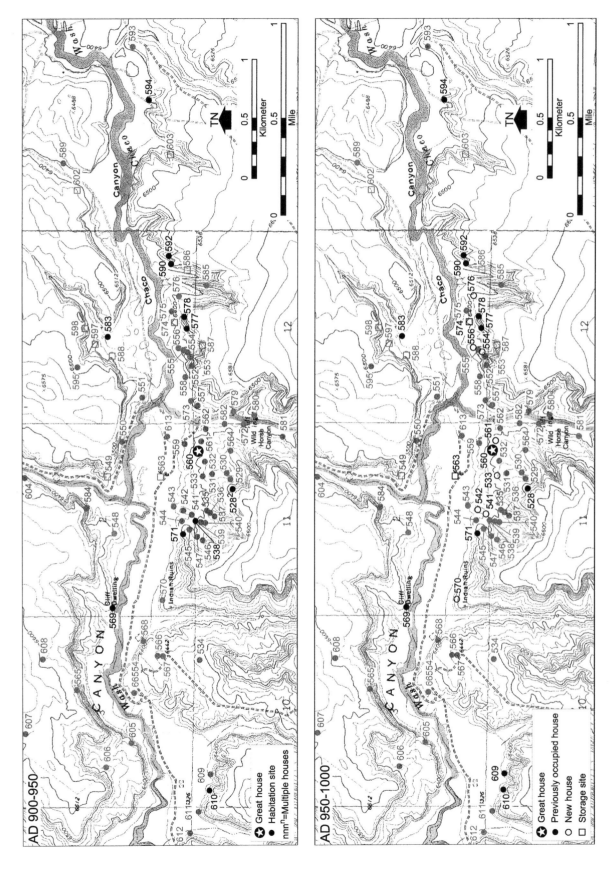

Figure 4.3. The Chaco East Community: initial occupations in the A.D. 900–950 period (*top*) and 950–1000 period (*bottom*).

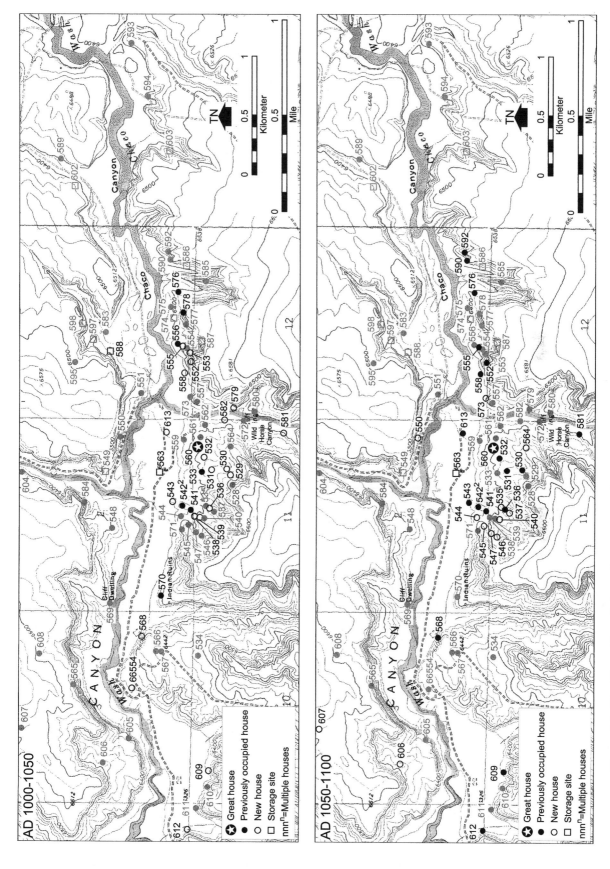

Figure 4.4. The Chaco East Community: house occupations in the A.D. 1000–1050 period (*top*) and 1050–1100 period (*bottom*).

[47]

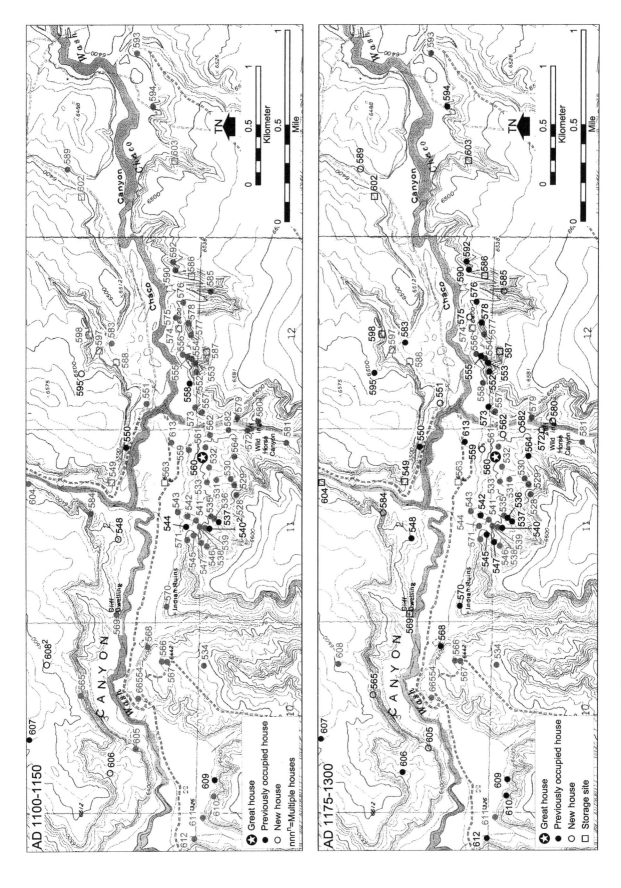

Figure 4.5. The Chaco East Community: house occupations in the A.D. 1100–1150 period (*top*) and 1175–1300 period (*bottom*).

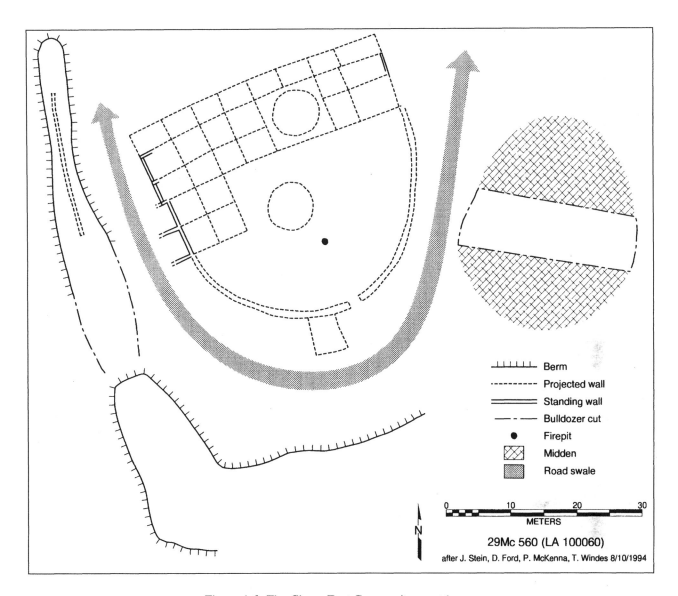

Figure 4.6. The Chaco East Community great house.

was intentional. For instance, 29Mc 607 on the high north horizon, first occupied in the late 1000s, is uniquely positioned to observe the contemporary Bis sa'ani great house 9.8 km (6.1 miles) to the north, Pueblo Pintado 9.5 km (5.9 miles) to the east, and the East Community great house 2.8 km (1.7 miles) to the southeast. The difference between the Chacoan and Mesa Verdean visual links, however, is not statistically significant unless an unreasonably wider area is considered.

Community integration, as a possible measure of social and political control, might also be inferred by the distance between small houses and the great house. Tight integration would be indicated by the placement of every house relatively close to the great house,

whereas loose integration would be suggested by a more widely scattered population. We might expect that through time, new house locations would have been forced farther away from the great house since the closer, more ideal areas had already been taken, thereby increasing variability in the overall spacing and increasing distances through time. Yet, mean spatial distance between those small houses within 2 km of the great house does not vary much temporally (ranging from 722 m to 852 m for different periods). Consideration of a larger area, however, shows a dramatic increase after A.D. 1100. Unfortunately, the varied landscape and lack of survey makes use of a perimeter greater than 2 km unrealistic.

After the hiatus in the mid-A.D. 1100s, the last occupants in the area (Mesa Verdean) would have had unlimited access to house locations, but they chose to reoccupy many of the older sites, including the great house, and to build in areas farther removed from the great house. There was a clear break between the occupations, as observed in the ceramics and by the fact that the new late domiciles were built over earlier ones. Both visibility to the great house and small-house spacing patterns of the late occupation differed from earlier periods but were difficult to statistically test reliably. It is clear, however, that the late occupation reflected a greater preference for both sides of Chaco Canyon rather than the dominant south side preferred by Chaco-era inhabitants. In the late period there was also a marked shift to the use of cliff ledges for habitation and isolated storage rooms.

SETTLEMENT PERMANENCY

The East Community illustrates a radical departure from the perception of Chaco as a permanently settled landscape. The nature of community permanency is an important one (Mills 1994; Nelson 1994), for it impacts models that consider scarce resources, competition, and the distribution of power as critical variables for understanding Chacoan communities. Because of the constricted nature of the canyon chosen for habitation, the response to the environment and topography for house placement provides important clues and a good test case to determine the kinds of occupation, intermittent or year-round, during the life of the community. The setting of the East Community brings these variables into sharp contrast, whereas houses in wide-open areas are generally less affected by the topography and related solar exposure. Three factors of house construction are pertinent to shedding light on this behavior: the landform, the house orientation, and the skyline.

Canyon Landform

Despite the narrow confines of the canyon, ample land was available for any type of seasonal or year-round settlement. Settlement around Fajada Butte and Pueblo Bonito was concentrated in the side rincons and the open gaps through Chacra Mesa. In the East Community, it was located primarily along the many ridges and talus slopes within the main canyon, where the inhabitants chose a variety of topographical locales. Houses were situated along the north side of the canyon on the flats, ridges, and in the cliffs, receiving the maximum advantage of winter sunlight and some shading in the summer. Houses on the south side received full summer sunlight but had reduced exposure during the winter when the cliffs behind them shortened the day. In fact, a number of habitations were built at the base or within the north-facing cliffs and ledges, ensuring reduced winter sun. These shaded locations were also favored for storage facilities.

House Orientation

House orientation is critical for maximizing or minimizing the amount of sunlight received (Olgyay 1963). Ideally, year-round houses are best sited due south (180° ± 30°) with the living quarters positioned on the south side (Schepp and Hastie 1985: 60; Total Environmental Action and Los Alamos National Laboratory 1984: 20–21). Many Chacoan houses were so oriented, with 54 percent of the contemporary houses in the nearby Fajada Gap community, down canyon, placed exactly within this quadrant (Windes 1993a: 378). This position maximized solar gain during the coldest season, but minimized wall exposure during the hottest season. In addition, the use of adobe and stone in wall construction provided 25 to 30 percent of the annual interior heating needs, boosting the room temperature between 2° and 5° (Johnson 1987). Considering the climate in Chaco for the past 63 years of record, where the average coldest day of the year is –14°F, with lows of –37°F (twice) and –38°F recorded since 1960 (Windes 1993a, Table 2.2 footnote), and the hottest day is 99°F, house orientation and attention to the skyline must have been major considerations for occupation.

Cliff houses built facing south maximized the winter solar advantage, the passive solar exposure of the heated surrounding rock, and the shade provided against the high summer sun, perfect for year-long occupation (Christenson 1991; Harper 1993). The Gallo Cliff Ruin in the Chaco campground perfectly illustrates this strategy, where the winter sun strikes directly into the site at sunrise, a strategy also common to Tsegi-phase Kayenta cliff occupation (Dean 1969: 22). The majority of room blocks at present-day pueblos such as Acoma (Knowles 1974) and most others (Ortiz 1979; Stubbs 1950) face south, with the exception of the southeast-facing Hopi villages.

Seasonal occupations (except for winter) impose a different strategy. An east-facing position (90° ± 30°) maximizes the early-morning sunrise in the warmer months but minimizes the heat to the long-axis of the house during the hotter hours. An east-facing position was popular down the canyon in the Fajada Gap community (45% of the houses). Although there is a common perception that prehistoric Puebloan houses were oriented haphazardly along an arc between east and south, this was far from true in Chaco Canyon (Windes 1993a: 378–382).

In the East Community, we calculated house orientations by taking an angle 90° from the house's back wall alignment toward the midden and pit structure area; we considered one-room and two-room units as field houses and did not include them in this study. The East Community house orientations revealed a wide selection of choices (Fig. 4.7), except in the southwest quadrant where there were no houses. Nearly half of the houses were oriented roughly east, followed by south, southeast, and north orientations, with each representing 15 to 17 percent of the sample. A mere four houses (4%) faced west or northwest. Only 17 percent faced south, and at best 34 percent (including southeast-facing houses) were positioned (121°–225°) for maximum winter solar advantages.

Surprisingly, many houses faced north. This is no mistake, for all were built against the canyon's north-facing cliffs, ledges, and talus slopes. Clearly, the occupation comfort-zone in these locales precluded permanent (including winter) occupation (Harper 1993). They would also certainly have been hot places for summer use, so they likely represent spring or fall occupations instead. It is these locales that were heavily favored by the majority of the initial house builders in the late A.D. 800s or early 900s (Fig. 4.3, *top*). Through time, the basic house orientation was *not* south facing, although there was a trend toward an increased southern orientation. But even during the last period of occupation, the majority of the ten new houses built by Mesa Verdeans faced east (60%), with only two facing south (20%).

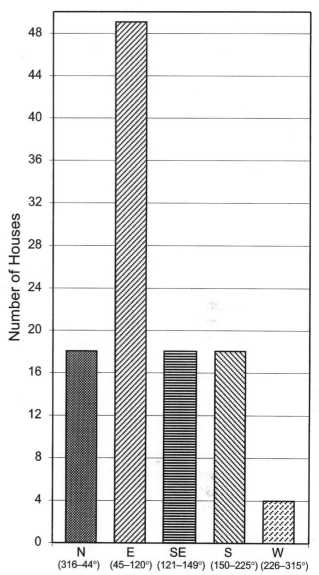

Figure 4.7. House orientation in degrees for the Chaco East Community sites.

The Skyline

Skyline limitations considerably influenced the impact of solar radiation on a house, particularly those skylines shaped by the cliffs and mesas bordering the East Community. Skylines for all habitations were mapped, and the amount of radiant energy available per house by season was calculated in British Thermal Units (BTUs) per square foot. The amount of exposure is critical for increased or decreased interior house temperatures. Figures 4.8 and 4.9 illustrate the departures

from the ideal, which here is considered to be a south-facing house without skyline obstructions. For example, a south-facing Mesa Verdean habitation (29Mc 565) and the great house (29Mc 560) were ideal, whereas those structures facing to the east with no skyline restrictions and to the north were less than ideal (Fig. 4.8). Overall, through time, the general character of the houses in the community was substantially below ideal for fall and winter solar advantages and at or above ideal for the spring and summer, a time optimal for farming.

COMMUNITY DYNAMICS

House location and orientation denote different occupational strategies for the people utilizing the area. If south-facing houses were inhabited all year and others were seasonal, then room counts help to quantify the permanent versus seasonal populations. Southeast-facing houses pose a problem to a clean dichotomy, so their rooms were added as potential counts to both group options (Fig. 4.10). Through time, estimated seasonal room counts always exceeded permanent ones (excluding southeast-facing houses), except in the early A.D. 1100s, when estimates are nearly equal. In the 1175 to 1300 period, seasonal rooms outnumber permanent rooms by nearly three to one. Although the indeterminate southeast-facing rooms could tip the balance, the general trend is that the majority of rooms were associated with seasonally oriented houses, except between 1050 and 1150, when the Chacoan network might be considered the most strongly integrated.

It was expected that permanently occupied houses would exhibit more rooms for a fuller range of activities and additional storage than their seasonal counterparts. On the average, permanent, south-facing houses were larger than seasonal ones, with a steady increase in room numbers through time (Tables 4.2, 4.3). Generally, southeast-facing houses tended to have more rooms than seasonal houses and their average number of rooms was similar to that of permanent houses; on this basis they might therefore also be considered year-round houses. This relationship was less evident, however, by the late A.D. 1000s, when southeast-facing houses were approximately the same size as seasonal houses. After 1175, the two southeast-facing houses contained fewer than five rooms each, a number smaller than in contemporary permanent and seasonal houses. The largest houses (14 to 35 rooms), however, did not generally meet the criterion of permanent as defined by orientation: five faced south, two southeast, and nine east (of the last, eight were oriented tightly between 97° and 108°). Additionally, the locations for permanent, south-facing houses were not random. Of the 16, half (29Mc 536, 541 through 547) were clustered next to each other along three adjacent ridges just west of the great house. The remainder were scattered, but the majority (five) of these were located on the north side of the canyon, where permanent occupation would have been more favorable.

T tests comparing the average number of rooms for various group house orientations of inferred seasonality were not conclusive for differences at the .05 level of

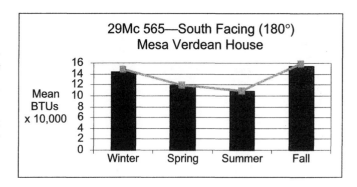

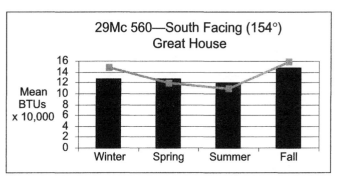

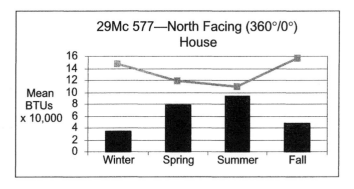

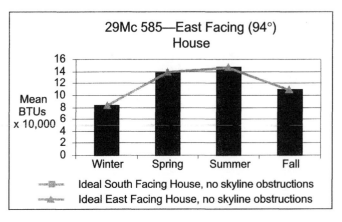

Figure 4.8. The effects of solar radiation in mean BTUs per square foot on a vertical wall for house examples in the Chaco East Community. Gray line represents an ideal setting for a house facing due south (180°) or due east (90°), without skyline obstructions.

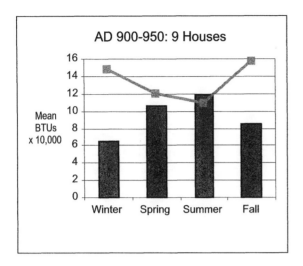

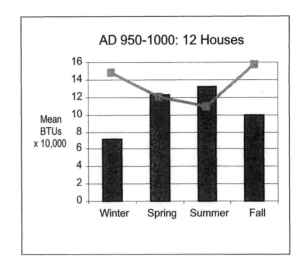

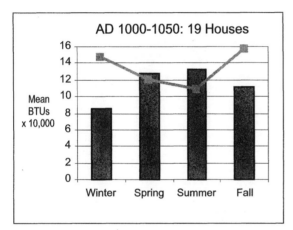

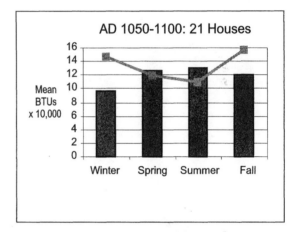

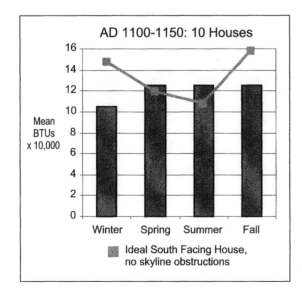

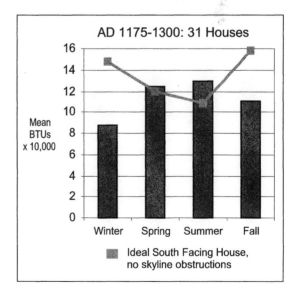

Figure 4.9. The effects of solar radiation in mean BTUs per square foot
on a vertical wall for houses through time in the Chaco East Community.
Gray line represents an ideal setting for a house facing due south (180°),
without skyline obstructions, representing a year-round occupation.

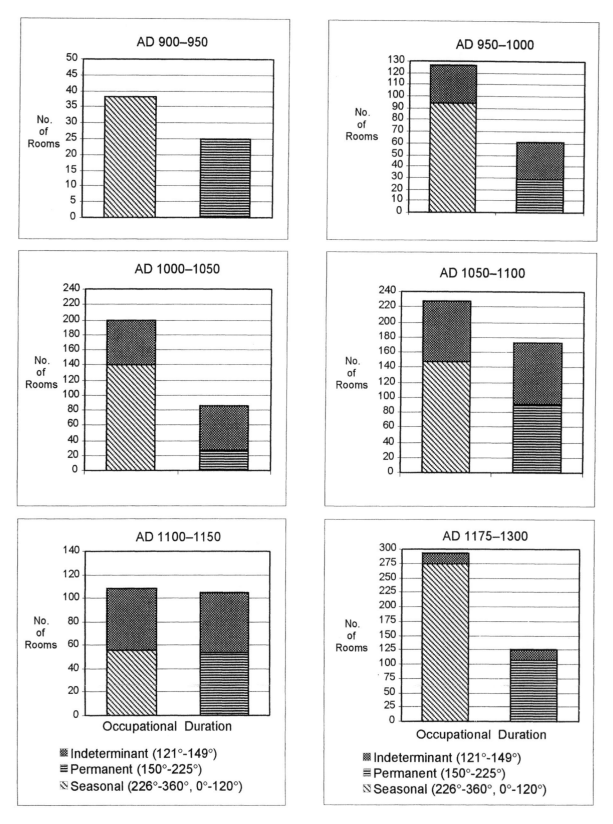

Figure 4.10. Occupational duration of house rooms in the Chaco East Community by period, A.D. 900–1300, based on house orientation. If the indeterminant southeast-facing rooms belonged solely to either the seasonal or permanent option, it could change conclusions regarding community permanence in some cases.

Table 4.2. Frequency of Houses with Three Rooms or More in the Chaco East Community

No. of Rooms	3	4	5	6	7	8	9	10	11	12	13	14	15	17	18	20	23	24	25	35
No. of Houses	8	12	4	14	6	3	3	3	4	6	1	8	3	1	1	2	1	1	3	1

Table 4.3. Orientation of Houses with Three Rooms or More in the Chaco East Community

Orientation Ceramic Assemblage	No. of Houses	Mean No. of Rooms	Standard Deviation	Coefficient of Variation	Min.–max. No. of Rooms
Orientation: 226°–0–120°					
Red Mesa (A.D. 900–1050)	12	5.7	3.7	66	3–17
Gallup (A.D. 1050–1100)	11	10.5	6.2	59	4–25
Chaco-McElmo (A.D. 1100–1150)	4	11.5	9.0	78	3–23
Mesa Verde (A.D. 1175–1300)	21	9.5	5.7	60	3–25
Orientation: 121°–149°					
Red Mesa (A.D. 900–1050)	3	9.7	2.1	22	8–12
Gallup (A.D. 1050–1100)	5	11.4	5.2	46	6–20
Chaco-McElmo (A.D. 1100–1150)	4	13.0	10.5	81	4–24
Mesa Verde (A.D. 1175–1300)	2	3.5	0.7	20	3–4
Orientation: 150°–225°					
Red Mesa (A.D. 900–1050)	2	14.5	14.8	102	4–25
Gallup (A.D. 1050–1100)	4	11.3	1.9	17	10–14
Chaco-McElmo (A.D. 1100–1150)	3	17.7	15.1	86	7–35
Mesa Verde (A.D. 1175–1300)	8	8.3	4.0	48	3–14

T Test

Number; Mean; Standard Deviation	50; 8.94; 5.83	14; 10.35; 6.67	17; 11.35; 7.98
House Orientation	226°–0–120° (W, N, E) Seasonal?	121°–149° (SE) Permanent?	150°–225° (S) Permanent
226°–0–120° (W–N–E)		$p_1 = 0.222$	$p_1 = 0.095$
121°–149° (SE)	$p_1 = 0.222$		$p_1 = 0.360$
150°–225° (S)	$p_1 = 0.095$	$p_1 = 0.360$	

NOTE: For the *t* test, the equal variances null hypothesis was true, thus equal variances SAS PROC TTEST was used. Direction of the significant difference is predicted (permanent houses have more rooms), therefore one-tail probability (p_1) values were appropriate.

significance (Table 4.3). Similar results were obtained when southeast-facing and south-facing houses were combined to compare with the remainder of the sample. Nevertheless, the trend for different house sizes between the two groups based on orientation approached significance ($p = 0.095$), with the difference occurring by chance alone at just 9.5 percent. Least significant difference *t* tests (which control for comparison-wise error rates) for the series of *t* tests run for orientation and time were not significant for differences in house size by orientation and through time based on ceramic assemblages.

In summary, landform selection, house orientation, and the impact of skylines strongly reflect a population that either ignored the solar advantages for its households or one that did not spend the fall and winter in residence. Although some year-round residence is undeniable, the majority of houses appear to have served as part-time residences in the spring and summer. It would be worthwhile to see if house cultural materials are indicative of these same differences (Monks 1981), although an architectural setting makes the strongest case for or against occupational permanency (Harper 1993: 79–93).

A number of A.D. 900s-1000s east-facing houses were excavated in the Fajada Gap community down canyon, but seasonal indicators, particularly of botanical and faunal remains, were inconclusive. Although evidence for spring and summer activities was common, it was not possible to determine a specific winter occupation at these sites. Faunal remains at one site, however, seemed predominantly from warm weather hunting (Gillespie 1993: 392) and, therefore, raised the possibility of seasonal occupation. Burial remains from Gillespie's site and an east-facing one nearby were not normally distributed by age and sex, considering the lengthy house occupations (Windes 1993c: 400-401); perhaps seasonal occupations also explain these discrepancies.

COMMUNITY ORIGINS

If the people in the East Community were highly mobile, then where did they come from and where did they go? Both at Pueblo Pintado and the East Community, the ceramic and chipped stone assemblages are not the same as those observed in the main lower canyon or, for that matter, in any areas beyond the canyon. These classes of artifacts also differ between these two communities. An examination of sherds and chipped stone at 4 of the 12 earliest East Community house sites reveals few ties beyond the local vicinity (Table 4.4). For instance, imported Chuska (trachyte-tempered) and Red Mesa Valley (chalcedonic-tempered) ceramics were far less prevalent in the local assemblages than in down-canyon communities (Toll and McKenna 1997: 89–90, 94–96, Table 2.38), where ties to the west and south appear to have been strong. Pottery of northern origins, exhibiting crushed igneous rock temper from the north, was also rare at the early East Community houses but relatively common in early houses at Pueblo Pintado.

Chipped stone in the East Community reveals only trace amounts of the exotic material prevalent at down-canyon sites (see Cameron 1997a); again, ties beyond the local area seem to have been tenuous. We recently studied lithics from two communities of Pueblo I sites 10 km (6 miles) south of Chaco Canyon (at the head of Kin Klizhin Wash and at the south fork of Fajada Wash). Evidence of Pueblo I settlement in and around Chaco is sparse, and these two communities may represent areas of origin of the inhabitants who founded the Pintado and East communities. In contrast with the Pintado and East communities, however, these lithics showed high frequencies (20% to 40%) of an exotic yellow-spotted chert originating in the Zuni Mountains

(LeTourneau 1997), suggesting strong southern origins or ties instead. Evidence of this southern link is practically nonexistent in the Pintado and East communities. Analyses of the wood used in construction at Pueblo Pintado also indicate an absence of ties to the timber resources used in lower canyon sites; instead, the use of local species was common for building the Pueblo Pintado great house.

Thus, there is no clear origin for the populations that first inhabited the East and Pintado communities, but it is apparent that their resource acquisition was different and primarily local compared to down-canyon communities. There were no occupations to the east or north that might have contributed to upper-canyon populations, unless their rise can be attributed to the collapse of the great Pueblo I communities north of the San Juan River (Wilshusen and Ortman 1999), a possibility that is strongest for the early occupation at Pueblo Pintado.

REINTERPRETING COMMUNITIES IN CHACO CANYON

The East Community represents one of the later Anasazi seasonal expansions into marginal areas in the Chaco region, a pattern that has been noted as early as Basketmaker III times with the huge pit house settlements at Shabik'eshchee Village and near Peñasco Blanco (Wills and Windes 1989). The East Community area was home to an early small Basketmaker settlement, perhaps as a seasonal venture, but then was unoccupied for several centuries afterward. Forces driving the latest colonization may have stemmed from a number of factors, including socioeconomic and political conditions around the periphery of the San Juan Basin, the vastly improved environment, and, perhaps, the wide-scale abandonment of much of the northern San Juan during late Pueblo I times (Wilshusen and Ortman 1999).

Specific explanatory "push-pull" factors (Cameron 1995: 114–115) that promoted movements in and out of the area are difficult to pinpoint without first clearly identifying the possible areas of population origin. Although the wetter A.D. 900s allowed horticultural expansion into more marginal areas, it is difficult to believe that many factors stimulating migration (like depletion of resources and demographic pressures) would have had an effect on the relatively small Pueblo I populations located along the peripheries of the San Juan Basin where resources were more abundant. These factors, however, would have been relevant to populations from the interior of the basin and perhaps beyond the peripheries. The early Basketmaker settlement may

Table 4.4. Exotic Ceramic and Chipped Stone Materials Represented at Early Small Houses, A.D. 875–925

East Community[1] Sites 29Mc:	528	569	577	578	Totals	%
CERAMICS[2]						
Temper in wide neckbanded:						
unclassified sand (presumably local)	21	21	11	9	62	30.4
chalcedonic sand (exotic–nonlocal)	0	2	1	0	3	1.5
trachyte (exotic–nonlocal)	1	2	0	1	4	1.9
igneous (exotic–nonlocal)	1	1	0	0	2	1.0
Temper in Early Red Mesa Black-on-white:						
sherd-unclassified sand (presumably local)	40	30	23	28	121	59.3
chalcedonic sand (exotic–nonlocal)	0	1	0	2	3	1.5
trachyte (exotic–nonlocal)	0	4	0	1	5	2.5
igneous (exotic–nonlocal)	1	2	0	1	4	1.9
Sample Totals	*64*	*63*	*35*	*42*	*204*	*100.0*
CHIPPED STONE						
Morrison Formation chert (1040)	0	0	0	0	0	0.0
Zuni Mt. spotted-yellow chert (1072)	1	0	0	0	1	0.2
Washington Pass chert (1080)	0	0	0	0	0	0.0
obsidian (3500)	0	0	1	0	1	0.2
quartzose gray chert (2221)	0	3	0	0	3	0.5
Site Totals	*219*	*241*	*46*	*55*	*561*	

Pueblo Pintado[1] Sites 29Mc:	765	766	769	770	Totals	%
CERAMICS[2]						
Temper in wide neckbanded:						
sherd-unclassified sand (presumably local)	0	0	0	2	2	0.5
unclassified sand (presumably local)	46	15	22	43	126	30.1
chalcedonic sand (exotic–nonlocal)	2	1	1	1	5	1.2
trachyte (exotic–nonlocal)	1	0	0	0	1	0.2
igneous (exotic–nonlocal)	3	0	1	1	5	1.2
Temper in Kiatuthlanna/Early Red Mesa Black-on-white:						
sherd-unclassified sand (presumably local)	114	30	44	41	229	54.8
chalcedonic sand (exotic–nonlocal)	4	2	1	3	10	2.4
trachyte (exotic–nonlocal)	4	0	1	0	5	1.2
igneous (exotic–nonlocal)	20	6	7	2	35	8.4
Sample Totals	*194*	*54*	*77*	*93*	*418*	*100.0*
CHIPPED STONE						
Morrison Formation chert (1040)	0	0	0	0	0	0.0
Zuni Mt. spotted-yellow chert (1072)	0	0	3	0	3	0.2
Washington Pass chert (1080)	0	0	0	0	0	0.0
obsidian (3500)	0	3	0	2	5	0.3
quartzose gray chert (2221)	4	8	33	17	62	4.0
Sample Totals[3]	*140*	*310*	*337*	*776*	*1563*	

NOTE: Ceramics examined with 20x microscope; totals may differ from Table 4.1. Chipped stone material codes after Warren 1979.
Sources of exotics
   Eastern or southeastern San Juan Basin: obsidian (3500) from the Jemez Mts. or Mt. Taylor.
   Southern San Juan Basin: chalcedonic temper; cherts from the Zuni Mts. (1072) and the Morrison Formation (1040).
   Western San Juan Basin: trachyte temper; cherts from Washington (Nabona) Pass (1080) and the Morrison Formation (1040).
   Northern San Juan Basin: igneous temper.
   Quartzose gray chert (2221) is locally abundant only at nearby Pueblo Pintado community sites and to the north.
1. East Community, 4 of 12 earliest house sites sampled. Pueblo Pintado, 4 of 6 earliest house sites sampled.
2. Sherd sample totals represent about 40% of wide neckbanded and 15% of Kiatuthlanna/Early Red Mesa Black-on-white sherds on the surface of the 4 East Community and 4 Pueblo Pintado Community house sites.
3. Chipped stone samples represent about 50% of all surface chipped stone at sites 769, 770; 100% at site 766; 9% at site 765.

have established familiarity and use-rights (Cameron 1995: 111; Schlegel 1992) for groups that later returned for a more substantial occupation. Nevertheless, mobility is necessary for a successful horticultural adaptation in the northern Southwest (Cameron 1995: 112–113; Lekson 1995: 102–103; Nelson 1994: 4); from a Native American perspective, it is simply a necessity of life (Naranjo 1995).

The wide extent of the expansion throughout the San Juan Basin and beyond in the A.D. 900s may support a peer-polity model of organization (Kintigh 1994; Renfrew and Cherry 1986). Certainly at this time, Chaco Canyon was not a "center" and the many communities were not "outliers," at least not to Chaco Canyon. Roads and communication shrines served to link communities and also assisted the regional mobility of peoples across the San Juan Basin. Whether these roads were formal or not beyond the community areas (Kantner 1997; Roney 1992) does not negate their value as transportation or communication routes to the greater region. Roads, or, perhaps more properly "routes," could be construed as signs of centralized power or, conversely, of independence (Vivian 1997b: 58–59) for the many Chacoan communities. Turquoise craft activities were widespread in small houses in many, if not all, the communities, but the lack of caches suggests that centralized control of distribution was not important and that the turquoise may have been associated with local ritual activities.

Clearly, something did occur in the lower canyon to set Chaco Canyon apart from the rest of the San Juan Basin by the middle and late A.D. 1000s. This change was mirrored to some degree in the East Community; there were more houses through time, but in the 1000s houses proliferated, particularly near the great house. Extensive refuse deposits containing some ceramics and lithics revealing ties to the west and south accumulated at the great house, a sign of intermittent, perhaps ritual, activity, although there was little outward evidence of the massive building modifications that accompanied this intensity of trash deposition elsewhere. Line-of-sight connections and house spacing seemingly indicate close integration of the small-house community with the great house, although by the early 1100s, there was a notable decline in occupied houses. Breaking tradition, there was also a major expansion to the north side of the canyon and a dissipation of small houses away from the great house. This shift to the north side of the wash after 1100 set a trend that lasted until the area was deserted by 1300, a significant departure from earlier house location preference ($\chi^2 = 5.34$, $\rho = 0.02$, df = 1, n = 92).

Whether the last, Mesa Verdean, occupation reflected continuity of the Chacoan tradition or not is still open to debate (Fowler and Stein 1992; McKenna and Toll 1992; Stein and Lekson 1992; Wilcox 1996; Windes 1997). Surface evidence suggests a temporal break in occupation, and the population was more scattered. Much of the occupation was now on the north side, although this pattern was not quite statistically significant ($\chi^2 = 2.90$, $\rho = 0.08$, df = 1, n = 90) between the two groups with a Chi-square test unless early A.D. 1100s houses were excluded. Line-of-sight connections to the great house also seem to have been less relevant than during Chacoan times. The prevalent reuse of earlier house sites, however, complicates the picture and may or may not imply cultural continuity. A seasonal use of the area still predominated, although this might be linked to the occupation on top of Chacra Mesa to the east of Pueblo Pintado Canyon. Overall, there is much in common between the East Community's late occupation and the coeval occupation down the canyon, including the reuse of great houses and small houses (Windes 1997). Nevertheless, the contrast between the two areas is stark in terms of material acquisition sources except for turquoise.

This focus on community dynamics emphasizes the duration of house occupation, spatial and visible relationships to the great house, and house spatial distribution through time. It shows that perhaps many of the community dynamics were seasonal, with a large part of the community shifting residence to outside the canyon, a possibility that may also characterize other communities in Chaco Canyon and a basic strategy for many historic western Pueblos (Nelson 1994: 4). The concept of "outliers" (Marshall and others 1979; Powers and others 1983) should accordingly be reevaluated, along with the role of the lower canyon as the center of a hypothesized Chaco "system" (Grebinger 1973; Kintigh 1994; Sebastian 1992; Vivian 1990) or the focus of "the Big Idea" (Stein and Lekson 1992: 87–92).

The East and Pueblo Pintado communities must be considered residential settlements lacking enough people for internal population reproduction (Mahoney, this volume). Only by grouping the separate communities in Chaco Canyon could an overall sustainable community be maintained, *if* mobility was not an option. Otherwise, the importance of the peripheries of the San Juan Basin must be considered when explaining Chaco organization, particularly if large masses of people were shifting residence seasonally. In part, some of this movement in the late A.D. 1000s may be explained by influxes of people for ritual activities (Judge 1989;

Renfrew 1999; Toll 1985), at least at the great houses, but the entire question of mobility is much more complicated (Saitta 1994), particularly for the surrounding communities. Mobile populations increase the difficulty of applying explanatory models that rely on the expansion of authority, power, and leadership by local elites (Kantner 1996a; Sebastian 1992), because the basis of control cannot be anchored to local plots of land and resources. This research supports notions of disparate groups residing or connected to Chaco (Kantner 1996a; Renfrew 1999; Vivian 1990), but the identity of and origins of these groups is unclear, as are the forces that prompted the migrations.

Although the East Community did reveal some connections to the greater region, archaeological manifestations of integrative facilities within the community were centered on the great house. The role of the great house in the community was undoubtedly important and appears to be coeval with the first small-house use of the East Community area. At least initially, the great house was probably linked to storage and community integration. The primary use of the area must have been agricultural with local wild plant and faunal resources being of secondary importance. By the mid-to-late A.D. 1000s, however, open access to the great house plaza was restricted by a masonry wall. The main midden area, resembling others studied in downtown Chaco (Toll 1985), may have received periodic deposition, with the great house now being the focus of increased ritual activity (Renfrew 1999). Whether local inhabitants or outsiders or both were responsible for the shift in func-

tions at great houses is unknown, but this research does support other findings (Van Dyke 1999b) that emphasize the surprising heterogenous nature of Chacoan great houses and their associated communities. Only more intensive study can hope to reveal the changing complexities of these great house communities and their role in the overall Chacoan settlement pattern.

Acknowledgments

We wish to thank the many people who helped with the fieldwork and analytical parts of this project. First and foremost are the many sessions of Sierra Club volunteers, led by Bonnie Sharpe and her assistants, Cheryl Srnka, Jim Ilchuck, Tom Meehan, John Fries, Chuck Buck, and Reid Earls, III; they accomplished prodigious amounts of fieldwork. Bonnie Sharpe, in particular, is recognized for organizing and running the crews every year. We also extend appreciation to Bill Doleman for his statistical expertise; to Karen Hunt, Erik Niemeyer, and Ron Stauber for graphics production and assistance; and to Jeremy Moss and Randi Gladwell for field assistance at Pueblo Pintado. Peter McKenna and Eric Blinman did the microscopic analysis of the ceramic temper sample. Brian Johnson, P.E., computed the solar data used for this report. Finally, without the able assistance of Art Ireland, Ron Brown, John Schelberg, and Connor Windes, this community would not have been rediscovered in 1988.

Part 2

The Relationship Between
Great House Communities
and Chaco Canyon

Figure Part 2. Computer reconstruction of the Edge of the Cedars
great house positioned on the site in southeastern Utah.
(Photograph by Winston Hurst, reconstruction by John Kantner)

CHAPTER FIVE

Chaco Outlier or Backwoods Pretender?
A Provincial Great House at Edge of the Cedars Ruin, Utah

Winston B. Hurst

The period of culture history termed "Pueblo II" by archaeologists (about A.D. 900–1150) witnessed cultural developments of profound and fundamental significance in the development of the so-called "Anasazi" cultures of the American Southwest. These developments, often subsumed under the term "Chacoan Phenomenon" (Irwin-Williams 1972), are archaeologically manifest in the rise of large and spectacular architectural complexes ("great houses") in the Chaco Canyon and Aztec areas of New Mexico's San Juan Basin and similar but generally smaller great houses or "outliers" scattered around the basin and beyond. Wherever they occur, great houses are commonly associated with surrounding communities of dispersed, smaller, residential structures, extraordinarily large pit structures ("great kivas"), and formally constructed "roads" ("great trails" might be a more apt term for these features) that extend sometimes for kilometers or tens of kilometers from the great houses (Crown and Judge 1991; Kincaid 1983; Lekson 1984; Lekson and others 1988; Marshall and others 1979; Powers and others 1983; Sebastian 1992; Vivian 1990; and a host of other references cited therein).

Questions concerning the functions of these "great" features and their relationships to both their associated communities and to the larger great houses of the Chaco-Aztec core have become a major focus of discourse in southwestern American archaeology. It is increasingly apparent that the rise and demise of the Chaco centers and contemporaneous outlying communities were developments of such salient importance that understanding them is key to understanding much of puebloan culture history, both leading up to and following the Chacoan florescence (Adler 1996b; Lekson 1996a, 1996b; Lekson and Cameron 1995). Intelligent investigation of these questions is dependent on the accumulation of fundamental data regarding the identification and distribution of great features and associated communities: How do we identify them, where do they occur, where do they not occur, and what patterned variability can we recognize among them both through time and across space?

This chapter contributes in a small way to that dialogue by focusing on Edge of the Cedars pueblo (42SA700), a late Pueblo II period ruin in southeastern Utah. Specifically, it addresses several questions: First, what defines a "great house"? Second, is there a *bonafide* great house at Edge of the Cedars? Third, if Edge of the Cedars is a qualified great house, to what degree is it "Chacoan" and what is implied about its relationship to the cultural centers to the southeast? This review of the evidence at Edge of the Cedars shows that its main structure had the characteristics to warrant identification as a great house by most definitions, but in a scaled down, rather unimpressive, less-than-grand version.

WHAT MAKES A GREAT HOUSE?

Development of a good working definition of what constitutes and identifies a great house is a challenge that was discussed and debated at great length during the 1970s. Is there even any substance or reality to the term "great house"? Is there really a category of structure that served some kind of special function distinctly different from normal houses, and can structures of this category be identified by a discrete series of evident archaeological properties? The debate has tended to take form in patterns eerily following modern political discourse: Were the large and formal structures scattered about the Four Corners region built by communities of humble and peaceful farmers who happily donated their time and resources to the creation of large community centers in which they could gather for religious occasions and perhaps pool their surplus resources to be redistributed to households or communities in need? This gentle vision was in vogue during the ascendancy of the Democratic Party during the 1970s, when Jimmy Carter was in the White House, and can be termed (with tongue in left cheek) the "Democrat" hypothesis. Or were these structures simply the elaborate residences of those families who had the intelligence and ambition to garner wealth and power, as opposed to the less industrious masses who occupied all those other less impressive houses? This point of view attained some popularity during the Reagan presidency and the ascendancy of the Republican Party in the 1980s, and can be termed (tongue parked in right cheek) the "Ayn Rand" or "Republican" hypothesis.

The questions and alternate hypotheses are obviously vastly more complex and diverse than that, but this silly caricature of the debate is sufficient to illustrate the point, which is simply that the concept of great house may be more a product of our desperate drive to classify things than a true reflection of any cultural institution in ancient puebloan society. Classifying phenomena helps us to create the illusion of understanding by allowing us to label them with names. Was there ever really a category of structure that stood functionally apart in the same sense as, say, a cathedral, a school, a County Courthouse, or a ruling family's palace? Or were there just houses and pueblos of varying degrees of wealth and architectural sophistication?

After a century of archaeological investigation and three decades of focused academic discourse around these inquiries, we have not really answered the fundamental question. What we have done is this: We have reified the concept of great house by discussing it for so long that it has achieved the status of given truth. More and more, we have come to focus our discourse not on the question of *whether* there were such things as functionally specialized great houses, but rather on what constitutes a great house, how we can identify a real one, and what specialized roles and functions great houses and their occupants served in the societies that created them.

I offer here no answer to this problem. In the interest of clear thinking and discourse, however, I feel compelled to state it, prior to moving ahead on the basis of some explicit assumptions. For present purposes, I am following my intuition and the predominant sentiment of my contemporary archaeologists, that there is a category of site that stands qualitatively apart from "normal" habitation sites of the 10th to 13th centuries, and

that sites of this category can be identified by certain archaeologically observable properties.

I use the term "great house" here as a descriptive category for any prominent structure with certain formal attributes reminiscent of the classic Bonito phase structures in the San Juan Basin of northwestern New Mexico (Lekson 1984; Vivian 1990; and a library of other sources cited therein). I avoid use of the term "outlier" (Powers and others 1983) with reference to these structures outside the San Juan Basin because of its *a priori* connotations of a hierarchical relationship between them and their analogues in the Chaco area.

For the same reason, I try to differentiate between the term "Chacoesque," by which I mean having attributes similar to or reminiscent of those that we have become accustomed to thinking of as being at home in San Juan Basin sites but not elsewhere (Morris 1939: 205), and the term "Chacoan," which I use to refer to items or attributes that can be confidently ascribed to direct importation from the San Juan Basin. Classic Chaco Black-on-white pottery, for example, is "Chacoan" wherever it appears, whereas Mancos Black-on-white pottery with a Chaco-style paint job is "Chacoesque" and possibly Chaco-inspired, although probably not "Chacoan" in the strict sense. I also use the term "Chaco era" as a relatively clean modifier for developments contemporaneous with the Classic Bonito phase expression in the San Juan Basin (roughly A.D. 1000–1150).

What constitutes a qualified Chacoesque or Chaco-era great house? If there is a functional reality to the category, there should be a set of observable traits by which we can identify a great house. Unfortunately, few discrete properties are common to even the most seemingly obvious and outstanding candidates. A number of properties commonly occur among great house candidates in various combinations, however, and a general consensus has emerged among Southwestern archaeologists that a structure can be called a great house if it exhibits a majority of these features. They include multistory or high-roofed single-story construction with large rooms; one or more blocked-in, above-grade kivas; an associated great kiva; evidence of one or more associated roadlike features; and an associated "community" of scattered, smaller, less formally constructed unit pueblo or multiunit pueblo habitation sites (Powers and others 1983).

Great houses commonly share a number of architectural properties or features (Lekson 1984), including massive, core-and-veneer or solid core masonry walls faced with the most tabular sandstone available; adobe-

and-rubble-filled foundation or footing trenches; and (at least sometimes) "intramural beams" or logs incorporated into masonry walls. Associated great kivas often have an entry antechamber on the north and may have a complete or discontinuous ring of surrounding, surface, "peripheral" rooms. Many great houses have at least one nearby, prominent mound of midden, imported fill, or construction debris. These mounds are distinctly more prominent and sharply mounded than the low-relief "trash mounds" commonly associated with typical habitation sites. At many of the western great houses, the mounds are part of an intermittent, surrounding berm or *nazha* (Fowler and others 1987; Stein and Lekson 1992).

Although not fundamentally essential to identification of a great house *per se*, some discussion of the formal attributes of "round rooms" (Lekson 1984), or standard household or "clan" kivas, is germane to the following discussion. Standard kivas throughout the northern and eastern San Juan country share certain common attributes, including a generally circular ground plan, a central firepit, and various floor features including a small *sipapu* pit (symbolic spiritual passageway to and from the underworld) north of the firepit.

There is a patterned difference, however, between typical "Chacoan" kivas in the San Juan Basin of New Mexico and "Mesa Verdean" kivas north and northwest of the San Juan River. The San Juan Basin kivas are typically ventilated by a subfloor shaft that passes under the kiva wall and rises from the floor south of the firepit, thus requiring no deflector to buffer floor draft, whereas the northern kivas are almost universally ventilated by a shaft that penetrates the south wall above floor level, thus requiring a deflector to control draft. Chacoan kivas also commonly have a large floor pit or "subfloor vault" to the west of the firepit (Judd 1964: 177; Lekson 1984: 52).

Even less germane to identification of a great house, but interesting and worthy of mention, is a recurrent pattern of reoccupation and secondary reuse of great house structures. Most excavated great houses were abandoned during the middle A.D. 1100s and then reoccupied during the A.D. 1200s. The reoccupants often subdivided the large rooms into smaller rooms by the addition of partition walls and effectively lowered the high ceilings by laying new floors over 25 cm to 50 cm or more of trash or imported fill. Burials were sometimes interred in abandoned rooms and postoccupational debris of great houses (Bradley 1974, 1988; Irwin-Williams 1972: 14; Judd 1954; Lekson and Cameron 1995: 190; Morris 1919; Pepper 1920).

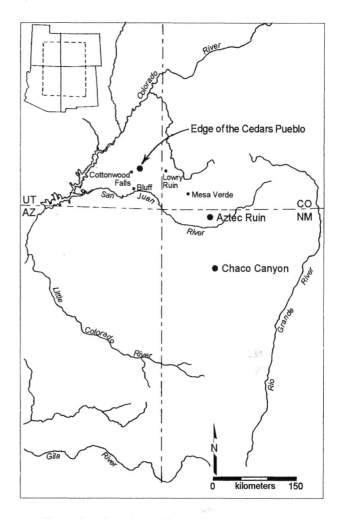

Figure 5.1. Location of Edge of the Cedars pueblo.

EDGE OF THE CEDARS PUEBLO: "YOU CALL THIS A GREAT HOUSE?"

North of the San Juan River and west of the Montezuma Canyon drainage, there are about a dozen great houses with problematical characteristics. Two of them include the structures in the Cottonwood Falls and Bluff communities (Mahoney, this volume; Jalbert and Cameron, this volume); the others have not been documented. Edge of the Cedars pueblo is the smallest and least impressive of these, one of the northernmost, and one of the farthest from Chaco Canyon. The ruin is a focal attraction of Edge of the Cedars State Park and museum, located at the northwest edge of the town of Blanding, in San Juan County, Utah (Fig. 5.1). This area is near the west edge of the "great sage plain" (Gregory 1938), in the northwestern reaches of the San Juan drainage, comfortably within the northern San Juan or "Mesa Verdean" province of the ancient Southwestern world. The northwest edges of the San Juan Basin and Chaco Canyon are approximately 100 km (60 miles) and 240 km (150 miles) to the southeast, respectively.

The Edge of the Cedars site consists of the remains of two superimposed villages dating to the late Pueblo I period (late A.D. 800s) and late Pueblo II period (about A.D. 1050–1150). Here I discuss the later village, which consists of six rubble mounds and eleven associated depressions (Fig. 5.2). Five of the Pueblo II room blocks are single- or double-kiva household units with surface room blocks on the north or west sides of circular depressions, presumably marking the locations of partially filled household kivas or "round rooms" (Lekson 1984: 50). The sixth room block (Complex 4) is a centrally located, two-story structure of approximately 12 ground-floor rectangular rooms, two enclosed kivas, and a contiguous, exceptionally large (14 m diameter) and deep, kiva depression.

Architectural details indicate that the structure grew in several construction stages into a block of six relatively large rooms and two blocked-in kivas. Subsequently, three of the four largest rooms, which formed a rectangular structural core, were each subdivided into two smaller rooms, and the fourth was made host to one of the enclosed kivas. A small suite of tree-ring dates attests to a construction or remodeling episode between A.D. 1109 and 1117 and another about 1215 (Laboratory of Tree-Ring Research Accession Number A–451, "Archaeological Date Report" on file, Edge of the Cedars State Park; ceramic information based on observations by the author). A near absence of diagnostic 13th-century potsherds in the assemblage suggests that the later dates represent a middle Pueblo III period remodeling effort that failed to culminate in significant reoccupation.

Most of Complex 4 at Edge of the Cedars pueblo (Fig. 5.3) was excavated between 1969 and 1973 by a Weber State College field school and a changing assortment of Weber State and Brigham Young University graduate students, under contract to a series of local development-oriented agencies. Some of their findings are documented in a small stack of student notebooks, a few maps and diagrams, and several rolls of photographs. Field documentation is completely missing for all 1972 excavations (about half the rooms in Complex 4 and the only excavations conducted to date in the large kiva). Extant notes, photographs, and preliminary analytical data from the early excavations are on file in the museum at Edge of the Cedars State Park, which was created in 1974 and opened in 1977.

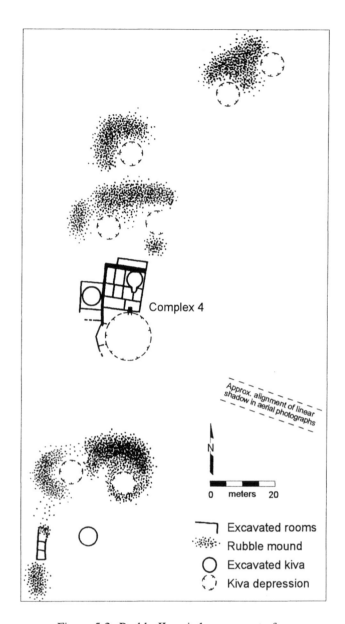

Figure 5.2. Pueblo II period component of Edge of the Cedars pueblo (42Sa700).

Except for a brief preliminary statement summarizing the first year's work (Green 1971), no report on these excavations has ever been written, and the ruin remains largely uninterpreted in the Edge of the Cedars museum exhibits. Aside from some preliminary artifact sorting, no systematic analysis of the collections was ever undertaken prior to 1997. Since the opening of the museum, additional small-scale excavations have been conducted in and around Complex 4 by a series of museum curators, mostly in connection with ruins stabilization projects. These investigations have not been published because of time limitations and conflicting staff priorities.

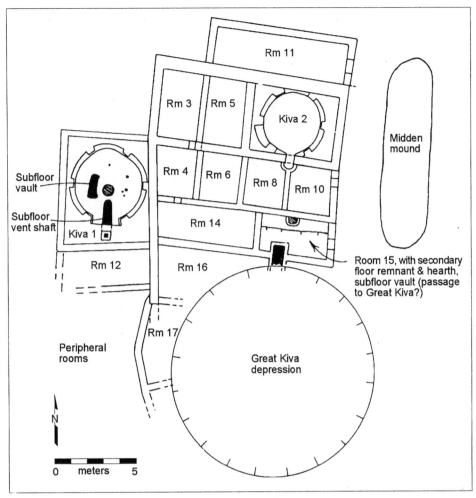

Figure 5.3. Features in Complex 4 at Edge of the Cedars pueblo.

For the reasons discussed in the introductory paragraphs above, some of the most critical questions for understanding the Edge of the Cedars Pueblo II community concern the function of its dominant central room block, that structure's relationship to other structures and settlements in the area, and the relationship between the Edge of the Cedars community and contemporaneous developments in New Mexico. Does Complex 4 at Edge of the Cedars have properties that identify it as a Chaco style great house? If so, do its "Chacoesque" properties imply some degree of formal connection between the Utah community and the power centers in Chaco Canyon? Or was the Utah community essentially independent and self-sufficient, informally sharing broad cultural forms and customs with other communities throughout the Four Corners region, with those forms and customs being most elaborately developed in the communities of the Chaco–Aztec area of the San Juan Basin? Complex 4 at Edge of the Cedars does

exhibit Chacoesque properties, albeit on a relatively small scale, contrasting with the monumental scale and relative architectural sophistication of the classic Chacoan great houses of the San Juan Basin.

Multiple-Storied Core Room Block

The Complex 4 rubble mound at Edge of the Cedars rose more than 2.6 m above the surrounding ground surface at its highest point. Excavation of the mound revealed intact masonry rising several courses into a second story. The volume of rubble in the mound shows that a central block of four large, original rooms once rose to two full stories, though the second story walls were not necessarily as tall as those of the first story. The second story roof would have provided a panoramic view of much of the northern San Juan country, with line-of-sight visibility east to Colorado's beanfield country, the Rocky Mountains, and the Mesa Verde escarpment; south to Shiprock, the Carrizo–Lukachukai–Chuska Mountains, and the Black Mesa scarp; west to Cedar Mesa and Elk ridge; and north to the Abajo Mountains.

Blocked-In, Above-Grade Kivas with Chacoesque Floor Features

Complex 4 encloses two standard-size round rooms, both constructed mostly or entirely above ground within rectangular, walled spaces (Fig. 5.3). Kiva 1, which was completely excavated (and somewhat crudely restored), was built into a rectangular enclosure that was added onto the west side of the central room block core. It appears to have had a high, domed roof with an exterior platform surface approximately on level with the second-story floors to the east. In addition to the usual kiva features, Kiva 1 has a subfloor ventilation shaft and no deflector as well as a subfloor vault west of the firepit, the two standard features of a Chaco-style kiva. Kiva 2 was never completely excavated and its floor feature configuration is unknown. It is unclear whether Kiva 2 had a second-story room over it or an exposed rooftop at the same level as Kiva 1. It may have been built as a remodeling of the northeast room of the core block.

Core-and-Veneer Walls

Most of the walls in Complex 4 appear to have been constructed with interior and exterior facing stacks separated by a core of rubble and mud. The primary back wall of the structure clearly exhibits core-and-veneer construction and is notably wider than the other walls (75–80 cm; Fig. 5.4). Although its original morphology has been modified by several generations of stabilization and restoration, unmodified exposures of the west wall of the original room block also reveal core-and-veneer construction with an original thickness of 50 cm. The east wall of the room block and the east-west wall extending between rooms 3–5–Kiva 2 and rooms 4–6–8–10 are also relatively thick and most likely contain core-and-veneer construction obscured by early stabilization errors.

Tabular Sandstone Wall Facing

There is virtually no tabular sandstone within any reasonable pedestrian catchment area from Edge of the Cedars ruin. Rocks in this region are Dakota Sandstone and ancient stream gravels, ranging from irregularly

Figure 5.4. Core-and-veneer back wall of Complex 4, 80 cm thick, looking east.

chunky to subrounded. These rocks are rarely rectanguloid on any face, and even more rarely form slabs. Not surprisingly, most of the walls at Edge of the Cedars reflect the nature of the local rock, with masonry consisting of irregular sandstone rocks and occasional cobbles set with a smooth face to the exterior, in mortar joints that were tightened by chinking with numerous small sandstone spalls (Fig. 5.5). Yet there is clear evidence that the builders exerted considerable energy in an effort to construct its blocked-in kiva walls of tabular sandstone stacked with minimal mortar joints, in a style that seems to be struggling toward Judd's Chaco type IV (Fig. 5.6; Lekson 1984: 17). There is no evidence of any effort to produce the formal banding exhibited at some of the Chaco Canyon and Aztec structures.

Figure 5.5. North façade of the core-and-veneer back wall, showing typical masonry at Edge of the Cedars pueblo. Approximately 80 cm of the lower part of the wall is newly exposed and retains the original chinking.

The source of the tabular rock used in the kiva walls has not been determined. It appears to have been sufficiently remote, or the supply sufficiently limited, that the builders gave up the effort before completing the walls of Kiva 1 to bench level. The masonry quality, or at least the quality of the stones utilized in the masonry, deteriorates about halfway up the walls, with carefully selected and tightly stacked slabs giving way to more blocky, irregular stones set in increasing amounts of mud chinked with sandstone spalls. The tabular sandstone masonry was apparently not intended to be seen, as the walls of at least one kiva were completely covered with thick, unpainted plaster when first excavated (Fig. 5.7).

Foundation Trenches

A 40-cm-deep footing trench filled with adobe and rubble was documented under the core-and-veneer back wall (Fig. 5.8), and evidence for smaller foundation trenches was recorded in association with the long room added onto the north side of the room block. These trenches were filled with adobe and rock. There is no information as to the presence or absence of foundation trenches elsewhere in the structure, but the early excavators at Edge of the Cedars were not attuned to them, and their excavations generally terminated at the base of the walls.

Unfortunately, it is impossible to be sure that foundation trenches are not common in Utah or in the northern San Juan in general. Few excavators have looked for them. What we have is not a documented absence of foundation trenches, but rather a near-absence of documented ones. This is an important distinction, brought home to me by my own documentation of a footings trench at the base of a Pueblo II wall in a small, unimpressive structure of several rooms a few miles northwest of Edge of the Cedars (Hurst 1985: 7-27 and 28). This trench was not typical of trenches found at Chaco Canyon great houses, but rather served to seat a foundation course of large stones. These large, basal-course stones are unlike the narrow slabs commonly

Figure 5.6. Tabular sandstone masonry in the west wall of Kiva 1, 1989. Note change from tabular sandstone to unshaped blocks in upper reaches of the wall.

Figure 5.7. Original plaster in the east wall of Kiva 1, 1969.

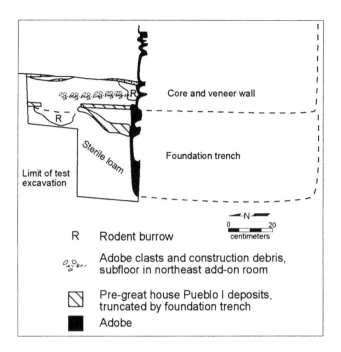

Figure 5.8. Profile of foundation trench under the core-and-veneer back wall; partial exposure in 1989 test pit.

found in Basketmaker and early puebloan structures, and this trench illustrates the need for caution in the use of foundation trenches as diagnostic features of Chacoan or Chacoesque great houses.

Intramural Beams

It is not clear why incorporation of logs into masonry walls would be a hallmark of architectural sophistication, because wood is far less structurally sound than stone and would be expected to weaken a stone masonry wall. Nonetheless, the use of "intramural beams" is an architectural trait well documented in the great houses of Chaco Canyon (Lekson 1984: 16, 24) that has not been commonly reported from ruins of the northern San Juan region (except for some informal occurrences in "backwoods" cliff houses in the far western San Juan). Although this apparent pattern may be due in part to sampling error (remarkably few substantial Pueblo II–III period ruins in the north have been excavated and thoroughly described), presently available data indicate that intramural beams may be a Chacoan, or at least a Chacoesque, architectural trait. Intramural beams do occur at Edge of the Cedars pueblo and are a possible indicator of great house status.

At least one wall of Complex 4 incorporated intramural horizontal logs into the masonry. The early exca-

Figure 5.9. Basal course of wall, showing stone façades with rotted logs in core. Trowel points north.

vators documented two horizontal logs built into the southern wall of the great house, either butted to or tied into the primary western wall (east wall of the Kiva 1 enclosure). These logs were offset from one another, one higher and built into the south half of the wall, the other lower and built into the north half. The only photograph of these beams failed to produce a publishable image, but the wall and beams were sketched before the excavators removed the wall almost to the basal course, presumably because decay of the wood had left it too weak to stand. In 1986, additional stabilization-related excavation reexposed the basal course (Fig. 5.9) and revealed it to be 35 cm thick, with horizontal logs laid longitudinally between exterior veneers of sandstone rock. Though not noted in the written documentation, Gary Parker reported to me in 1997 that an early 1980s stabilization effort also exposed logs incorporated into masonry in the perimeter of Kiva 2.

Great Kiva

Extraordinarily large kivas or kivalike structures were not always present at great house settlements and were sometimes located well away from great houses. These "great kivas" occurred widely in the northern Southwest long before the construction of great houses. By the late Bonito phase, however, great kivas appear to have been incorporated into the great house settlements and have been found in close association with most great houses.

The great kiva at Edge of the Cedars was contiguous to the south edge of the Complex 4 room block (Fig. 5.3). It has not been excavated except for three test trenches for which there is no documentation beyond several fuzzy photographs. Its depression is clear, however, and measures approximately 14 m in diameter and at least 2 m deep. Several photos taken prior to backfilling of the test trenches show that the walls of the great kiva were masonry lined but they reveal little significant detail about the masonry. There is no information on the presence or absence of a bench or floor features. A low but distinct berm bordered the south and east sides of the depression but it is now obscured by a concrete walk. Remnants of masonry surface rooms bound the depression on its north and west sides.

I conducted supplemental excavations at the northwest edge of the great kiva preparatory to wall stabilization in 1986; they revealed remnants of what appeared to be a series of peripheral rooms connected to the southwest part of the great house and wrapping around at least the west edge of the great kiva (Figs. 5.3, 5.10). The outer wall consisted of several courses of masonry with little associated rubble, suggesting that this part of the structure was either unfinished, later stone-robbed, or never built more than about 1 m high. (Early Blanding residents are known to have robbed rock from the ruin for use in foundations. This part of the ruin would have been easily accessible by wagon and is likely the area most heavily robbed.) Basal remnants of masonry room-dividing walls extended from the outer wall to the edge of the great kiva depression. The limited excavation showed that the outer wall of the western peripheral rooms continued to curve southeastward beyond our excavations, though there was no evidence for it on the surface. Perhaps the low berm

Figure 5.10. Peripheral rooms at the west edge of the great kiva depression, looking north, 1986. Note the encircling wall and partition wall remnants. Features in the floor are actually subfloor, in the Pueblo I period component.

around the south and east sides of the depression conceals additional peripheral masonry, though little rubble was evident even before the State Park built a concrete walkway over it. The full extent and configuration of the peripheral rooms are therefore unknown at this time. They appear to have been constructed on the surface immediately adjacent to the kiva pit or perhaps partly onto the kiva roof platform. Collapse and filling of the kiva and decay of its upper edges have destroyed all but the outer portions of the exposed rooms.

Photographs show that the early excavations exposed an unexplained concentration of rubble at the north edge of the great kiva, inside the south edge of one of the great house rooms. The 1986 excavations revealed a rectangular, masonry-lined passage into the floor of the room in that location, extending beneath or through the room's south wall. Though it was not fully excavated and its depth and nature are unknown, this feature is almost certainly an entry passage into the great kiva. If so, that makes this room of the great house analogous to the entry antechamber commonly situated on the north side of Chacoan great kivas.

Large Rooms

If wall ties and abutments reflect construction episodes (see Fig. 5.3), the initial Complex 4 structure at Edge of the Cedars consisted of two large, two-story room columns, each measuring nearly 6 m long by about 4 m wide, with the west wall extending south beyond the rooms for nearly 10 m. Two more large, two-story room columns were then added to the south side to create a rectanguloid, two-story core. The structure assumed its final form with the addition of two more relatively large rooms (about 5 m and 7 m long by about 2 m wide) onto the south side; a single, 9-m long by 2-m wide room on the north side; the enclosed, above-grade Kiva 1 on the west side; a small kiva inside one of the four core rooms; room-dividing partitions inside the other core rooms; and the great kiva complex.

Late Modifications and Intrusive Burial

The history of room subdivision, floor raising, and burial interment in Complex 4 is not fundamentally germane to the structure's candidacy as a great house. However, the changes are interesting in that they closely parallel the patterns of late reuse of Chaco-era great houses throughout the Four Corners region. Sometime during the structure's occupational history, three of the large original rooms were each subdivided into two smaller rooms by the addition of a single-course ("simple," in Lekson's terminology) partition wall. Kiva 2 may have been built into the fourth room at this same time, although the dating of its construction is not clear.

Excavation records are confusing as to the nature of the floors in Complex 4 (notes are entirely missing for about half the rooms), but there is no question that at least the southeast room was remodeled by raising the floor with imported fill to a height of approximately 20 cm above the original floor. The extant excavation notes make clear reference to two distinct floor surfaces, one

significantly higher than the other. Fortunately, the early investigators failed to complete their excavation of this room, leaving an untouched balk of sediment standing against the north wall. Photographs taken near the end of excavation show this balk, with the secondary floor and an associated ash lens clearly visible. The upper portion of the balk later slumped away, burying and preserving the bottom portion, including the remnant of the secondary floor. Stabilization-related excavation in 1986 and 1989 explored these balk sediments, exposing a well-preserved portion of the final floor, including a firepit with an adobe rim coping against the north wall of the room. These excavations also revealed that the floor surface had been raised and replastered and the firepit had been moved or remodeled several times. When finally abandoned, the floor level of the room had been raised about 25 cm by these successive remodelings, and the firepit was filled to overflowing with charcoal and ash. It is impossible to be certain from the early notes whether raised secondary floors were present in all other rooms, but there is clear evidence of such remodeling in one other room for which documentation is available (Room 5).

The timing of the partitioning of the large core rooms and the raising of the floors is unclear. Some of the remodeling may be associated with early A.D. 1200s tree-ring dates from Kiva 2. These dates are anomalous in that the distinctive Pueblo III period Mesa Verde White Ware pottery (McElmo Black-on-white and Mesa Verde Black-on-white) that normally dominates ceramic assemblages in this area after the late A.D. 1100s is rare at the great house. If remodeling was undertaken during the A.D. 1200s, the structure appears never to have been actually reoccupied.

Only one formal burial, a child, was documented from the Edge of the Cedars site. Unfortunately, the sketchy surviving notes fail to describe the burial fill or its relationship to surrounding sediments. It was adjacent to the exterior of the east wall of Complex 4, in either postabandonment rubble fill or the bottom of a swale between the wall and the midden berm.

Mound or Berm

There is good evidence for a topographically prominent refuse pile reminiscent of those associated with other described great house sites located close to the east side of Complex 4 (Fig. 5.3). The early excavators ran a long trench along the outside of the east wall, leaving a prominent sediment mound to the east that still stands, albeit somewhat eroded by weather and ob-

Figure 5.11. Enlarged section of USGS aerial photograph 2–33 GS–VIQ (8–22–55) showing Edge of the Cedars pueblo and what may be an ancient road approaching the great kiva from the east-southeast. The track of an abandoned wagon road, trending southeast-northwest intersects the older feature at right center. The top of the photograph is north.

scured by a concrete park walkway. The notes on that excavation are minimal and fail to describe the sediment matrix or the presence or density of building rubble. No clear mound at this location is visible in the few extant preexcavation photographs, but both the photographs and the preexcavation contour map show a distinct benching and possibly a slight hump on the east slope of the Complex 4 mound. Several 1972 slides show the sediments in the east wall of the trench to be nearly devoid of building stone.

In 1984, museum curator Sloan Emery dug a test pit in the mound east of the early trench and encountered midden sediments with little rubble. A broken corrugated pot recovered in the test pit appears to have been set or tossed onto the mound sometime prior to abandonment and structural collapse. Sediments from the early trench produced a large number of artifacts, including an abundance of late Pueblo II ceramics.

These observations strongly suggest that there was a prominent midden mound close to the east side of the Complex 4 room block, near enough to the structure

that the space between was largely filled by rubble during the decay of the structure, thus masking the existence of the midden mound. This feature may have been continuously or discontinuously aligned with the low berm that surrounds the east side of the great kiva (although such berms are normal features of pit structures and not usually connected to great house berms). Sketchy documentation and subsequent State Parks surface modifications, including the overlying concrete sidewalk, make assessment of this feature difficult.

There is no clear evidence of a berm or *nazha* around the Complex 4 structure. The great kiva crowds it closely on the south, however, and a double-unit pueblo crowds it closely on the north, leaving little room for a berm.

Road?

A 1955 government aerial photograph (Fig. 5.11; Dept. of the Interior GS–VIQ, 2–33, 8–22–55) clearly shows a shadowy, straight, linear feature approaching the south edge of the Edge of the Cedars great kiva from the east-southeast, through what was then a plowed field. It aligns roughly with the south edge of the great kiva. This feature has not been identified on subsequent government aerial photographs, but it matches a subtle, linear stripe of slightly lighter-colored sediments that is evident in low-level aerial photographs of the site taken prior to excavation in 1969. It also aligns precisely with a 30-m-long, shallow, linear depression located approximately 200 m east-southeast of the great kiva that remains visible enough to appear on the Blanding City orthophoto contour maps.

This swale is roughly 10 m wide, with low, diffuse, amorphous suggestions of lateral berms. The remnant swale and the linear patterns in the photographs define the track of an old road leading into the site, still detectable after nearly nine decades of repeated plowing. This feature may well be an ancient road trace, but its identity is clouded by poorly documented historic usage of the site, including removal of wagon loads of building stone, probably from that portion of the ruin lying directly in line with the swale (Lyman 1972: 4–5). This swale could therefore be either a prehistoric or a historic Anglo feature, or possibly both. The width of the remnant swale and the fact that it is not oriented directly toward the earliest part of the Blanding settlement enhance the likelihood that it may be an ancient feature. If it was, its full extent and points of destination and origin are unknown. No trace of it has been found along its projected alignment through town or beyond.

The Surrounding Community

The Edge of the Cedars Complex 4 room block and great kiva are located amidst a tight cluster of five smaller, unit and double-unit house mounds. These unit houses are arrayed in file along the ridge crest to the north and south of the great house, within a space of about 150 m. According to local lore, more "kivas" and presumably associated house mounds were obliterated during construction of several modern houses along the ridge extending south. Other small habitation sites of the appropriate age are known to have existed at various locations within the present limits of Blanding, and some are still in the area surrounding the town. Though the extent of this associated community has not been determined, it seems clear that a surrounding community did, in fact, exist.

Some Words About Trade

Exotic trade items appear to occur with greater frequency at road-associated great houses than at other great house settlements (Lekson and others 1988: 108; Powers and others 1983: 337). Does that pattern hold true at Edge of the Cedars? That question cannot be conclusively answered yet, for two reasons. First, the collections from the Edge of the Cedars excavations are only now being analyzed, so quantitative data regarding the occurrence of imported versus local material are not yet available. Second, even if such data were available, there are few comparable data sets from contemporaneous habitation sites in the region. Such data are unavailable even from other household room blocks within the Edge of the Cedars site, as excavations there have been mostly restricted to Complex 4. Although a number of contemporaneous habitation sites have been excavated throughout the region, few of their collections have been rigorously or thoroughly analyzed, and the analysts have varied tremendously in their competence and the structure of their data. This makes meaningful, broad comparisons extremely difficult and of limited usefulness. Until wider data sets of competently generated and comparable data become available, we are stuck with intuitive observations.

Although quantitative data are not yet available, imported trade goods are certainly present in significant quantities at Edge of the Cedars ruin. Perhaps the most notable exotic artifacts are three copper bells (Fig. 5.12), probably imported from Mexico (Palmer 1994; Vargas 1995), and a number of olivella shell beads from California (at least some of the latter were from Pueblo I period pre-great-house deposits).

Figure 5.12. Copper bells from Edge of the Cedars pueblo.

Analysis of ceramics from the excavations is still in progress. In initial tallies and rapid surveys of the unanalyzed collections from Complex 4, I have identified a significant representation of imported pottery (some 10% to 15% of decorated wares). Most of this material is Tusayan White Ware and Tsegi Orange Ware from the Kayenta-Navajo Mountain region, about 150 km (90 miles) southwest of Edge of the Cedars. Identified types include Black Mesa Black-on-white, Dogoszhi Black-on-white, Sosi Black-on-white, Tusayan Black-on-red, Citadel Polychrome, Cameron Polychrome, and Tusayan Polychrome. Occasional sherds of Cibola White Ware with Chacoan attributes also occur, including remnants of one heavily worn Chaco Black-on-white vessel. Also present are rare bits of Chuska White Ware and even an occasional fragment of Woodruff Smudged from the Mogollon area. Chacoan ceramics are less easily recognized in northern San Juan Pueblo II period assemblages than are those from the Kayenta region, and more intensive and thorough analysis is expected to raise the percentage of recognized imports from the southeast. Nevertheless, imported artifacts appear to be significantly represented at Edge of the Cedars, although, thus far, they do not bespeak a major connection to the San Juan Basin.

THE CHACOAN QUIDDITY AT EDGE OF THE CEDARS RUIN

Complex 4 at Edge of the Cedars has many of the properties of a great house, including a two-story core of large, high-ceilinged rooms; core-and-veneer walls with foundation trenches; an attempt to utilize tabular sandstone in an area where tabular sandstone is not readily acquired; logs incorporated into the wall masonry; a great kiva complete with northern entry and peripheral rooms; probably a road; and a distinct, high-relief trash mound. Like some other northern great houses, the floor in at least one of the rooms was raised and its large rooms were subdivided, possibly during the early A.D. 1200s, as indicated by a small suite of anomalously late tree-ring dates. Like some other great houses, it may have been used as a postoccupational burial place.

Although it may be an embarrassment in contrast to its more impressive analogues to the southeast, Edge of the Cedars is certainly a *bonafide* great house, or we have to alter and narrow our criteria in order to exclude it. Despite its comparatively "backwoodsy" and provincial qualities, the Edge of the Cedars structure boasts most of the common great house traits, lacking only the magnitude, sophistication, and flexed posturing of the classic great houses and related features in New Mexico. But classifying it as a great house only brings us to the difficult questions.

Does the presence of a great house complex at Edge of the Cedars, even on so poor a scale, imply a *formal* connection to Chaco Canyon? Are these features really "Chacoan" or just "Chacoesque"? The answer depends on definitions, and any clear answer is inevitably tautological. If we define "Chacoan" with reference to these features, then they are by definition Chacoan and their presence in Utah bespeaks strong Chacoan influence if not actual colonization or political or religious interference. If we define these features as being generic puebloan characteristics during the Pueblo II–III period, with a "Chacoan" variant being more narrowly and exclusively defined (analogous to the way we have viewed ceramics and other dimensions of regional variability within puebloan culture since the 1930s or before), then their presence in Utah only bespeaks influence from Chaco to the degree that these features precisely conform to a narrowly defined Chacoan stylistic and architectural canon. By adjusting our definitions, we can probably make the local Chacoesque features as "Chacoan" as we want them to be.

So we must drop labels and get back to specific questions. Exactly how did the great house and associated developments in Utah relate to the more spectacular developments in the Chaco-Aztec centers? Do the Utah expressions represent population intrusion of lineages or elite representatives from the uptown centers of the San Juan Basin? Was there actual Chacoan colonization, in some sense, of the villagers in the "boondocks," or is this just the local version of what everybody was doing at that time throughout a vast cultural sphere of interaction, with the fanciest and most complex expression occurring in the Chaco-Aztec belt? Did the Utah expression represent simple local emulation of the power and glory of more affluent and powerful population centers to the southeast, or was it a franchise arrangement, with local communities buying into a Chacoan ceremonial-political-economic system and formally authorized to use its symbols? In what way and at what scale were commerce and redistribution of resources involved? Did it involve any degree of coercive or punitive power from Chaco or Aztec? Was there a formal military component? Were the roads used for commerce, communication, resource redistribution, military logistics, ritual, architectural expression of sacred landscape and reenactment of mythological events, or something entirely different that we have not yet considered? Were the great houses actually occupied by resident lineages, or did they function in some other fashion, as community structures that were not permanently occupied or perhaps occupied by serial inhabitants?

These questions have been explored by an army of Chacoan archaeologists since the 1970s, resulting in a library of discourse (Vivian 1990) too vast to be summarized here. Let it suffice to point out that the most intriguing of the Chacoesque features at Edge of the Cedars are those that would not have been evident to the casual observer. Local builders trying to emulate the power and grandeur of the Chacoan communities of the San Juan Basin might be expected to copy the external appearance of great house structures, but would probably not be concerned with replicating hidden architectural details, if they were even aware of them. Yet the builders of the Edge of the Cedars great house appear to have gone to some effort to conform to a Chacoan canon of architecture, even in its *hidden* structural details. Such hidden details include rubble-cored masonry, plastered-over tabular sandstone wall facings, intramural beams, and foundation trenches. These characteristics tell us of a greater-than-casual familiarity with, and commitment to, the details of mainstream Chacoan architecture. That in turn seems to imply interaction at a higher level than a simple sharing of ideas or local emulation of the outward trappings of Chacoan power expressions. It suggests that the local builders had previously observed or participated in the actual construction of Chacoan structures elsewhere or were privy to significantly detailed "down-the-line" information regarding architectural details appropriate for a truly Chacoesque great house.

Do these hidden Chacoesque details reflect overt intrusion of an expansionist Chaco system into the northwestern provinces of the San Juan country or simply local adoption of symbolically loaded architectural attributes as argued by Van Dyke (this volume) for the Red Mesa Valley? Although the Edge of the Cedars data provide no specific answer to that question, they do clearly show that the local community was an active participant in widespread communication and ideational systems rather than an isolated province on the fringes of the Anasazi world. There can be little doubt that the central Chacoan communities were known to and spoken of by the inhabitants of Edge of the Cedars. It is certainly possible that Edge of the Cedars hosted at least an occasional visitor from the San Juan Basin, and quite likely that some residents of the Edge of the Cedars community visited the awesome and no doubt legendary communities of Chaco Canyon. More solid insights into the frequency, intensity, and nature of such interactions are maddeningly elusive.

Perhaps there is a message in the deterioration of the masonry quality during the construction of Kiva 1. It could imply simply a flagging commitment related to a threshold in the relationship between labor cost and perceived value. Alternatively, it could imply a stronger degree of external involvement and oversight at the planning and early construction stages than in the later stages of construction. There might be a similar whispered hint in the nature of the foundation trenches. These features often fail to precisely underlie the constructed walls and have no apparent architectural or engineering function; perhaps they were more of an on-ground plan than an actual foundation system *per se* (Lekson 1984: 15). The foundation trench documented under the east wall of the northeast room at Edge of the Cedars Complex 4 follows this pattern, with the actual wall only partially overlapping the foundation trench. Although this feature need not necessarily imply anything beyond local planning, it could be part of an instructional launching package reflecting some degree of outside consultation or oversight in the initial stages of planning and construction. It will be interesting to see whether other great house structures in the far provinces exhibit similar evidence of initial planning and commitment to a Chacoesque architectural canon, with deteriorating commitment in the later stages of construction.

Some discussion of the relationship of the Edge of the Cedars great house community to its Pueblo I period predecessor is warranted. Van Dyke (this volume) points out that the frequent appearance of Chaco-era great houses in sites having earlier components is evidence for local development of great houses, perhaps driven by a process of "competitive emulation" rather than expansion of a truly Chacoan presence into uninhabited areas. It does not, however, preclude the possibility of a direct Chacoan connection and even physical presence in the local community, if the local community sought to expand its prestige and power by attaching itself in some direct political, ceremonial, or symbolic way to the central Chaco great houses. Outside "interference" can occur by local invitation as well as by imposition, coercion, or invasion. For present purposes, it bears noting that the Edge of the Cedars great house was established over the ruins of a substantial Pueblo I period village and that this placement is a recurrent pattern among Utah's candidate great houses, as it is in the Red Mesa Valley (Van Dyke, this volume) and elsewhere. That pattern may mean that *if* direct Chacoan intrusion was involved in the "outlier" great houses, it represented an invitation by long-established communities rather than the establishment of daughter colonies in new territories by an expanding Chacoan population (compare Vivian 1990).

In the final analysis, is there anything about Edge of the Cedars that bespeaks a direct Chacoan presence? In the absence of any "smoking gun" evidence one way or the other, we are left to intuitive conclusions, and the intuitive answer at this time is "no." This conclusion is based on the rustic qualities of the Edge of the Cedars great house. Its Chacoesque properties seem more *pro forma* than pretentious. It is simply not in the same league, either in scale or in architectural investment, as its upscale analogues in the San Juan Basin. Although scale does not necessarily preclude a direct involvement in the great house development, or even occupation by Chacoan inhabitants, it certainly gives the impression of homespun provinciality and is what one might expect in an emulative great house far removed from the lights of the big towns.

In summary, Edge of the Cedars is a qualified great house, but a poor version compared to great houses in the San Juan Basin. Although the possibility of direct Chacoan involvement in its establishment remains an open possibility, this particular structure *feels* like a local attempt at a small-scale great house by people with some detailed knowledge of how a Chaco-style great house was supposed to be constructed. It will be interesting to see whether other far-northwestern great houses share these properties, if others are more strongly and confidently "Chacoan," and what patterned variability exists among them.

Much more work must be accomplished before we can hope to approach an understanding of the role of great houses and related features in Utah and the relationships of their occupants to those of other great houses elsewhere. There is a tremendous need for careful examination and documentation of great houses, roads, and related structures in this region, and some of that work is ongoing by Severance at Cottonwood Falls and elsewhere, by Cameron and Lekson at Bluff (Cameron 1997c; Cameron and others 1996, 1997), and by Mahoney in the Cottonwood Falls extended community (this volume). We need many more tight, clean dates from well-controlled excavation contexts. We need good, strong, well-provenienced ceramic assemblages from a variety of candidate great houses and other contemporaneous communities, carefully assessed by competent analysts. We need detailed temporal and descriptive information on the Chaco-era roads and associated artifacts and features. And we need to see more intact masonry. The dedication by Marshall and others in their landmark 1979 volume on the San Juan Basin Anasazi communities remains as pertinent now as it was two decades ago: "To Alden C. Hayes, who told us to find out *what* happened before we started writing our explanations of *why* it happened."

Acknowledgments

This chapter is a preliminary product of an ongoing effort by the author and curatorial staff at Edge of the Cedars State Park, funded in part by the State of Utah, to compile a synthetic report on the excavations at Edge of the Cedars. Cooperation of the Utah Division of Parks and Recreation and various early excavators is gratefully acknowledged.

CHAPTER SIX

Chacoan and Local Influences in Three Great House Communities in the Northern San Juan Region

Joseph Peter Jalbert and Catherine Cameron

The northern San Juan region is best known for the spectacular 13th-century cliff dwellings and towers at Mesa Verde and Hovenweep, but this expanse also harbored numerous Chaco-era great houses beginning in the late 11th century. The Bluff great house, located in southeastern Utah, was one of these structures. Reports on the few great houses in the northern San Juan region that have been excavated are meager and we know little of the communities that surrounded the great houses. Excavations at the Bluff great house between 1995 and 1998 and a survey of the Bluff community in 1997, undertaken by the University of Colorado, provide a glimpse of a Chacoan community on the northern frontier of the Chacoan world.

The San Juan River forms the southern boundary of the northern San Juan region, which extends from Pagosa Springs on the east to Cedar Mesa on the west (Lipe 1995). Historically the University of Colorado (CU) has been involved in studies of great houses in this area. In the 1950s, Robert Lister, then a CU faculty member, excavated a number of sites surrounding the Far View great house as part of the university's first Archaeological Field School (Lister 1964, 1965, 1966). The great house itself had been excavated at the turn of the century by Jesse Walter Fewkes but was only briefly reported (Fewkes 1917). During the 1970s, another faculty member, Frank Eddy (1977), conducted an extensive survey and excavations at the Chimney Rock great house community at the northeastern edge of the Chacoan world.

The Bluff Great House Project continues this tradition of great house exploration on the northern frontier. Operating as the University of Colorado Field School, project excavations have revealed a lengthy occupation at the great house, including at least two episodes of construction. The structure was almost certainly in use until the early A.D. 1200s and was likely initially built toward the end of the Chaco era (late 10th and early 11th centuries). The area around the great house has been heavily disturbed by modern development and by the meandering San Juan River, but a significant number of Chaco-era communities have been identified and recorded. The Bluff Survey worked in cooperation with a similar project undertaken by Nancy Mahoney of Arizona State University (Mahoney, this volume). She conducted an intensive survey of sites surrounding the Cottonwood Falls great house, approximately 30 km (18.6 miles) north of Bluff. The combined efforts of the two university surveys covered approximately 80 percent of the canyon between the two great houses. Although no road segments were identified within the survey boundaries, one extends north up Cottonwood Canyon from the Bluff great house and another segment heads south from the Cottonwood Falls great house, so the two communities may have been connected by a prehistoric road.

This chapter reports on both the Bluff great house excavations and the results of the study of the surrounding community, and comparisons are made to the earlier work at Far View and Chimney Rock. Of the three, the Chimney Rock great house most closely mimicked the masonry style, kiva roof construction methods, and other architectural attributes of Chaco Canyon. Both the Bluff and Far View great houses appear to have been more local in architectural style. It is noteworthy that significantly different patterns in the organization of surrounding structures occurred at each of the three communities. Both settlement layout and architecture were different, with local architectural styles persisting in each of the three communities. Apparently only the Chimney Rock layout was directly influenced by the presence of a great house. In each community, topography and the location of arable land were probably the most important determinants of settlement layout.

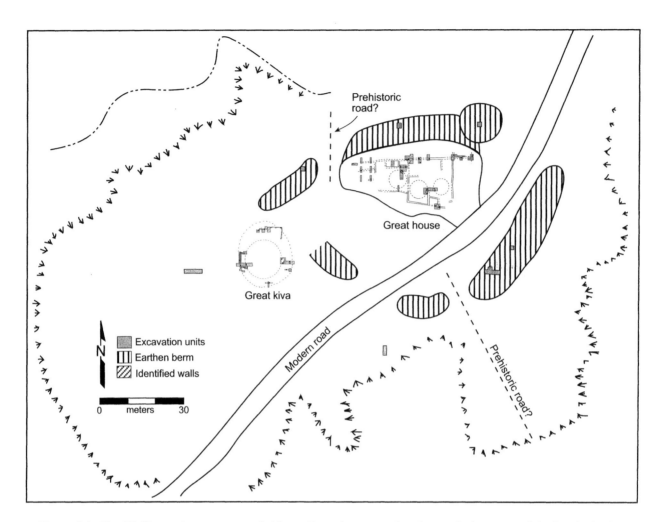

Figure 6.1. The Bluff great house, surrounded by a discontinuous earthen berm. At least two of the breaks in the berm were entry points for prehistoric road segments. The circular great kiva is outside the berm to the southwest.

THE BLUFF GREAT HOUSE

The Bluff great house is located on a prominent, gravel-capped hill overlooking the San Juan River. Backed by cliffs of Bluff Sandstone, the setting provides a wide view of the river drainage to the east, south, and west, as well as up Cottonwood Canyon, which enters the San Juan from the north. Local residents have been aware of the site since the town of Bluff was first settled in the late 1800s, but its possible connection to the Chaco "system" was only recognized in the early 1980s. In addition to its prominent location, the site has other Chacoan characteristics: the great house itself, a great kiva, prehistoric road segments, and a berm, or low earthen mound, surrounding the great house (Fig. 6.1).

Between 1995 and 1998, the University of Colorado conducted excavations at the Bluff great house as part of an archaeological field school (Cameron 1996, 1997b,

1997c, 1997d, 1998). The site revealed an intriguing mix of local ceramics and Chacoan architectural features constructed with a local masonry style. Although ceramic evidence indicates use of this location beginning at least by A.D. 500, the majority of the ceramics throughout the site represent late Pueblo II period types (1050–1150), coinciding with the height of cultural developments in Chaco Canyon. Abundant Pueblo III period pottery suggests continuing use of the great house into the 1200s. Apparently few ceramics were imported to Bluff (Kantner and others, this volume), but ceramicist Eric Blinman said in 1996 that some pieces may have been locally made copies of Chacoan styles, including a fragment of a Chaco Black-on-white pitcher.

The great house mound is about 50 m long and 30 m wide (Fig. 6.2). Excavations focused on a program of wall-clearing, especially at the west end of the site and along the rear (north) wall. A deep test unit (1 m by 2 m)

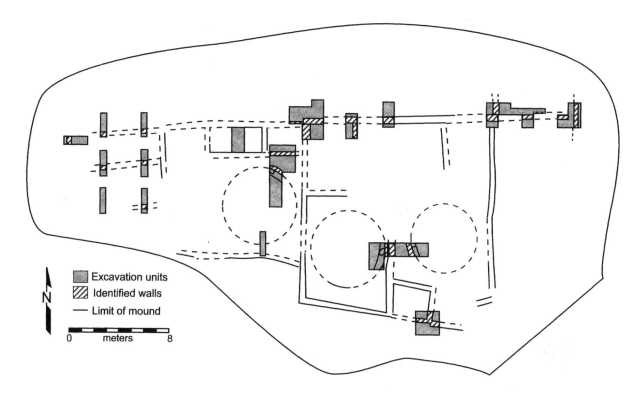

Figure 6.2. The Bluff great house, showing excavation units completed through 1998. Hatched areas indicate masonry walls. Three kivas are located along the front of the structure; a pilaster and bench were identified in each.

was excavated into one of the rear rooms (Feature 2), and similar tests were made into each of the three blocked-in kivas that front the structure. Wall clearing showed that the great house was constructed in at least two and possibly three stages. The westernmost end of the mound is low and may have been only a single story high. Feature 2, in the central part of the site, was once two stories; it was built of single-coursed, scabbled masonry typical of other Pueblo II structures in southeastern Utah. The eastern half of the great house was built of wide core-and-veneer walls similar to construction in Chaco Canyon but not nearly as well executed. Blocks were poorly shaped and sometimes set in abundant mortar. The lack of attention to architectural detail is most obvious where the east and west parts of the structure join. When the east part of the structure was built, an additional north-south wall was simply built up against the easternmost wall of the earlier structure, creating a double wall simulating the core-and-veneer technique.

Masonry at Bluff contrasts sharply with the finely crafted Chaco-style stone work at Chimney Rock and is also different from the pecked-face masonry construction at Far View (Rohn 1977: 58). It seems more similar to the masonry at Edge of the Cedars (Hurst, this

volume), although the tabular sandstone masonry Hurst describes for Kiva 1 has not been found at Bluff. The quality of the building stone near Bluff is poor, however, and may have limited the mason's ability to emulate Chaco-style construction. Foundation trenches and intramural beams like those observed at Edge of the Cedars have not yet been found at Bluff.

The three blocked-in kivas are similar in construction, but interestingly they do not show obvious Chacoan characteristics. Each is about 6 m in diameter, slightly smaller than the average blocked-in kiva in Chaco Canyon (Lekson 1984: 32), and has a high pilaster and bench. None have the radial-beam pilasters typical of Chacoan kivas. Instead, pilasters rise about 70 cm above the bench like those in Mesa Verde-style kivas. Because excavations were limited to a small trench, however, the presence of other Mesa Verde characteristics, such as six pilasters and a southern recess (Ferguson and Rohn 1987: 28–29), could not be observed. The kivas are slightly smaller than the kiva excavated by Frank Eddy at Chimney Rock, which was about 8 m in diameter and which did have radial-beam pilasters (Eddy 1977: 38). At Far View, one kiva is larger than the kivas at Bluff (about 8 m in diameter),

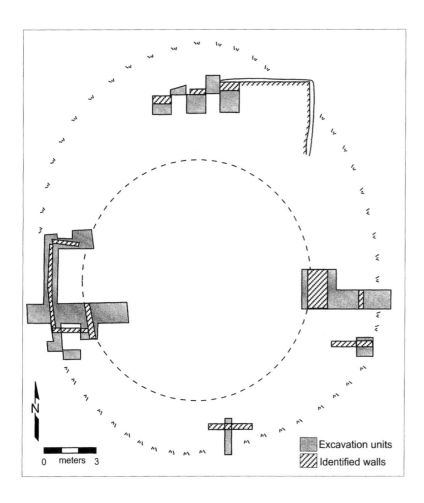

Figure 6.3. The great kiva, showing excavations through 1998. The single partially excavated antechamber room is to the west. A number of walls and a bench likely form another antechamber to the north. Walls to the east and south may indicate additional antechambers.

but three others are smaller (about 4.5 m in diameter). The pilasters in the Far View kivas are like those at Bluff; none are Chacoan in style (Fewkes 1917).

The Bluff great kiva is a deep, masonry-lined structure about 13 m in diameter and partly surrounded by peripheral rooms or antechambers (Fig. 6.3). The interior wall consists of sandstone slabs and blocks set in abundant mortar. The wall extends down about 3 m to a stone- and clay-covered surface that is probably the bench. The floor of the structure may be another meter below this, but was not examined. Our limited test excavations encountered no roofing elements.

Located along the west side of the great kiva, the single excavated antechamber is almost 4 m long (parallel to the edge of the great kiva) and 2 m wide. It has a packed clay surface that was level with the top of the interior wall of the great kiva (about 1 m below modern ground surface). Test excavations showed that the great kiva may have had antechambers at least in all four cardinal directions.

Vivian and Reiter (1960) noted that antechambers were common at great kivas in Chaco Canyon and were often points of access into the main chamber, especially from a north antechamber. Many great kivas in Chaco Canyon and in the northern San Juan area (like Edge of the Cedars, Hurst, this volume) have additional peripheral rooms, but only at the Aztec great kiva, about 160 km (100 miles) southeast of Bluff, do these peripheral rooms surround the entire great kiva. Most peripheral rooms seem to have been an "afterthought" and were often poorly constructed (Vivian and Reiter 1960: 94–95). At Chimney Rock, an excavated great kiva (Structure 17, 5AA88) exhibits a series of stone "cists," many with large plank lids, arranged along the *inside* of the structure. Although Eddy compared them to the rooms outside the great kiva at Aztec Ruins, these cists seem functionally different from features that others have called antechambers. At the Far View community, a great kiva was, until recently, misidentified as a reservoir (Ferguson and Rohn 1987).

The Bluff berm is a low, discontinuous earthen mound that surrounds the great house and forms a platform against the north (rear) wall. At least two of the breaks in the berm served as entry points for a prehistoric road that passed between the great house and the great kiva. The road extended southeast toward Chaco Canyon and north up Cottonwood Wash toward the Cottonwood Falls great house. Other breaks in the berm may have been caused by modern earth-moving activities (especially construction of the access road to the Bluff town cemetery), but discontinuous earthen mounds around great houses have been recorded elsewhere (Kintigh and others 1996; Warburton and Graves 1992; Windes 1982). Similar structures have not been found surrounding either the Chimney Rock or Far View great houses, but both were excavated before such features were commonly recognized. It is also possible that the limited space on Chimney Rock's pinnacle precluded the construction of a berm.

The densest trash deposits were in the area of the berm southeast of the great house. We placed a long trench there with the intent of bisecting the entire mound. The trench was more than 5 m in length, but the top of the mound had apparently been truncated by erosion and the trench revealed only eastward-sloping strata. Sediments were more than 1.5 m deep with several distinct layers. Near the base of the berm was a thick, black layer that seemed to consist primarily of burned vegetal material that may have been discarded roofing. Radiocarbon dates of corn cobs from this layer were highly variable, but record deposition in the A.D. 1100s and early 1200s. Ceramics from the berm were predominantly of the late Pueblo II period, although Pueblo III styles were represented in the upper levels and Pueblo I pottery was noted. One layer produced numerous sandstone spalls that may have come from construction of the great house or great kiva. A thick layer of burned daub was originally interpreted as discard from wattle-and-daub houses, but it may instead represent discarded roofing material, perhaps from the great kiva.

North and west of the great house, cultural material in the berm was not as dense but just as deep. The platform north of the great house was clearly a substantial construction consisting of at least 1.5 m of building debris and other cultural material. A piece of charcoal from this area produced a tree-ring cutting date of A.D. 1120, supporting a late date for the construction of the berm or at least of the platform behind the great house. West of the great house, cultural material in the berm was even sparser but still deep; this area produced a great deal of burned wood.

The Bluff great house was probably built in the early A.D. 1100s and continued to be used into the middle 1200s. Although it has many Chacoan characteristics, masonry and ceramics are predominantly local. Bluff contrasts sharply with Chimney Rock, where architecture was definitely Chacoan and at least some ceramics were imported from Chaco Canyon. In some aspects of kiva construction, Bluff is similar to Far View, although masonry is cruder.

GREAT HOUSE COMMUNITIES IN THE NORTHERN SAN JUAN REGION

In their overview of cultural developments in the northern San Juan region, Varien and others (1996) report an interval of low population in the 10th and early 11th centuries, followed by significant population increases in the late 11th century. Varien and his colleagues (1996: 96) think that great houses built during the 11th and the 12th centuries were constructed within existing communities (see also Kane 1993). Although many great houses have been recognized in the northern San Juan region, there has been little study of the surrounding communities of small habitations that presumably used these structures. The Bluff great house community survey provides an important look at the small sites that surround one of these great houses. Survey and excavation conducted decades ago at the Far View and Chimney Rock great house communities provide data for comparison with Bluff. The three communities permit an initial assessment of the nature of the Chacoan community in the northern San Juan region.

The Bluff Great House Community

The Bluff community survey archaeologists recorded nine sites that were at least partly contemporary with the great house. The sites ranged between 0.8 km to 9.6 km (0.5 to 6.0 miles) from the great house (Fig. 6.4). Although dating by surface ceramics provides only limited accuracy, most of the sites could be assigned to the middle to late Pueblo II period or to the early Pueblo III period.

Individual unit pueblos constitute the most common site type, followed by multiple household sites and "talus sites" (defined below). The sites recorded during the survey probably represent only part of the original prehistoric community; intermittent flooding along the

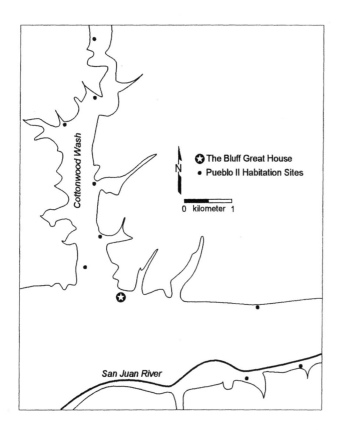

Figure 6.4. The Bluff great house community, showing the great house and other sites recorded during the 1997 survey.

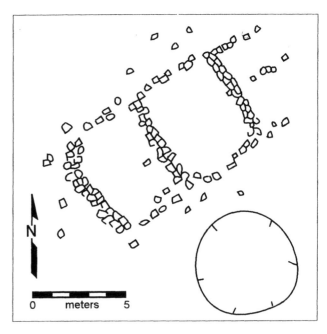

Figure 6.5. Site CU 97-9 (42 SA 23746), a typical Bluff community unit pueblo. The midden is located on a slope approximately 20 to 25 m to the east-southeast.

San Juan River and the development of the modern town of Bluff have likely destroyed or obscured a number of sites.

Individual unit pueblos are the primary features at four sites. An additional site, CU 97-5 (42 SA 23040), includes two unit pueblos from two different periods (Pueblo I and Pueblo II). The structures in these sites were built primarily of roughly shaped sandstone slabs that were occasionally supplemented with cobbles (Fig. 6.5). Placement appears to have been dictated primarily by access to arable lands; four settlements were located on terraces along Cottonwood Wash, and the fifth was placed on a terrace above the San Juan River. All five sites were relatively isolated, with the next nearest sites ranging from 0.7 to 1.3 km (0.4 to 0.8 mile) away. Surface ceramics date these sites to the middle Pueblo II to early Pueblo III periods.

Three community sites are large enough to have housed the residences for multiple households. Site CU 97-7 (42 SA 23744) has a minimum of 20 rooms divided between two pueblos. The sizable number of ceramics recovered date to both the Pueblo II and Pueblo III periods, but the visible structures are probably remnants from the later component. The two other multiple household sites consist of aggregations of unit pueblos along terraces of the San Juan River. Site CU 97-10 (42 SA 23747) has as many as 10 unit pueblos. It is atop a small terrace surrounded by heavy talus on the north side of the San Juan River. Unlike other habitations in the Bluff great house community, many of the structures at CU 97-10 appear to have been constructed with upright slabs. Although slab architecture is frequently associated with the Pueblo I period, Rohn (1977) indicated that some Pueblo II unit pueblos on Chapin Mesa had large upright slabs that served as the footing for jacal structures.

The Dance Plaza site (CU 97-11; 42 SA 23748) is also multihousehold. It is located along the south side of the San Juan River and contains a minimum of 17 room blocks aggregated around one of the most unique examples of public architecture in the northern San Juan (Fig. 6.6). This "Dance Plaza" is a 10-m by 22-m structure consisting of an open plaza surrounded by low, 1-m thick walls with what appear to be two room blocks on its east and west ends. Almost no wall fall is associated with the structure; the masonry walls must not have been very high, although jacal construction may have extended their height. Speculations about this structure's function include a dance plaza, ball court, and square great kiva. Regardless of the Dance Plaza's func-

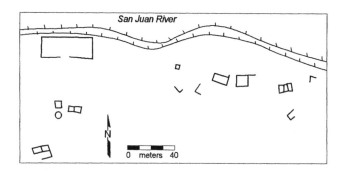

Figure 6.6. Plan of the Dance Plaza site (42 SA 23748), with a large rectangular community structure in the northwest corner and a minimum of 17 associated room blocks.

tion, the settlement is significant in that it is the Bluff community's only other example of community architecture besides the Bluff great house and great kiva. Because the settlement likely dates between the early and middle Pueblo II period and does not appear to have been contemporary with the Bluff great house (late Pueblo II to early Pueblo III), it may have served as a community focus *before* the great house was built.

An additional multihousehold site was identified but designated as a "talus site," a term borrowed from Rohn's (1977) Chapin Mesa survey. He used it to describe anomalous sites that were situated among the talus at the base of canyon walls. Site CU 97–3 (42 SA 23741) is the only site in the Bluff community area that fits this description. The architecture appears to represent three unit pueblos and two additional structures located among boulders along the cliffs of Cottonwood Wash. Just as Rohn struggled to determine the nature of the talus sites that he encountered on Chapin Mesa, we had difficulty discerning the function of this settlement. Interpretation was further hampered by severe site disturbance in the form of erosion and looting.

The Chimney Rock Great House Community

An overview of the data compiled during community studies at Chimney Rock pueblo provides a perspective of a community on the opposite side of the northern San Juan region. Chimney Rock pueblo is on top of a steeply dipping *cuesta* or mesa overlooking the Piedra River (Eddy 1977) in one of the few areas along the river where there is a broad and open floodplain (Mobley-Tanaka 1990). The Chacoan architecture is on the upper portion of the mesa and habitations are clustered on the

lower mesa and on the river terraces at the mesa's base (Eddy 1977).

The barriers imposed by topography are important in considering the organization and settlement layout exhibited in the Chimney Rock community. Differences in elevation segregated the community into three distinct zones (Fig. 6.7). Uneven terrain on both the mesa and the river terraces combined with other factors such as arable land to further divide the community into seven distinct habitation clusters. On the upper and lower mesa, flat terrain appears to have been the determining factor for structure location (Mobley-Tanaka 1990). On the terraces around the base of the mesa, room blocks and pit structures clustered around patches of arable land along the Piedra River and its tributaries. Isolated unit pueblos were often built on smaller patches of arable land (Mobley-Tanaka 1990).

Some 64 residential settlements with a combined 217 habitations were documented around Chimney Rock (Eddy 1977). Most of the structures were classified into one of three distinct architectural styles that corresponded with one of the three topographic areas. The river terraces were dominated architecturally by room blocks with recessed floors. More traditional unit pueblos without recessed floors and pit houses were present but in smaller numbers. Most structures were built of cobbles or jacal but sandstone masonry was also used (Mobley-Tanaka 1990). These structures were similar to the predominant architectural style seen at late Pueblo I and other early Pueblo II period sites encountered in the Navajo Reservoir District located down the river from Chimney Rock (Eddy 1966). Large pit depressions surmised to be great kivas were also interspersed among the smaller sites.

The sites on the lower mesa exhibited marked differences from those located on the terraces below. Rather than reflecting the predominant architectural styles of the Piedra region, houses were built in a style peculiar to Chimney Rock. The structures consisted of circular living rooms with smaller rectangular storage rooms attached to their north sides. Additional circular rooms were often added together during multiple building episodes, giving the structures a honeycomb appearance (Fig. 6.8; Mobley-Tanaka 1990). Walls were two to three courses thick and consisted of flaked sandstone slabs cemented by mud mortar (Truell 1975). Large pit depressions located on the lower mesa are indicative of the presence of great kivas. The upper mesa structures consisted of the Chimney Rock great house and other associated community architecture that exhibited a distinct Chacoan style.

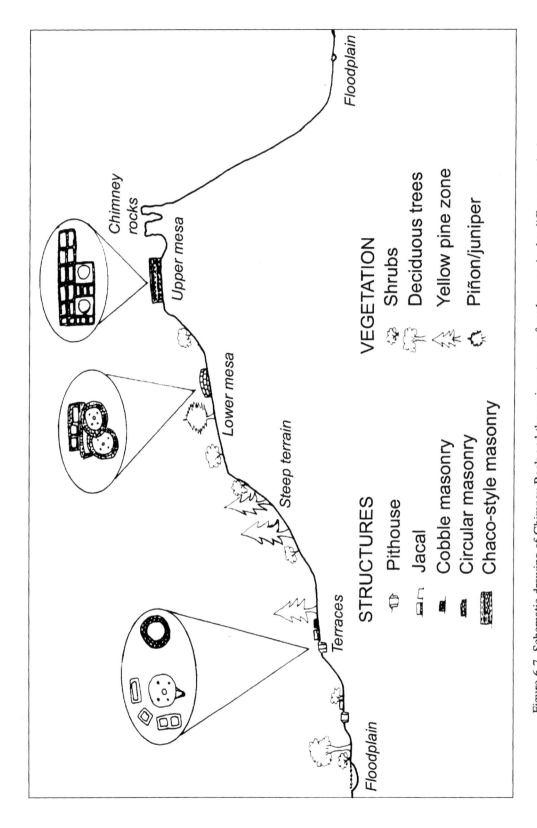

Figure 6.7. Schematic drawing of Chimney Rock and the various types of settlements in the different vertical zones: room blocks and pit structures on the river terraces, "honeycomb" residential structures unique to Chimney Rock on the lower mesa, and a Chaco-style great house on top of the mesa (adapted from Mobley-Tanaka 1990: 2).

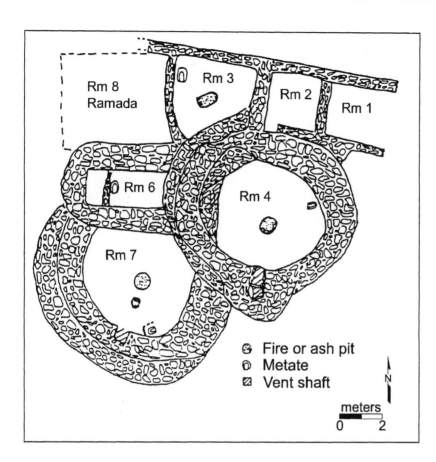

Fire or ash pit
Metate
Vent shaft

meters
0   2

Figure 6.8. A honeycomb structure on the lower mesa of Chimney Rock. The circular rooms appear to have been used for habitation and the rectangular rooms for storage. The architecture of these structures is unique to the Chimney Rock community (adapted from Mobley-Tanaka 1990: 96).

The Far View Great House Community

The Far View community on Chapin Mesa at Mesa Verde National Park, located in the central section of the northern San Juan region, provides the third view of a great house community. Three sites excavated by the University of Colorado during the late 1950s were described by Lister (1964, 1965, 1966) as having "typical" Pueblo II and early Pueblo III period domestic architecture and they provided a model for changes in community settlement patterns for these periods.

The Far View community began in the early Pueblo II period as a cluster of 14 settlements. During the middle of Pueblo II, the Far View great house was constructed and the community expanded to 36 settlements (Rohn 1977). Two of them, Site 866 and Site 875, were excavated by Lister (1965, 1966). Site 866 consisted of 10 single-story rooms with 3 associated pit structures. Masonry was one course thick, with "chipped edge" sandstone slabs (Lister 1966). Site 875 had two separate structures representing two different occupations, one in the early Pueblo II period and the other in middle to late Pueblo II. The later structure had a single tree-ring

date of A.D. 1047 (Lister 1965). The earlier occupation was represented by a block of 17 rooms with 3 kivas. The second occupation was built on top of the remnants of the first, and one of the original kivas was remodeled and reused during the second occupation. The later structure was also eventually remodeled and expanded; what started as an inverted U-shaped structure with 9 rooms and a central kiva became a rectangular structure with 15 rooms and an enclosed central plaza with a kiva (Fig. 6.9). Although this late structure was at least partly contemporary with occupation of Site 866, it differed in masonry style; the walls at Site 875 were double-coursed and consisted of sandstone blocks whose faces were shaped by grinding and in some cases by pecking (Lister 1966: 67). Other habitation structures in the Far View community were comparable in size to those at Sites 866 and 875 or were smaller, one- to two-household unit pueblos (Rohn 1977).

The end of the Pueblo II period was a time of important changes in the Far View area. Larger habitations and the construction of towers were among the more significant developments. The number of settlements in the community shrank to 18 during the late Pueblo II period, but there was still a distinct amount of diversity

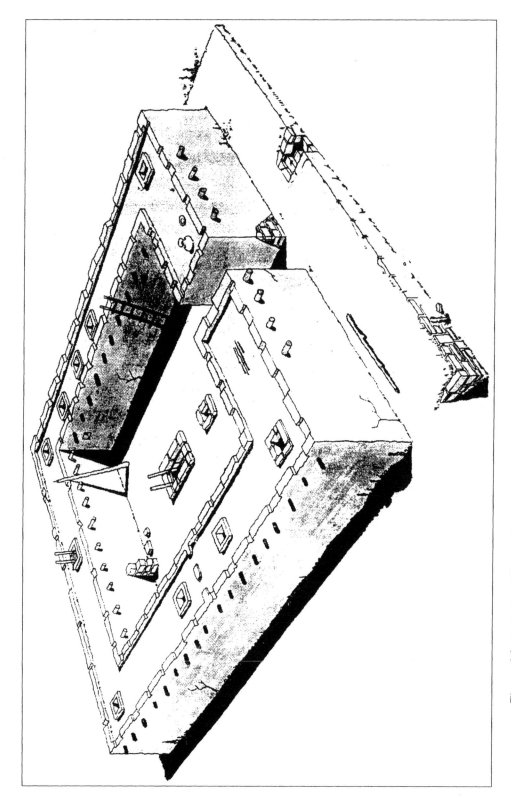

Figure 6.9. Artist's rendition of the second stage of the middle to late Pueblo II period pueblo at Site 875 in the Far View community. The structure is comparable in size and style to a number of other Far View community structures of this period (from Lister 1965: 61; reprinted with permission of the University Press of Colorado).

in the community structures (Rohn 1977). Two smaller unit pueblos dated to this time period but larger structures predominated, including some with 50 rooms. Site 499, of late Pueblo II to early Pueblo III period date, consisted of a series of 12 ground-story rooms enveloping a plaza with two central kivas (Lister 1964). Lister (1966) speculated that there might have been six additional second-story rooms. Apparently a two-story tower was attached to the room blocks and connected to the kivas by subterranean passages. The masonry was double coursed and consisted of pecked and ground sandstone blocks.

INTRA- AND INTERCOMMUNITY COMPARISONS

The Bluff, Chimney Rock, and Far View great house communities exhibited a number of differences in settlement layout and architecture that might have been the result of local conditions, including topographic and environmental constraints. Other factors may have included social organization and agricultural strategies. The similarities among the three communities might have reflected influences of the Chaco "phenomenon" or characteristics common to northern San Juan communities or even pan-Anasazi community traits.

Topography clearly created differences among the three communities with regard to settlement location. The Bluff community encompassed two settlement patterns. Habitations in Cottonwood Wash followed a dispersed pattern with distance between them averaging 0.1–0.8 km (up to half a mile), and individual unit pueblos constituted the majority of the habitations. This pattern may have been dictated by the narrow canyon and the area of land necessary for household agriculture. Varien (1997) suggested that the placement of residences was a means by which households claimed land. The distance between habitations means that each household would have had almost a whole kilometer along the narrow canyon available for agriculture. Household members may have maximized their claims to arable land by placing their unit pueblos at or proximate to the mouths of side canyons. A different Bluff settlement pattern is evident along the broad San Juan River floodplain, where two of the three settlements consisted of aggregations of unit pueblos located on terraces of the river. The habitations around the Cottonwood Falls great house appear to have had a similar dichotomy in settlement pattern. Habitations in the narrow canyon were more dispersed than the closely aggregated habitations on the mesa top.

The Chimney Rock community pattern was tightly clustered, with rugged topography as the main factor determining distance between groups of habitations. Location on the upper and lower mesa related to the availability of level ground. Settlements along the terraces appear to have been clustered around areas of arable land. Social factors also may have influenced the layout of the Chimney Rock community. Locations of habitations on the upper and lower mesa perhaps were dictated by the social phenomena centered around the Chimney Rock great house. Only the strong pull of the great house, an important community structure, could have compensated for the mesa's inaccessibility, poor or nonexistent soils, and distant water sources. The placement of the community as a whole was significant, because Chimney Rock is one of the few areas along this stretch of the Piedra River Valley where cold air drainage does not drastically reduce the growing season (Eddy 1977).

Habitations within the Far View community were also tightly clustered. During the middle of the Pueblo II period, 36 of them were located within less than 2 km (1.2 miles) of the Far View great house (Rohn 1977). Rohn viewed Mummy Lake as a central reason for aggregation in the area prior to the construction of the great house, based on the assumption that the lake was some sort of water control feature. However, that function of Mummy Lake has recently been challenged and the notion was raised by Lekson in 1997 that it was the remnant of a community structure (a great kiva) rather than a reservoir. Agriculture may have been another factor in settlement layout at Far View. The tight clustering evident there was not uncommon in other areas of Mesa Verde, where small concentrations of habitations and communities clustered around the limited areas of higher-quality soil on the mesa tops.

Although the communities had different layouts, improving agricultural productivity was probably the main reason for settlement patterning. It is not surprising that in Bluff, Chimney Rock, and possibly Far View, subsistence appears to have been a primary factor affecting community layout. Even if the communities had major changes in ideological or political systems, they had to maintain a community layout that stressed agricultural sustainability.

There is considerable intercommunity and even intracommunity diversity in the remains of small site masonry and architectural design. Unlike the great houses, there does not seem to have been a Chacoan influence on small domestic architecture. Instead, each of these communities reflects building styles that were predominant within their particular area of the northern San Juan. Variations of the Prudden unit pueblo as seen at Bluff are common in southeast Utah (Varien 1997). The diversity of structures and masonry types in the Far View community is evident at Pueblo II period sites all over Mesa Verde (Smith 1988). The above-ground circular structures on the lower mesa at Chimney Rock are unique both within the Piedra region and the northern San Juan (Eddy 1977; Mobley-Tanaka 1990; Truell 1975). An absence of comparable designs near Chimney Rock may mean that the circular structures were a local development that failed to spread because of the isolation of the Chimney Rock community.

Chacoan versus Local Influences

The Bluff great house and the domestic structures surrounding it formed a dispersed community during the Chaco and post-Chaco eras. The great house was built in a local style that included some Chacoan attributes, such as wide walls and multiple stories. Prehistoric road segments and the berm are additional features that hint of a Chacoan world view. On the other hand, ceramics and other artifacts from both the great house and the surrounding community were largely locally made and showed little evidence of interaction with Chaco Canyon. Similarly, at Far View, although the community was more tightly nucleated around the great house, the structure itself and some of the surrounding habitations were constructed of pecked-face masonry, which was common in the northern San Juan but less common in Chaco Canyon. In their local flavor, Bluff and Far View followed a pattern comparable to many other great houses in the northern San Juan region such as Yucca House, Yellow Jacket, Lancaster, and Escalante Reservoir. Kane (1993) proposed that for communities that were established prior to the Chaco era and then "captured" by an economic system centered on Chaco Canyon, Chacoan architectural elements might have been added to the local construction style.

The Chimney Rock great house and its surrounding community are unusual. The great house was built with a masonry style similar to that used at great houses in Chaco Canyon, but unique circular structures characterize the surrounding habitations. Of the three communities, Chimney Rock seems most likely to have been closely connected to Chaco Canyon. Eddy (1977) has suggested that it was an outpost established by priests from Chaco Canyon. Kane (1993) agreed and further

proposed that the outpost was established so that the people of Chaco Canyon could exploit the abundant timber in the area. In comparison, the Bluff and Far View communities in all probability were established by local people adopting elements of a Chacoan style.

The preliminary review of these three communities leaves us with the notion that certain aspects of their residents' day-to-day lives were largely unchanged by the construction of great houses. We think that shelter and subsistence differed little from settlements not associated with great houses. Furthermore, changes in politics or religion are not archaeologically evident nor recognizable in the smaller households, although these changes are more clearly reflected in integrative community architecture. Further clarification of the extent of Chaco Canyon influence on these three communities must await test excavations at domestic sites around the Bluff great house and more intense scrutiny of the data from the Far View and Chimney Rock communities.

Acknowledgments

Excavation of the Bluff great house was jointly sponsored and funded by the University of Colorado and the Southwest Heritage Foundation, and co-sponsored with Abajo Archaeology. Funds were also generously provided by the National Geographic Society and the National Center for Preservation, Technology, and Training of the National Park Service. The Bluff Community Survey was funded by the University of Colorado and the University of Colorado Museum. Our abundant thanks go to the people of Bluff who were so supportive of the project, including Skip and Alex Lange, Bill Davis, Charlie Delorme, Gene and Mary Foushee, Vaughn and Marcia Hadenfeldt, Maggie Lasakow, Kelly McAndrews, Joe Pachak, Jonathan Till, Jean and Dan Treece, Debbie Westfall, and Jay Willian. At the Bureau of Land Management, assistance was provided by Dale Davidson and Nancy Shearin. Appreciation is expressed to Steve Lekson, co-director of the Bluff Great House Project; Mark Bond, field foreman; Winston Hurst and Jonathan Till of Abajo Archaeology, who led excavations on the great house; and University of Colorado graduate students Caryn Berg, Dan Falt, Chris Ward, and Eden Welker, who served ably as crew chiefs. Finally, the project could not have been completed without the skillful efforts of the more than 40 field school students who worked cheerfully despite heat, bugs, and fugitives.

CHAPTER SEVEN

Chacoan Ritual Landscapes
The View from Red Mesa Valley

Ruth M. Van Dyke

An investigation of great house community autonomy requires an understanding of the relationships between the communities and Chaco Canyon. Great house communities have been primarily defined by virtue of the presence of Bonito-style (Chacoan) architectural forms, yet the processes underlying the spread of this architecture throughout the San Juan Basin are poorly understood. Because the largest and most impressive concentration of Bonito-style architecture is in Chaco Canyon, the canyon is usually assumed to be the hub from which the architecture emanated. Bonito-style architecture at great house communities could have been built by migrants carrying masonry traditions from Chaco into new or existing communities. It could have been constructed by masons from Chaco Canyon as part of a physical manifestation of canyon-imposed control or influence. Canyon masons could have been consulted or invited to undertake construction by local leaders. Canyon-based scenarios usually place the appearance of Bonito-style architecture in great house communities during the Classic Bonito phase, about A.D. 1050 to 1120, when canyon activities would have been in full swing.

It is possible to conceptualize alternatives to Chaco-directed construction scenarios, however. Local people may have been emulating Bonito-style architecture observed either at Chaco Canyon or in neighboring communities. A rationale for local emulation of Chacoan architectural forms is suggested by Renfrew and Cherry's (1986) peer-polity interaction model, in which neighboring communities observe and compete with one another in the absence of a strong political authority. Kintigh (1994: 134–136) notes that peer-polity interaction may explain the appearance of quasi-Bonito-style great kivas at post-Chacoan communities as Cibolan groups sought prestige by emulating the Chacoan past. Could prestige also have been gained by emulating the Chacoan present?

In a recent large-scale comparative study, I focused on the origins of Bonito-style architecture in outlying communities throughout the greater San Juan Basin (Van Dyke 1998, 1999b). The results of the study show that substantial regional diversity is contained under the rubric of the Chacoan "system." Although some outlying communities may have interacted intensively with Chaco Canyon, others may have interacted rarely with the canyon or not at all. Great house architecture in outlying communities need not signify an expansionist Chacoan presence. In the Red Mesa Valley, three lines of evidence (early great house dates, architectural differences with canyon great houses, and insular patterns of artifact distribution) suggest that at least some great houses were constructed under the auspices of local rather than Chaco Canyon direction. As both ritual settings and symbols, these great houses could have been constructed in competitive emulation among neighboring communities as part of the creation and legitimation of local social inequality.

RED MESA VALLEY GREAT HOUSES AS LOCAL PHENOMENA

The Red Mesa Valley is a topographically defined area south of the Dutton Plateau located approximately 65 km to 90 km (40 to 56 miles) south of Chaco Canyon and stretching approximately 80 km (50 miles) from east to west. The valley contains at least 10 communities dating from the Chacoan era and containing Bonito-style architectural features (Fig. 7.1): Andrews (Marshall and others 1979; Van Dyke 1997b, 1999a), Casamero (Harper and others 1988; Marshall and others 1979; Powers and others 1983; Sigleo 1981), Coolidge (Marshall and others 1979), Coyotes Sing Here (Marshall and others 1979), El Rito (Allan and Gauthier 1976; Powers and others 1983), Fort Wingate (Marshall and others 1979; Peckham 1958), Haystack (Marshall

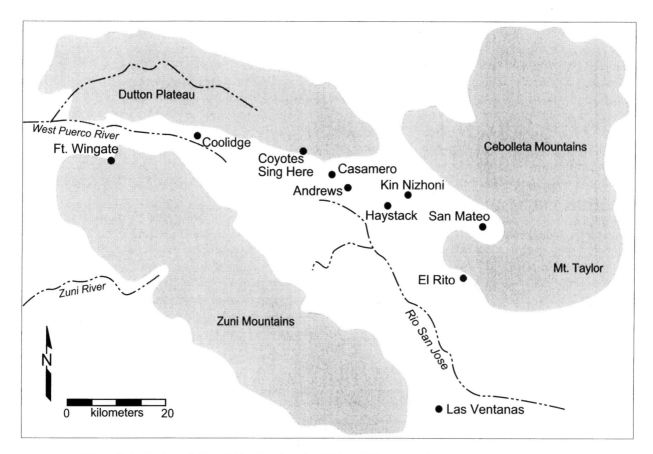

Figure 7.1. Early and Classic Bonito phase Red Mesa Valley great house community locations.

and others 1979; Powers and others 1983), Kin Nizhoni (Marshall and others 1979; Powers and others 1983), Las Ventanas (Marshall and others 1979), and San Mateo (Marshall and others 1979). Great houses in these communities were variable in terms of size and layout (Fig. 7.2). Most communities also contained one or more great kivas, and some contained earthworks and road segments. Early dates, architectural diversity, and insular artifact distribution support the impression that some Red Mesa Valley great houses were locally constructed.

Early Dates

Many Red Mesa Valley great houses, including Andrews, Casamero, Coolidge, El Rito, Fort Wingate, Haystack, and Las Ventanas, appear in the midst of communities where occupation dates from the Late Pueblo I period or earlier. Kin Nizhoni is the only one of the Red Mesa Valley group that resembles what Marshall and others (1982: 1231) would term a "scion outlier," founded *in toto* during the Pueblo II period and lacking a Basketmaker III or Pueblo I period substrate.

Recent research at the Andrews community (Van Dyke 1997b, 1999a) supports the long-held contention among Chacoan scholars that the Red Mesa Valley great houses are themselves relatively early. The Andrews great house and associated great kiva are dated by ceramics to around A.D. 1000 and were constructed at the location of an intense Late Pueblo I to Early Pueblo II period occupation. Five middens are in the vicinity of the Andrews great house and associated great kiva. The nearest, Midden 1, yielded a mean ceramic date of 1017 ± 90. In contrast, mean ceramic dates for Middens 2 through 5 cluster between 919 ± 56 and 930 ± 60. The Early Pueblo II period component of the surrounding community included two additional isolated great kivas with associated mean ceramic dates of 924 ± 60 and 941 ± 74. The overall picture is one of a thriving Late Pueblo I–Early Pueblo II period community with several community centers, of which the great house was but the latest.

This pattern is not unique among the Red Mesa Valley communities. Mean ceramic dates and ranges for 10 additional Red Mesa Valley great houses (Table 7.1) were calculated using ceramic data collected by other

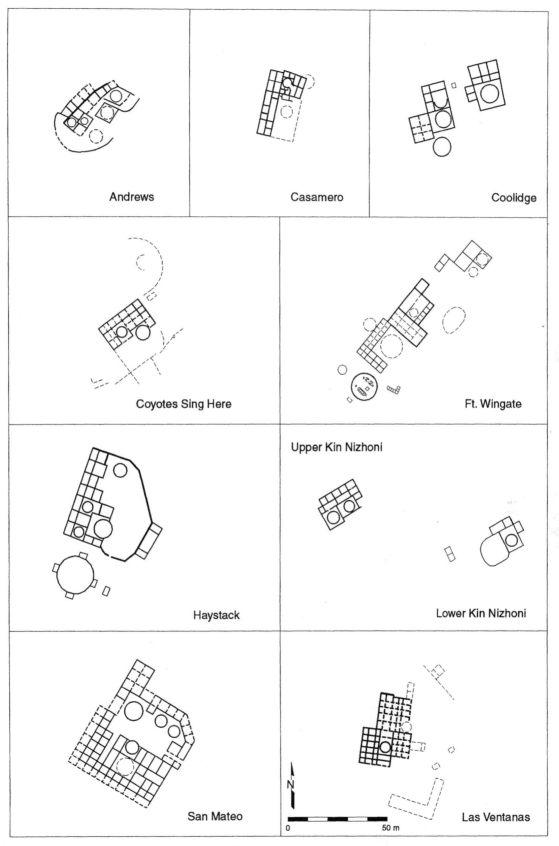

Figure 7.2. Plans of ten Red Mesa Valley great houses. (All plans except Andrews are based on Marshall and others 1979: 135–196.)

Table 7.1. Ceramic Dates for Red Mesa Valley Great Houses

Great House	Mean Ceramic Date (A.D.)	Date Range (A.D.)
Fort Wingate	992	948–1036
El Rito	1000	925–1075
Andrews	1017	927–1109
Coyotes Sing Here	1044	990–1098
Lower Kin Nizhoni	1044	992–1096
San Mateo	1049	991–1107
Coolidge	1060	1008–1112
Upper Kin Nizhoni	1076	1039–1113
Casamero	1078	1033–1123
Las Ventanas	1079	1037–1121
Haystack	1080	1050–1110

NOTE: Mean ceramic dates and ranges for all great houses except Andrews and El Rito were calculated using ceramic tallies listed in Marshall and others (1979) and following procedures set forth in Van Dyke (1997b). Mean ceramic dates for Andrews are from Van Dyke (1997b); El Rito dates are not mean ceramic dates but are based on the ceramic date range given by Powers and others (1983: 222).

researchers (Marshall and others 1979; Mills 1988; Powers and others 1983). The great houses cluster into three groups. Two structures (Fort Wingate and El Rito) appear to be even earlier than Andrews, with mean ceramic dates of A.D. 992 ± 44 and 1000 ± 75, respectively. Four great houses (Coyotes Sing Here, Lower Kin Nizhoni, San Mateo, and Coolidge) have mean ceramic dates that cluster between 1044 and 1060, and the remaining four (Upper Kin Nizhoni, Casamero, Las Ventanas, and Haystack) have mean ceramic dates that cluster between 1076 and 1080. These dates are derived from surface ceramic assemblages that in some cases are small (for example, 30 diagnostic sherds from Las Ventanas), but they are in line with the temporal assignments discussed by the researchers (Marshall and others 1979; Powers and others 1983). A pattern of early great houses established in existing communities calls into question the long-standing assumption that outlying great houses were founded as part of a program of Chacoan expansion in the mid-eleventh century (Vivian 1990: 184).

Architecture

I designed a large-scale comparative architectural study (Van Dyke 1998, 1999b) to determine whether outlying great houses were constructed under the influence or direction of Chaco Canyon residents or whether the structures were local manifestations. Chaco Canyon great houses provided an archetype against which I compared outlying great houses. Seven Canyon great houses dating from the Early and Classic Bonito phases were used as the baseline for comparison: Chetro Ketl, Hungo Pavi, Peñasco Blanco, Pueblo Alto, Pueblo Bonito, Pueblo del Arroyo, and Una Vida. Data came primarily from Lekson's (1984) architectural synthesis. No attempt was made to separate brief construction episodes, because most outlying great houses in the comparative sample remain unexcavated, so dates cannot yet be similarly refined. Analysis was based on the premise that external architectural characteristics could be easily imitated by outsiders, but internal precepts of Bonito-style construction could not. Considering the constraints imposed by the limited data from the largely unexcavated outlying great houses, a set of "internal" variables were formulated that presumably would have been difficult for outsiders to emulate. These variables included core-and-veneer masonry, banded facing, symmetry, elevated kivas, and kiva-to-room ratio. If internal variables exhibited little diversity with respect to each other and to Chaco Canyon, then the outlying great houses might be interpreted as Chacoan in origin, and vice versa.

Results of the analysis indicated that a variety of relationships existed between outlying great house communities and Chaco Canyon. The Red Mesa Valley emerged as a topographic subregion that contained substantial great house diversity, illustrated particularly well by two of the internal variables: kiva-to-room ratio and banded veneer style.

Kiva-to-Room Ratio

Kivas are commonly considered to have been used for ritual purposes at least some of the time (Adler 1989; Lekson 1988). Steward (1937) and Lipe (1989, 1995) used kiva:room ratio as a means of gauging changes in the composition of the groups who used kivas and the social functions served by kiva activities. Steward (1937) contended the characteristic puebloan habitation site kiva:room ratio of 1:6 or 1:5 indicated that every lineage constructed its own kiva and conducted its own ceremonies. A shift to kiva:room ratios of 1:15 to 1:25 was interpreted as reflecting a change in the organization of ritual and a concomitant emphasis on kivas as settings for integrative social activities. Lipe (1989: 56, Table 1) estimated a kiva:room ratio of 1:15.2 for nine Chacoan great houses in the Mesa Verde area, but local "Mesa Verde Anasazi" pueblos exhibited kiva:room ratios of 1:6.5. This pattern was interpreted by Lipe (1989: 59) to mean that Chacoan great house kivas functioned at a large-scale, integrative level, whereas kivas in local pueblos were more likely used by households or extended families (Lipe 1989: 64).

If social structure was organized in similar ways and if great house kivas served similar functions in both Chaco Canyon and outlying great houses, then kiva: room ratios of both should be similar, regardless of other differences in overall structural size. Instead, there are marked differences in kiva:room ratio between the Red Mesa Valley great houses and Chaco Canyon great houses. Kiva:room ratios from the Red Mesa Valley great houses are variable, ranging between 1:4 (Andrews) and 1:30 (Las Ventanas), with an average of 1:7. Contemporaneous Chaco Canyon great houses, by comparison, exhibit an average kiva:room ratio of 1:22. A Mann-Whitney U-test calculated the differences between the two data sets as statistically significant ($\rho = 0.006$). This pattern suggests that differences existed between Chaco Canyon and Red Mesa Valley great houses in kiva function and in the size and composition of the groups who used the kivas.

Banded Veneers

Banded Type II or III veneers (Judd 1964; Lekson 1984: 17–19) were considered an internal variable based on the assumption that outlying great house veneers may well have been plastered (for example, Marshall 1982: 185, 187, Table 18; see Van Dyke 1998: 110–111, for discussion). Banded veneers are conspicuously absent from most Red Mesa Valley great houses with exposed masonry. This pattern does not appear to be entirely due to either temporal differences or the vagaries of raw material availability. Great houses at both Fort Wingate (Marshall and others 1979: 55) and El Rito (Powers and others 1983: 222) lack banding but do exhibit compound rather than core-and-veneer walls; because both aspects may be a figment of the relatively early construction of these buildings (Table 7.1), these two great houses were not included in this part of the study. Raw material availability does not appear to have dictated the presence or absence of banding. Although limestone figured prominently in the construction of several Red Mesa Valley great houses at Casamero, alternating layers of limestone and sandstone were used to heighten the banded effect (Marshall and others 1979: 133).

Among nine Classic Bonito phase Red Mesa Valley great houses for which information is available, only two, Casamero (Sigleo 1981: 3) and Kin Nizhoni (Marshall and others 1979: 171) are recorded as exhibiting banding. Fisher's exact test determined that the difference in presence or absence of banded veneers at Red Mesa Valley great houses as compared with Chaco Canyon great houses is statistically significant ($\rho = 0.021$). Without getting into a discussion of what the *presence* of banded veneers might mean at Casamero and Kin Nizhoni, the fact that banding is *absent* at seven Red Mesa Valley great houses indicates that the builders of these structures did not share the internal architectural precepts of construction endemic to canyon masons. In other words, the pattern supports an interpretation of these great houses as local manifestations.

Artifacts

Both ceramic and lithic artifacts from the Red Mesa Valley sites evoke a pattern of insularity rather than one of widespread interaction and exchange. The Red Mesa Valley surface ceramic assemblages are homogeneously Cibolan, with only 133 nonlocal sherds recorded out of a total of 19,563 among 10 great house communities. Of the nonlocal sherds, most (95%) are White Mountain Red Wares; unlike Chaco Canyon and the central San Juan Basin, the Red Mesa Valley does not appear to have received any significant quantity of Chuskan wares. Like Chuskan ceramics, Washington Pass chert is rare in Red Mesa Valley lithic assemblages. In the Andrews community, Washington Pass chert comprised only 42 out of 3,584 artifacts examined, or 1.2 percent. As might be expected, Chinle chert from the nearby Chinle Formation occurs in high frequencies at sites in the Red Mesa Valley (Brandi 1988; Powers and others 1983, Appendix D, Table 1). However, Cameron (1984) did not find as much Chinle chert in Chaco Canyon as was predicted by a linear regression analysis, and there is no clear pattern in support of the redistribution of Chinle chert from Chaco Canyon. Like the architectural evidence discussed above, the artifactual evidence from the Red Mesa Valley tends to support less rather than more interaction with Chaco Canyon during the Early and Classic Bonito phases.

LOCALLY CONSTRUCTED GREAT HOUSES AS RITUAL LANDSCAPE

If, based on the evidence summarized above, we accept that some Red Mesa Valley great houses were of local rather than canyon origin, what could have impelled locals to engage in this construction? What possible purposes might great houses have served in the context of local Red Mesa Valley communities? I contend that some outlying great houses and associated features may have been built as settings for ritual activities that both legitimated and constructed local power relationships.

The concept of a Chacoan ritual landscape originally was proposed by Stein and Lekson (1992: 87), who contended that Bonito-style architectural features constituted "a common ideational bond among what may be ethnically, linguistically, or culturally diverse populations." Bonito-style architectural features could have functioned as ritual setting as well as ritual symbol. The features may have been constructed as part of the legitimation and creation of local social inequalities within a context of competitive emulation among neighboring communities.

Ritual may be used to both legitimate and to construct social inequality. Ritual that legitimates an existing social order may be considered the behavioral manifestation of ideology in its pejorative sense, camouflaging social and economic inequalities (Cohen 1979; Godelier 1978) and ameliorating potential conflict between individual and group interests (Aldenderfer 1993). Following Foucault's (1980, 1982) insight that power is reflexively constituted, Bell (1992, 1997) and others (Bloch 1987; Cannadine 1987) have expanded the concept of ritual as legitimation, recognizing that ritual is not merely a mask for power, but also a means to power. By claiming exclusive access to ritual knowledge or the supernatural, for example, leaders not only legitimate but also construct their authority. Among the ethnographic Pueblos there is a strong relationship between social power and access to ritual knowledge (Cushing 1966: 12; Parsons 1939: 112; Whiteley 1986: 70). McGuire and Saitta (1996) contend that ritual provided an arena for negotiation of the struggle between communal and hierarchical aspects of Puebloan society.

McGuire and Saitta (1996) posit the concept of *complex communalism* to explain the apparent contradictions in Puebloan social organization. Although communities allegedly held land, tools, technical knowledge, and other resources in common, every individual did not necessarily have the same access to these resources. The first settlers in an area would have acquired the most productive farmland and would have been in the best position to produce and control surplus as well as ceremonies.

It is likely that the individuals or factions who controlled and directed construction of Bonito-style architecture would have also played highly visible roles in any ceremonial activities that took place there. If Bonito-style architecture was constructed to function as a ritual setting, social inequalities could have been legitimated and created through construction and through ceremonies or activities enacted in the facilities. For example, a ritual that involved redistribution of surplus would have ostensibly benefited the entire community but also would have increased the prestige of the donors of the surplus.

Following the tenets of a peer-polity interaction model (Renfrew and Cherry 1986), construction of Bonito-style architecture could have benefited local leaders seeking to bolster personal prestige through competition on a regional scale. Bonito-style architecture would have spread through observation and competition among neighboring communities. Great houses are impressive features; once they appeared in one community, leaders in a neighboring community might have had little trouble convincing their populace that competitive emulation of these dramatic structures was necessary. Everyone in the community would have contributed their labor or other resources, but the economically advantaged members of the community would have been able to contribute more. Such generosity would have specifically enhanced the status of those with economic resources to spare, while perhaps fostering an overarching rubric of a shared, egalitarian, community-wide endeavor. Those who had engendered the idea and who were able to contribute the most material support logically would have played a pivotal role in whatever activities were undertaken in the finished structure, thus furthering their own exclusive access to ritual knowledge. Individual or factional social power would have been reflexively created as well as expressed through construction of Bonito-style architecture.

The Andrews Great House as Ritual Setting

Andrews is a good example of a Red Mesa Valley great house that apparently represents a local development and that probably functioned as a setting for community ritual. The Andrews community was located on colluvial slopes at the base of a sandstone escarpment rising 156 m (512 feet) above the Casamero Valley (Fig. 7.3). The community included a great house with associated great kiva and other features, two isolated great kivas, and 39 small house structures (Marshall and others 1979: 117–129; Van Dyke 1997b, 1999a). It was founded in the Late Pueblo I period by 15 to 20 people but apparently quickly attracted additional settlers. Population estimates for the community during the

Pueblo II period range between 70 and 120 people, depending on how settlement contemporaneity is assessed and whether or not great house rooms are counted (Van Dyke 1998: 208–211). Fertility alone cannot account for a population that by conservative estimation tripled within 50 years. Settlement patterns revealed a situation in which original settlers retained control of the best farmland. Late Pueblo I and Early Pueblo II period habitations were clustered in the area of the great house, but although the great house and a few of the larger domestic structures continued to be occupied during the Late Pueblo II period, new Late Pueblo II households were established farther south along the escarpment (Fig. 7.3). A systematic examination of potential agricultural yields from the different areas is planned to help determine whether the Late Pueblo II period lands were actually less productive. Meanwhile, the settlement pattern supports the possibility that community social inequality existed and was associated with differential agricultural yields.

The Andrews great house exhibited a number of characteristic Bonito-style architectural elements (Fig. 7.4). The multistoried structure contained approximately 20 rooms and 5 enclosed kivas. Walls exhibited both core-and-veneer and compound construction and were built of local sandstone and limestone. Rooms averaged 15 square meters in area, nearly four times that of rooms in the surrounding small habitations. In contrast with canyon great houses, as discussed above, the Andrews great house lacked banding and exhibited a low kiva:room ratio. An associated great kiva southeast of the great house was 12 m in diameter and was oriented toward the northeast. The outlines of four to five attached rooms are visible in the rubble surrounding the great kiva.

Several lines of evidence support an interpretation of the Andrews great house locale as a stage for community ritual. The great house was constructed on a finger ridge in the same topographic situation as two earlier, community great kivas. If we assume that the earlier great kivas were used for community gatherings, the continuity in location suggests a similar use for the Andrews great house. As noted in the "early dates" discussion above, the great house was built in an area that ceramic evidence indicates was an important locus of the original community settlement, associating it with firstcomers and their descendants.

The location chosen for great house construction was visually dramatic and imposing. At 2,139 m (7,018 feet) above sea level, the great house would have been the highest structure in the community and would have afforded a view encompassing many surrounding habitations. This placement would have not only impressed onlookers but would have facilitated their observation of any events taking place atop the ridge outside the structure.

A modified swale in front of the Andrews great house may have constituted a ramp leading up to the southeast end of the great house. The ramp was flanked by a berm, now covered with artifacts, and it passed to the north of an associated great kiva before ending in what apparently was a passageway or masonry corridor leading between two kivas into the great house. A low retaining wall extended from the southwest side of the structure around the south end of the building. The retaining wall may have originally extended across an apparent 15-m gap to the beginning of the passageway.

These features indicate that movement into and around the great house was formalized, if not controlled. The retaining wall and swale did not represent physical barriers to access, but do provide evidence that space outside the great house was formally organized, which strongly suggests symbolic associations. The ramp provided a specific means of access to the structure and a highly visible route of entry for individuals or processions. Subsurface investigation is needed to confirm the existence of the passageway. If genuine, the passageway constitutes evidence of controlled access to the great house interior, an attribute associated with social inequality and ritual settings.

All of these attributes emphasize that the Andrews great house was a dramatic and highly visible setting charged with spatial symbolism and amenable to public spectacles. The Andrews great house might well have been the locus of ritual activities that simultaneously legitimated the standing of firstcomers and ameliorated tensions arising from social inequality within a rapidly expanding community.

ARCHITECTURAL EMULATION

The widespread distribution of great houses and other Bonito-style architectural attributes is not necessarily indicative of an integrated Chacoan system. Rather, a range of relationships probably existed between Chaco Canyon and the diverse entities that archaeologists have subsumed under the rubric of "outlier." Three lines of evidence (early great house dates, architectural differences, and local artifacts) indicate that Bonito-style architecture in some communities, such as Andrews in the Red Mesa Valley, may represent indigenous rather than Chaco Canyon-directed construction. Competitive

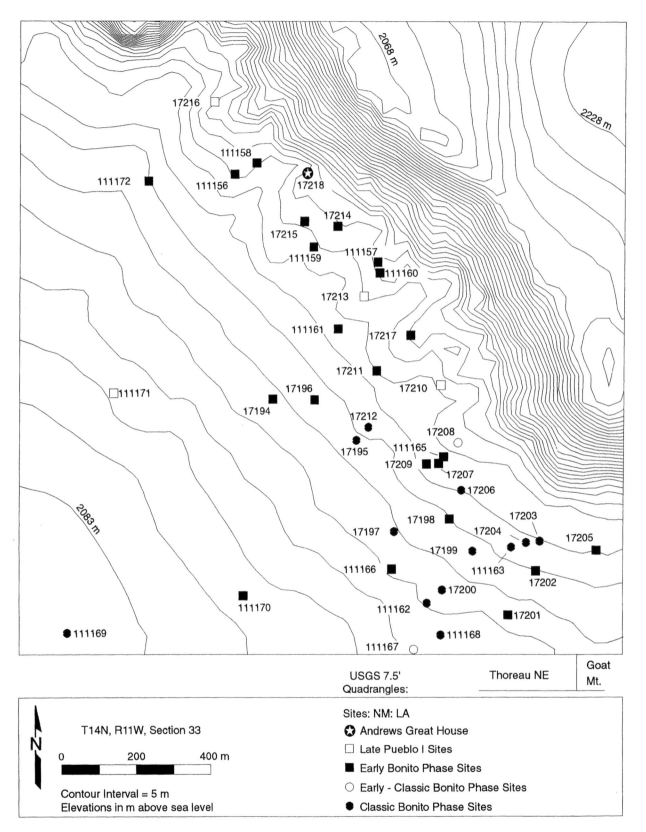

Figure 7.3. Locations of sites in the Andrews community.

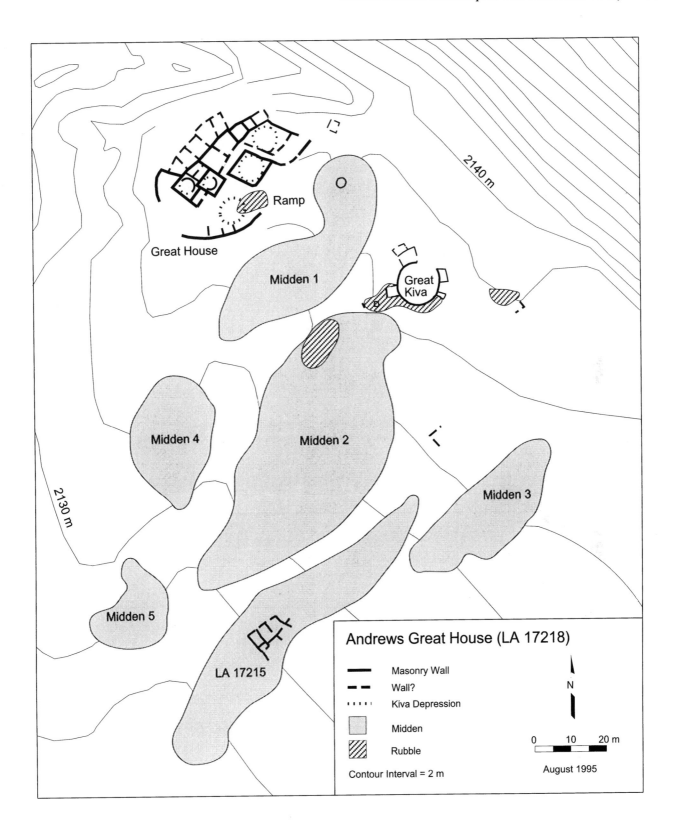

Figure 7.4. The Andrews great house and environs.

emulation as suggested in peer-polity models could explain the spread of superficially similar great house architecture to areas otherwise somewhat outside the scope of canyon influence. Bonito-style architecture constructed to function as a ritual setting could have assisted in the creation and legitimation of social inequalities within local communities.

Acknowledgments

Much of the information presented in this paper was gathered with the support of a dissertation improvement grant from the National Science Foundation (Gwinn Vivian, principal investigator). Fieldwork at Andrews was conducted with the able assistance of Sarah Herr and Joshua Jones and with the permission and encouragement of Jim Walker of the Archaeological Conservancy and John Roney of the Bureau of Land Management. I am grateful to an anonymous reviewer and to Chuck Adams, Jeff Clark, Patti Cook, Beth Grindell, Joshua Jones, Sarah Herr, Joan Mathien, Barbara Mills, Louise Senior, and especially Gwinn Vivian for specific suggestions and insightful comments on the ideas contained within this paper. Any errors are, of course, my own responsibility.

CHAPTER EIGHT

Notes from the Edge
Settlement Pattern Changes at the Guadalupe Community

Stephen R. Durand and Kathy Roler Durand

The current perspective on the Chacoan occupation of the San Juan Basin and beyond is that it represents a regional system. To date, however, it has been exceedingly difficult to understand the mechanics of the hypothesized Chaco system. The early formulation of Judge and his colleagues (Judge 1979; Judge and others 1981) that viewed Chaco as a regional redistribution system has been difficult to verify as scholars have looked closely at this model (for example, Mathien 1993; Toll 1991). Since then, there have been nearly as many views on Chaco as there are scholars in the Southwest (Vivian 1990: 391–418). Although we hold the somewhat unorthodox position that Chaco has been overinterpreted and is much less complex than is generally believed (Durand 1992; Roler 1999), we also feel that in order to understand the Chaco "phenomenon" it is important to first understand the variation in the communities and regions that were occupied within the San Juan Basin during the height of the developments in Chaco Canyon. We know a lot about Chaco Canyon itself because of the extensive research there; it is time that we understand, in detail, the other pieces of the Chaco puzzle.

In this chapter we describe the development and structure of the great house community of Guadalupe. Our bias is that the great house is only part of the story, and to understand the Chaco "phenomenon" on the edges of the Chaco region, it is necessary to understand the larger context in which the great house resides.

PREVIOUS WORK ON THE CHACO "PHENOMENON"

The idea that Chaco Canyon was the center of an organized system evolved from several extensive projects that began in the 1970s and the processual perspective that guided much of the research. Whereas some of these projects focused on sites within (for example, the Pueblo Alto community; Windes 1987) or near (the Bis

sa'ani community; Breternitz and others 1982) Chaco Canyon, others provided the first intensive work beyond Chaco Canyon (Irwin-Williams and Baker 1991; Irwin-Williams and Shelley 1980; Kincaid 1983; Marshall and others 1979; Nials and others 1987; Pippin 1987; Powers and others 1983). Among other things, these studies highlighted similarities in great house architecture across the San Juan Basin. As a result of this research, sites across and beyond the San Juan Basin were thought to be part of a broad system or phenomenon (Irwin-Williams 1972; Toll and others 1980). This Chaco "system" was viewed as more complex than earlier or later cultures and also more complex than the modern Pueblo cultures of the Southwest (Irwin-Williams 1980; Lekson 1984; Marshall and others 1979).

In recent interpretations, archaeologists have questioned the reality of the Chaco system models. Two reconsiderations have focused on communities in smaller regions within the San Juan Basin, the Totah region (McKenna and Toll 1992) and the Red Mesa Valley and the area north of Lobo Mesa (Kantner 1996a). In both cases, patterns within the region suggest that the communities in it were autonomous rather than part of a larger system, architectural similarities notwithstanding. McKenna and Toll (1992) note that the Aztec settlement complex in the Totah area (where the Animas, La Plata, and San Juan rivers come together) was approximately the same size as the Pueblo Bonito settlement complex as defined by Lekson (1988, the great houses of Pueblo Bonito, Chetro Ketl, Pueblo del Arroyo, Pueblo Alto, New Alto, Casa Chiquita, and Kin Kletso in central Chaco Canyon). They suggest that this large concentration of great houses in the Totah area would have comprised its own central place from approximately A.D. 1080 to the mid–1200s.

Kantner (1996a), on the other hand, discerned differences in the degree of centralization in the two regions he examined. Based on differences in the scale and dis-

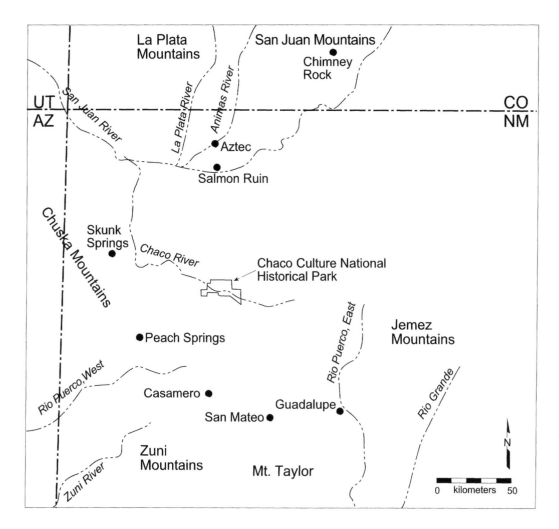

Figure 8.1. Guadalupe Ruin and other Chacoan communities in northwestern New Mexico.

tribution of great houses and great kivas in these areas (as well as differences in the availability of water, good agricultural land, and exotic trade goods), he concluded that more coercive and centralized power developed in the area north of Lobo Mesa than developed to the south in the Red Mesa Valley. The variability between these two areas and the evidence for political competition within them signify that communities in the region were not part of a larger system centered in Chaco Canyon. Instead, the construction of Chaco-style great houses in these regions was used by aspiring leaders in their competition for authority and power (Kantner 1996a: 92).

In a broader comparative study of Chaco Canyon and La Quemada in Zacatecas, Mexico, Nelson (1995) evaluated the level of organizational complexity reached by Chaco Canyon. Although he found that Chaco Canyon had been larger in scale, or areal extent, than La Quemada, the latter region had a higher level of hierarchical organization than Chaco Canyon. Evidence for hierarchical organization at La Quemada included an extensive road system leading to communities of all sizes,

large integrative structures that Nelson reported had a repressive function (pyramids and ball courts), and institutionalized violence (Nelson 1995: 614–615).

The results of these studies call into question the view that the Chacoans were organized into a San Juan Basin-wide system. The communities within Chaco Canyon may have been organized in some form of administrative system (see Sebastian 1992), but it does not necessarily follow that all settlements with Chacoan architecture were part of this system. Patterns within each subregion of the San Juan Basin (and beyond) should be evaluated before settlements within it are assumed to be part of the hypothesized Chaco system. It is to this end that this and other recent work on the Guadalupe Ruin community (Roler 1999) are directed.

THE GUADALUPE COMMUNITY

Guadalupe Ruin is a single-story masonry pueblo on an isolated mesa in the Middle Rio Puerco Valley (Figs. 8.1, 8.2). First reported in 1961 by Emma Lou Davis

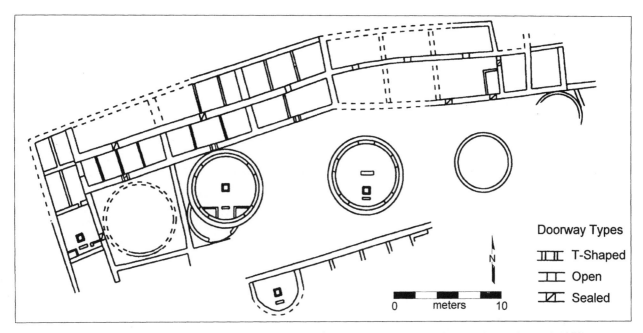

Figure 8.2. The ground plan of Guadalupe Ruin (adapted from Pippin 1987; Terrell and Durand 1979).

and James Winkler in an unpublished University of New Mexico survey (Pippin 1987), the site was excavated from 1973 to 1975 by Lonnie C. Pippin. The results of Pippin's work were published in 1987 and comprise one of the best-documented studies of a Chacoan site outside of Chaco Canyon. Pippin's research at Guadalupe was part of the larger Rio Puerco Valley Project conceived of and run by Cynthia Irwin-Williams during an 11-year period from 1970 to 1981 (Baker 1991a: 8). With the exception of the excavations at Guadalupe Ruin and at one other site, the primary fieldwork focus of the Rio Puerco Project was an extensive survey of the region.

Much of what we report here is discussed by Roney (1996) in his expansive analysis of the eastern San Juan Basin and the Acoma-Laguna area. Using the same primary data that we use here, Roney (1996: 148–149) defined the Guadalupe community as a much larger region than we do, with a total of 82 buildings. The local, small-scale patterns that we identify are consistent with those presented by Roney (1996) at a larger scale. Mahoney (this volume) considers the Guadalupe region at a scale similar to Roney. Our presentation is undertaken to provide a detailed description of one part of the Puerco region that others have described in a more general fashion (see Washburn 1974).

As part of the original research, the members of the Rio Puerco Project conducted an extensive analysis of the ceramics from the survey and test excavation collections and produced a ceramic seriation for the sites in the valley (Durand and Hurst 1991; Hurst 1991). The seriation segmented the ceramic sequence into 17 periods that spanned the puebloan occupation of the valley, about A.D. 800 to 1300 (Durand and Hurst 1991). The Rio Puerco Project also recorded site-size data for all sites surveyed, including an estimate of the number of rooms at each structure. More than 800 puebloan sites were recorded in the survey areas covered by the project (Baker 1991a).

Guadalupe Ruin is considered to be a Chacoan "outlier" by virtue of its architecture, site layout, and location. The east half of Guadalupe Ruin was constructed in about A.D. 960 (Pippin 1987: 100–105) and is the only example of Type I masonry (Lekson 1984) outside of Chaco Canyon. The west half of the building was constructed during the 1000s and was built with classic "core-and-veneer" masonry (Lekson 1984). Pippin (1987, Table 48) obtained only one tree-ring specimen from this portion of the building (A.D. 1112vv) and bases the 11th-century construction on ceramics and architecture. The Chaco-era ceramics from the site indicate that the occupation was continuous from 960 until the early to mid 1100s (Baker 1991a; Hurst 1991; Pippin 1987). The structure was extensively modified in the late 13th century and this is considered to be a San Juan–Mesa Verde reoccupation of the structure (Pippin 1987: 100, 114–128). The structural modifications are similar to those that occurred at the Salmon Ruin along the San Juan River to the north (Irwin-Williams and Shelley 1980). Pippin (1987: 114) is equivocal regarding occupation or abandonment of the structure during the post-Chaco era and pre-Mesa Verde period (A.D. 1130–1220), though transitional pottery forms do occur. For purposes of this chapter, we

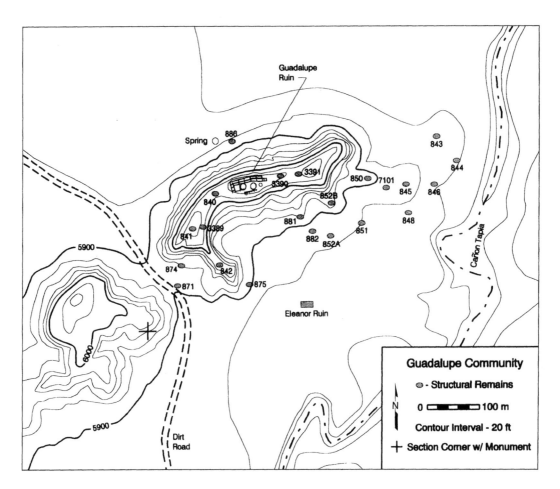

Figure 8.3. Distribution of all the structural remains in the Guadalupe community. Names and numbers correspond to those used in Table 8.1.

Table 8.1. Estimated Room Counts Through Time for Buildings in the Guadalupe Community

ENM Site Number	Period 1	Period 2	Period 3	Period 4	ENM Site Number	Period 1	Period 2	Period 3	Period 4
841	10	10	-	10	871	-	13	-	-
843	12	12	12	-	874	-	33	-	-
844	11	11	-	-	875	-	5	5	5
845	19	19	19	19	882	-	25	-	-
846	13	13	13	13	886	-	-	-	20
848	32	32	-	-	3389	-	24	-	24
851	27	27	-	27	3390	-	-	14	14
852B	4	4	-	-	3391	-	-	-	10
881	12	12	12	12					
Eleanor Ruin	9	9	-	19	Total no. of rooms	155	339	124	278
7101	6	6	6	6					
Guadalupe Ruin	-	29	29	50	N	11	21	10	16
840	-	38	-	38	Min. no. of rooms	4	3	5	3
842	-	3	-	3	Max. no. of rooms	32	38	29	50
850	-	8	8	8	Avg. no. of rooms	14.1	16.1	12.4	17.4
852A	-	6	6	-	Standard Deviation	8.6	10.8	7.3	12.6

NOTE: Numerical entries represent the estimated number of rooms derived from survey data and for buildings occupied during Period 1 (A.D. 900–960), Period 2 (A.D. 960–1130), Period 3 (A.D. 1130–1220), and Period 4 (A.D. 1220–1300).

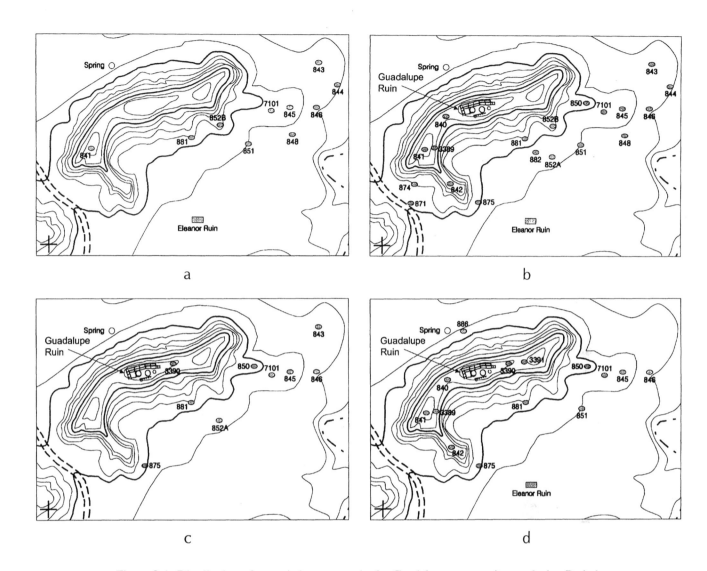

Figure 8.4. Distribution of occupied structures in the Guadalupe community: *a*, during Period 1, A.D. 900–960; *b*, during Period 2, A.D. 960–1130; *c*, during Period 3, A.D. 1130–1220; *d*, during Period 4, A.D. 1220–1300. For scale and position of section corner (+), see Figure 8.3.

assume that the structure was occupied during this intermediate period based on Pippin's observation of transitional pottery and the seriation that was conducted by the Rio Puerco Project (Durand and Hurst 1991).

The survey of the valley identified a number of structures (sites) at the base of Guadalupe Mesa, upon which Guadalupe Ruin sits. This grouping of structures is arbitrarily defined as the Guadalupe community and the locations of the structures are depicted in Figures 8.3 and 8.4. The 24 structures around Guadalupe Mesa are primarily located on the south side of the mesa and include rubble mounds that appear to contain architectural remains. There are other concentrations of artifacts (primarily ceramics and lithics) that were identi-

fied by the Rio Puerco Project that are not shown in Figure 8.3. With the exception of Eleanor Ruin, these structures were not excavated beyond testing in the trash middens. A preliminary report on Eleanor Ruin was produced (Flam 1974) and a full analysis of the Eleanor collection is being conducted by Proper (1997). An analysis of the faunal remains from Eleanor Ruin and from a number of other buildings in the community has been recently completed (Roler 1999).

Table 8.1 lists the number of rooms and the occupation history of the structures in the Guadalupe community. The time ranges for the periods were obtained by combining the seriation groups originally defined by the Rio Puerco Project (Durand and Hurst 1991). If a structure was considered to have been occupied in any one of the original seriation groups, it was considered to have been occupied during the longer combined period used in this chapter. Although the periods are not of equivalent length, they represent cultural stages in the life of the community. Period 1 (A.D. 900–960) was the occupation prior to the construction of Guadalupe Ruin, Period 2 (A.D. 960–1130) was the Chacoan occupation of Guadalupe and the surrounding community, Period 3 (A.D. 1130–1220) was the post-Chacoan occupation of the community, followed by Period 4 (A.D. 1220–1300), the terminal Mesa Verdean occupation of the community. Others (Baker 1991b; Baker and Durand 1991; Roney 1996) have described the large scale settlement pattern changes in the Rio Puerco Valley in terms of the original Puerco seriation. The present study was undertaken to evaluate the local community patterning in temporal periods that are consistent with cultural developments in the larger San Juan Basin region.

The room counts shown in Table 8.1 were based on wall alignments visible on the surface. Though in many cases the wall alignments were obvious, these counts are clearly estimates. Another problem with these data is that structure size, however defined, is only valid for the terminal occupation of each structure. For example, a building with an estimated 20 rooms (based on surface characteristics) that was occupied for 200 years probably did not start out with 20 rooms. Even though these totals may not be precise figures, we present this information to demonstrate general trends in community size through time and we feel that these general trends are worthy of discussion.

COMMUNITY PATTERNS

The initial observation that can be made regarding the Guadalupe community is that there was an established community around the mesa prior to the building of the Guadalupe great house. Figure 8.4a depicts the locations of the 11 structures that were present during Period 1. The structures were of modest size, averaging 14 rooms and ranging from 4 to 32 rooms per building. These counts and the total number of rooms (155) are probably overestimates for the reasons mentioned above. Interestingly, there was habitation at Eleanor Ruin during this period. The west portion of this structure contained core-and-veneer walls that would not have been out of place in Chaco Canyon, and the walls were nearly identical to the late Chacoan construction at Guadalupe Ruin. There was even a T-shaped doorway in this portion of the building (Flam 1974; Proper

1997; Roler 1999). All of these attributes support a later date for Eleanor than its initial ceramic date (A.D. 900–960). In contrast, Guadalupe Ruin does not date to Period 1 yet it had walls with an earlier architectural style than the walls at Eleanor Ruin that were exposed during excavation. Perhaps the unexcavated portion of Eleanor (the east half) was earlier than the excavated west portion of the structure.

The largest number of structures dated to Period 2 and, as noted, represented the Chacoan occupation at Guadalupe Ruin. Twenty-one buildings were occupied during this period with an average size of 16 rooms (Table 8.1, Fig. 8.4b). Whereas in the previous period the structures tended to concentrate on the east of Guadalupe Mesa, now the south side of the mesa was occupied as well. Though it is not obvious in Figure 8.4b, the structures were mostly located on shale bedrock remnants and not in the sandy colluvium that dominates this part of the valley (Baker 1991b; Nials 1991). The one exception to this pattern was Eleanor Ruin. The placement of all of the structures on the south or east side of the mesa was undoubtedly related to the solar efficiency of these locations (Windes and others, this volume).

One of the interesting buildings that was established during Period 2 is ENM 842. Though unexcavated, it appears to have been an isolated kiva. It cannot be classified as a great kiva in size, but there is an obvious depression with attached rooms and the diameter of the depression is clearly constrained by the top of the hill on which the structure was placed. This kiva may have functioned in a fashion similar to great kivas elsewhere in the Chaco region and may have been a community structure in the same sense as the great house itself at the height of the Chacoan occupation of the community. Certainly its location would have been dramatic and it was visible from the entire community.

The post-Chacoan occupation of the community (Period 3) witnessed a dramatic reduction in the number of structures used. Ten buildings were assigned to this period. The average number of rooms (12.4) was the lowest of the four periods and there were only four structures occupied at the base of the mesa with more than 10 rooms (Table 8.1, Fig. 8.4c). This period of flux seems to characterize much of the northern Southwest, and the settlement pattern changes observed at the Guadalupe community extended to the Puerco Valley generally (Baker 1991b; Baker and Durand 1991; Roney 1996).

During Period 4 the community increased in size again. The average number of rooms per building (17.4)

was the highest of the four periods (Table 8.1), partly as a result of remodeling at Guadalupe and Eleanor. At these buildings, the large Chaco-era rooms were subdivided, increasing the total number but not changing the overall structure size (Flam 1974; Pippin 1987; Proper 1997; Roler 1999). Although Eleanor was reoccupied and the rooms subdivided during this period, the distribution of the other structures on the south side of the mesa appears to have changed little from the preceding Period 3. The situation is quite different for the top of the mesa, however. Not only was the Guadalupe great house occupied during this period, but most of the available space on the mesa top contained structural debris dating to this time.

Structure ENM 886 was established on the north side of the mesa during Period 4. It is the only building located on the north side of the mesa, where it was situated adjacent to a spring (Fig. 8.4d). Considering the clear preference for the south side of the mesa, the north side location was undoubtedly related to control of the spring. This seep spring contains a substantial pool today despite modern ranching and well-drilling practices and certainly was an important water source during the prehistoric occupation of this area.

COMMUNITY HISTORY

In terms of size, clearly, the Chaco era (Period 2 in our scheme) was the height of the community. We propose that the establishment of the Guadalupe great house was an autochthonous development. To be sure, the Guadalupe great house shared many characteristics with other Chacoan great houses (for example, large rooms, T-shaped doorways, and core-and-veneer masonry). The Eleanor Ruin structure also shared these traits, but it was an exceedingly small building compared with other great houses (although the Guadalupe great house was small as well). Truell (1986) is clear about the presence of core-and-veneer architecture at the small houses in Chaco Canyon, though she also notes that this construction style is later than at the great houses by at least a century (Truell 1986: 308). It seems that at the Guadalupe community, core-and-veneer masonry was also present in at least one small-house structure. Considering the fact that only one small house structure was excavated and it revealed classic masonry and layout, it would be interesting to test other small houses in the Guadalupe community.

Guadalupe dated early for an outlying great house and contained the only known example of Type I masonry outside the central San Juan Basin. This masonry style extended from Kin Bineola (Powers and others 1983) and Peñasco Blanco to the west, through Chaco Canyon (Pueblo Bonito, Una Vida [Lekson 1984]), and to the East Community in the east (Windes 1993b; Windes and others, this volume). It can be argued that the 10th-century aspect of the Chaco "phenomenon" extended from Chaco Canyon to the southeast corner of the San Juan Basin. We are not arguing that this region is where the proposed Chaco system began; rather, we note the architectural similarity and the timing of that similarity. The parsimonious explanation is that the builders of the Guadalupe great house, the Guadalupe community inhabitants, had social and economic ties with the inhabitants of Chaco Canyon. It has always been our impression from Powers and others (1983) and Marshall and others (1979) that the 10th- and early 11th-century Chaco style (broadly defined) was a southern San Juan Basin phenomenon. The southern and perhaps the western great houses seem to have been built within an already established community (as at the Andrews community, Van Dyke 1997b) whereas at least some of the northern great houses were isolated buildings (like Salmon Ruin, Sterling, and Twin Angels). As Shelley (1983) remarked some years ago, "outliers" cannot be understood using the same explanation across the entire region in which they occur.

Why is a great house community located in the Puerco Valley? As Pippin (1987) and Irwin-Williams (1991) note, this region would have had significant agricultural potential. Pippin (1987) also documents the high environmental diversity of the region. In the space of a few kilometers, moving east to west, one traverses all the environmental zones from valley-bottom floodplains to ponderosa-pine forests. A few more kilometers to the west is the alpine zone on Mt. Taylor. The Puerco Valley is also a natural travel route from the south into the San Juan Basin. We have not quantified it here, but there does seem to be a significant amount of turquoise at Guadalupe Ruin (Mathien 1997b; Pippin 1987) and at Eleanor Ruin (Proper 1997). Subjectively, every ant mound that we have inspected on a midden in the Guadalupe community has had small flecks of turquoise. Judge (1989: 235–237) argued that the early date for Guadalupe may relate to control of the Cerrillos turquoise source. Although we consider Judge's characterization to be strongly worded, the turquoise present at Guadalupe Ruin indicates that the community was part of a large trading network that included Chaco Canyon communities.

The post-Chacoan occupation of the Guadalupe community is equally interesting. There is a dramatic decrease in occupied structures during the 12th and early 13th centuries. This decrease seems to have occurred at about the same time that there was a cessation in construction and decrease in population elsewhere in the San Juan Basin; the Chacoan adaptation changed and many structures were not used during this period. Whereas all of the values in Table 8.1 may be inflated, certainly so are the the values given for the post-Chaco era. Many of the structures assigned to that time were not continuously occupied throughout that interval (Baker 1991b; Baker and Durand 1991; Hurst 1991). In fact, the ceramics from Guadalupe Ruin are classified into only one of the post-Chaco seriation periods, and none of the structures were occupied during all of the seriation intervals that comprise our longer periods. The Guadalupe great house and all of the other community structures may have witnessed periods of abandonment. Much has been written about the post-Chaco era in recent years (Cameron 1995; Cordell 1997; Roney 1996), and the Guadalupe community seemingly fits the larger northern Southwest pattern. Coarsely, one can correlate environmental and climatic change with these events, though this is not necessarily a causal explanation.

Finally, in the last period (Period 4), there apparently was a substantial reoccupation of the community (Baker 1991b; Roney 1996). It is possible and even likely that this reoccupation was by immigrants from other regions. The entire character of the structures changed. The large rooms at Guadalupe Ruin (Pippin 1987) and Eleanor Ruin (Flam 1974; Proper 1997; Roler 1999) were subdivided. Kivas were added to these structures and the ceramic assemblage is both northern and eastern in character (Hurst 1991). Hurst (1991) recorded the presence of both Mesa Verde and Mesa Verde-like pottery and identified ceramic types that are associated with the Rio Grande region, indicating community ties to the northwest and east.

WAY OUT ON A LIMB

The patterns we describe in this paper could fit with the current model of development and decline of the Chaco system. Most Southwesternists consider the Chacoan era to be more complex than subsequent adaptations. For a different perspective on Chacoan developments we would like to suggest an alternative model, an explanation that considers the Chaco phenomenon to be the beginning of a pan-northern Southwest adaptation that reaches its peak immediately prior to European contact and not at A.D. 1100. In this model, the San Juan Basin developments are the first "experiments"

with sedentary agricultural village life and certainly not the last nor the most successful.

Plog made a similar argument in his insightful Keresan Bridge paper. Using the same term, "experiments," he suggested that food production may not have dominated the Anasazi landscape until after A.D. 1000 (Plog 1978: 366). Rather than considering the 10th and 11th centuries the peak of agricultural production, these centuries were the first attempts at aggregated village life based on food production. This adaptation was locally successful and permitted a period of population growth. The "experiment" ultimately failed, however, due to drought, or a failure of these agricultural practices to keep pace with a rising population, or depletion of sediment nutrients, or all of these factors. Further experimentation with full-time agricultural practices continued in the post-Chacoan era, when we see evidence of tremendous movements of populations across the northern Southwest and further intensification of agriculture.

Subsistence changes through time, from the Chacoan to the post-Chacoan era, are evident in the faunal and floral remains. Roler (1999) has documented a greater reliance on domesticated turkey for the meat component of the diet during the post-Chacoan era than during earlier periods at the Guadalupe community. Munro (1994) observed this pattern at sites across the northern Southwest during the post-Chacoan era. Pippin (1987: 139–141) notes an increase in the row number and cupule width for corn for the late assemblages from Guadalupe Ruin. Again, these patterns are not inconsistent with post-Chacoan assemblages from Chaco Canyon (McKenna 1991: 134–136) and beyond (Doebley and Bohrer 1980). We are not suggesting that there was a dramatic change in subsistence practices at the Guadalupe community. A slight intensification of subsistence practices, such as more productive corn or the addition of turkey, may have led to more substantial changes in the organization of the local community. Thus, the Chaco-era Guadalupe community may have been organized around food production and the seasonal exploitation of wild resources, whereas the post-Chacoan community may have been more dependent on food production with a diminished contribution from wild resources. These patterns likely recurred at communities across the San Juan Basin.

The population bulge in the Chacoan era at Guadalupe supports this alternative view, though the bulge may be more apparent than real. First, during the Chacoan era the community may not have been organized in the same way as during the subsequent periods of occupation. Windes and others (this volume) note that many of the Chaco-era structures at the East Community were not occupied year-round but rather represented a seasonal occupation. If Windes and his colleagues are correct and if this subsistence adaptation was widespread and not limited to the East Community, then the changes through time in the Guadalupe community may not have been the result of the collapse of a system but rather a change in the way Guadalupe community inhabitants used their landscape. The buildings that we have interpreted as habitation structures may have been used only seasonally or for other purposes. There is much environmental diversity in the region and the first villagers in the Guadalupe area may have been seasonally exploiting this diversity and may have been socially organized differently than the last villagers at Guadalupe.

The second reason why the population bulge in the Guadalupe community during the Chaco era may be more apparent than real is that, as Roney (1996) noted in citing McKenna (1991), we may not fully understand the systematics in the ceramic assemblages that have been used to define the post-Chaco era. In his summary of the Mesa Verde phase in Chaco Canyon, McKenna (1991: 129) listed only 10 absolute dates for the post-Chaco era and Mesa Verde periods (as we define them). This paucity of dates has made it difficult to understand the timing of the Mesa Verde phase ceramic changes in Chaco Canyon. McKenna and Toll (1991: 205) considered the ceramics in the late A.D. 1100s and 1200s to be a fusion of Chacoan and San Juan traditions. Hurst (1991) implied a similar situation for the Puerco region. McKenna and Toll (1991: 204) also did not see a substantial decrease in imported ceramics compared with earlier periods. The conclusion that we draw, perhaps naively, from these details is that the late 1100s and 1200s were not as dramatically different from the Bonito phase (pre–1120) as once thought. To be sure, the great houses were no longer being constructed, but the emerging picture of the post-Bonito phase is one of continuity rather than systemic transformation.

Finally, McKenna (1991: 130) stated that the early Chaco Canyon inhabitants placed trash in extramural middens and that this pattern changed after A.D. 1100 to disposal within rooms and kivas. McKenna (1991: 130–131) observed, then, that the quantities of later pottery in surface and extramural middens would be minimal. This pattern was represented at the Guadalupe community as well. Pippin (1987) described late trash-filled rooms at Guadalupe Ruin, and the pattern also occurred at Eleanor Ruin (Proper 1997; Roler 1999).

The seriation that was the basis for the patterns reported here used ceramics from surface collections and test excavations in extramural middens (Baker 1991a; Durand and Hurst 1991; Hurst 1991). Thus our notion of a lack of post-Chacoan occupation in the buildings in the Guadalupe community may be related to a change in trash disposal behavior rather than to a true abandonment of these structures.

Undoubtedly, something special went on in Chaco Canyon. We propose, however, that the rest of the San Juan Basin was not organized as an integrated system but rather represented a regional style and a similarity in local social organization. The outlying Guadalupe great house was a central place in the community and a focal point for ceremonial activities, but it was not connected to Chaco Canyon in any organized sense. If we assume that a Chacoan system existed, then the changes that occurred at about A.D. 1150 must signal the collapse of that system. On the other hand, if we do not posit a system it is possible to view Chacoan culture change in other and different ways. We have suggested, albeit briefly, a different model for Chacoan developments at the Guadalupe community that does not require us to view the Chacoan era as the height of social complexity in the northern Southwest. Rather, we propose considering the Chacoan era as the beginning of an adaptation that coalesced much later in time with the developments that characterized the terminal Pueblo IV period in the northern Southwest.

Acknowledgments

This chapter is dedicated to the memory of Cynthia Irwin-Williams, a mentor, an inspiration, and especially, a friend. She probably would not have agreed with our conclusions but she was the Puerco Project and would have supported us nonetheless. A huge cast of characters contributed to the Puerco research through the years and it is impossible to name them all. We thank each of you and especially acknowledge Larry Baker, Winston Hurst, Fred Nials, Lonnie Pippin, Mike Proper, and Phil Shelley. We are grateful to Linda Cordell, Keith Kintigh, Pete McKenna, Kate Spielmann, and Tom Windes for direct and indirect contributions to our understanding of the Chaco puzzle. Finally, we express appreciation to two anonymous reviewers for their insightful editorial suggestions and to the editors of this volume, John Kantner and Nancy Mahoney, for providing us the opportunity to contribute.

Part 3

Economic and Sociopolitical
Relationships Outside of
Chaco Canyon

Figure Part 3. Computer reconstruction of the Kin Tl'iish great
house positioned on the site in northwestern New Mexico.
(Photograph and reconstruction by John Kantner)

CHAPTER NINE

Household Economic Autonomy and Great House Development in the Lowry Area

James W. Kendrick and W. James Judge

During the Chaco era, household economic autonomy in the Lowry area created a social environment that allowed certain households to construct great houses. However, fundamental economic changes occurred at both the household and community levels at the end of the Chaco era (Late Pueblo II period, A.D. 1050–1150). These changes involved the inability of individual households to sustain a long-standing level of relative economic independence within their respective communities, and we believe larger corporate groups within the community gained greater control over household economic pursuits. As household mobility decreased and corporate groups within the community became larger during residential aggregation in the late 13th century, the capacity for overt competition among individual households diminished.

Recent investigations in the Lowry area, coupled with prior research that began in the 1920s, provide information with which to examine in detail Chaco-era community dynamics at various organizational levels such as the household, great house, and community. Household dynamics are addressed by considering the results of recent testing by Fort Lewis College (Judge 1998) at one small site, Puzzle House (5MT11787). Puzzle House is a multi-component Ancestral Pueblo site with documented occupations ranging from the Basketmaker III period (A.D. 450–700) to the Early Pueblo III period (A.D. 1150–1225). It is the only extensively tested small unit pueblo of the Lowry community. We examine community dynamics for Basketmaker III through the Pueblo III periods using information obtained by the Lowry Community Pattern Survey (Kendrick 1998; Kendrick and Judge 1996). We also review the developmental history of the Lowry Ruin, a great house complex partially excavated by Paul Martin (1936).

The Lowry Ruin and surrounding area have long been included in various discussions of great houses (or "outliers") and great house models (for example, Marshall and others 1979; Powers and others 1983; Vivian 1990). The ruin has been used to mark the northern boundary of the Chaco "system" (Judge 1989; Neitzel 1989), and, as this volume demonstrates, there are numerous models that attempt to explain its occurrence and function. Great house models can be grouped into two basic categories: colonization and local development (Kendrick and Judge 1996; Tainter and Gillio 1980). All colonization models focus on the nonlocal and intrusive character of Chaco-style architecture and material goods within outlying communities. These models propose the construction and use of great house complexes by persons or groups of persons from the Chaco "core." Colonization models, however, range from regarding these persons or groups as emigrants (Irwin-Williams 1972; Vivian 1990), missionaries (B. Bradley 1993), priests (Eddy 1972; Warburton and Graves 1992), and even armies (Wilcox 1993).

Local development models focus on local processes for the development of great houses, but within the regional context of the Chaco era. These models may emphasize local elites (Powers 1984; Powers and others 1983) or political competition (Kantner 1996a; Sebastian 1992). Other local development models stress the socially integrative and public aspects of great house complexes (Adler and Varien 1994; Fowler and Stein 1992; Lekson 1991; Marshall and others 1979; Mobley-Tanaka 1993; Toll 1985; Tucker 1993).

All these models add insight to our understanding of great houses and great house communities, but few of them incorporate the household and economic production at the household level as important elements in the development of outlying great houses. Households, as a basic constitutive component of ancestral puebloan communities, provide meaningful information regarding the nature of great houses such as the one at the Lowry Ruin. It is productive to study the development of great houses and great house communities from a local perspective based on household economic production, in addition to exploring the broad, overarching regional patterns.

We outline the development of the Lowry community by examining household, great house, and community dynamics. The relationships between households and great houses during the Chaco era may be investigated by considering these three main organizational levels through time. Our discussion incorporates the dynamics of economic autonomy with changes in community settlement patterns to better comprehend the Chaco era in the Lowry area. We then present a tentative model of community dynamics that focuses on changes in household economic autonomy from the 7th to the late 13th centuries and discuss its implications for understanding outlying great houses in the Montezuma Valley.

ARCHAEOLOGY OF THE LOWRY AREA

The Lowry Ruin is on the Great Sage Plain of the Montezuma Valley, 14.5 km (9 miles) west of Pleasant View, Colorado (Fig. 9.1). This area is typified by a gently dipping plateau that is deeply incised by canyons, resulting in numerous broad, flat mesas. Thick aeolian sediments conducive for maize agriculture cap these mesas. Springs and seeps are often located at canyon heads and within smaller drainages. A piñon-juniper woodland in a semiarid environment prevails across the area.

The Lowry Ruin is one of many Chaco-style great houses located throughout the Montezuma Valley (Fig. 9.2). These great houses became the dominant cultural features on the local landscape during the latter half of the 11th century. Though most of these structures have not been excavated, all have some form of Chaco-style architecture that typically defines a great house (multiple stories, enclosed or elevated kivas, Chaco-style masonry, great kivas, Chacoan material, and, in some cases, associated roads; Lekson 1991).

The great houses were impressive features within their communities. Entrances to the great house complexes via "roads" created formal landscapes. This built landscape, as it has been called (Stein and Lekson 1992), stood in stark contrast to nearby contemporaneous households that were typically much smaller (averaging less than 20 rooms) and had fewer nonlocal material goods. Yet at the Lowry Ruin, the incorporation of Chaco-style elements was brief and short-lived. A single generation could have easily built those por-

tions of the structure that comprised Chaco-style architecture, which date between the late A.D. 1080s and early 1100s (Ahlstrom and others 1985; Martin 1936). Occupation and use of the locality, however, extended back to the Basketmaker III period (450–700), and continued into the Pueblo III period (1150–1300).

The Lowry Ruin has long been recognized as an outlying Chaco-style great house (Martin 1936, Powers and others 1983). It was one of the first such structures investigated, and it extended the boundaries of possible Chacoan influence far beyond Chaco Canyon. The goal of our investigations in the area has been to provide context at the household and community levels to better understand the development of the Lowry great house.

HOUSEHOLD, GREAT HOUSE, AND COMMUNITY DYNAMICS

Definitions and Scales of Analysis

Our investigations in the Lowry area involve three primary scales of analysis: the household, the great house, and the community. We follow Lightfoot (1994) and Ashmore and Wilk (1988: 6) who define the household as "the group of people that shares in a maximum number of definable activities, including one or more of the following: production, consumption, pooling of resources, reproduction, coresidence, and shared ownership." We believe households are discernible in the archaeological record of the Chaco era as unit pueblos (Prudden 1903), typically comprising a kiva, surface rooms, and an associated midden. Prior to the Chaco era, we can identify households as pit houses and architectural suites of pit houses and surface rooms, such as those defined by Lightfoot (1994) at the Duckfoot site.

Great house buildings incorporated one or more of the following architectural or landscaping elements: multiple stories, enclosed or elevated kivas, and core-and-veneer wall construction (Lekson 1991). In some Montezuma Valley great houses, such as at Lowry, masonry styles resembled those in Chaco Canyon great houses. Others, such as at Escalante, did not incorporate Chaco-style masonry. Often, great houses occurred with great kivas, which were circular, subterranean structures typically with diameters greater than 10 m. Roads (linear swales) and other elements like earthen berms (*nazhas*) were sometimes associated with great houses. Together, these features formed great house complexes. Despite these similarities, Montezuma Valley great houses were also characterized by considerable variation in size, architecture, and chronology.

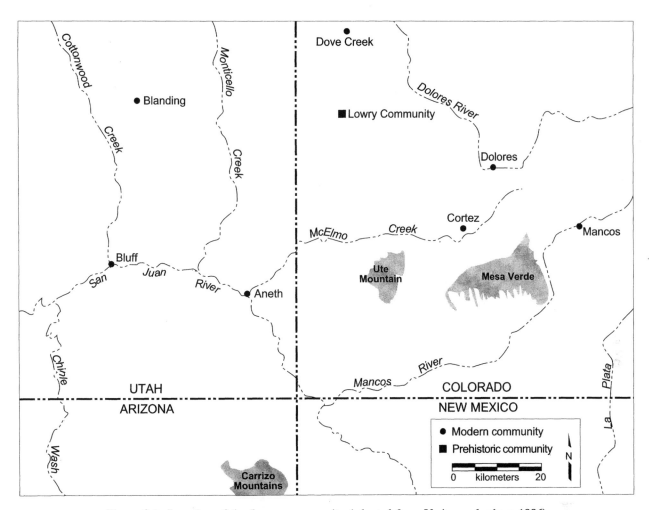

Figure 9.1. Location of the Lowry community (adapted from Varien and others 1996).

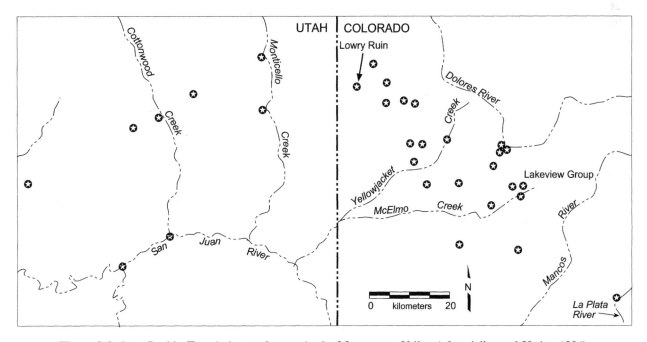

Figure 9.2. Late Pueblo II period great houses in the Montezuma Valley (after Adler and Varien 1994).

Communities are much more difficult to define as well as recognize in the archaeological record. Traditionally, communities have been defined by spatial proximity of contemporaneous residences (Rohn 1977). More recently, Adler (1990: 20) has defined a community as "an organizational entity with decision-making capabilities above the level of the primary economic unit, serving to define and reproduce resource access rights of smaller, constitutive economic units within the broader regional social system." We accept this definition for the Pueblo III period, when residentially aggregated communities may be identified, such as at Sand Canyon Pueblo, Goodman Point Ruin, or the Canyon Rim Ruin south of Lowry. Prior to Pueblo III, however, we believe basic economic pursuits, such as production, consumption, pooling of resources, and access to resources like productive land, were vested in the control of individual households. Individual households defined, controlled, and reproduced resource access rights, and that is what we mean by household economic autonomy.

It is likely that households prior to the Pueblo III period were integrated into some form of community organization, because large, nonresidential structures such as great kivas apparently functioned for purposes above the household level. Indeed, such structures may have facilitated integrative processes among different households or segments of the larger community. Great kivas, then, may have served as a forum for negotiation of resource access rights between household leaders. Such facilities would have become increasingly important as population increased, household mobility decreased, and the demand for access to productive resources intensified.

The scale of communities is difficult to identify within the archaeological record (as Mahoney notes in this volume). Adler (1996a) and Adler and Varien (1994) have discussed this issue for the Mesa Verde region. They discerned a bimodal distribution of great houses, with great houses either being located within 1 km (0.6 mile) of the next closest great house, or between 5 to 7 km (3.1 to 4.3 miles) from the next closest great house. The first mode represents multiple great house communities, and the second mode may indicate local community territories (assuming that great houses represented some form of community facility).

The Lowry Community Pattern Survey was conducted in a 14.5-square-kilometer (5.6-square-mile) area centered on the Lowry Ruin. We use the archaeological resources identified during the survey to examine the immediate community around the Lowry Ruin. Whether or not the entire community was actually included in the survey is impossible to say.

Pre-Chaco Era (Prior to A.D. 1050)

Community

Prior to the Chaco era, settlement of the Lowry area comprised dispersed households. The Lowry Community Pattern Survey grouped together sites of the Basketmaker III period (about A.D. 450 to 700) and the Pueblo I period (A.D. 700 to 900–930) because it is often difficult to distinguish them with only surface material. Using well-established ceramic chronologies, we would expect Basketmaker III sites to exhibit Chapin Black-on-white, the dominant ceramic type of the period (although it may have extended beyond 790) and Pueblo I sites to contain La Plata Black-on-white pottery. Typically, however, only plain gray body sherds are visible on sites of both periods. Additionally, most sites in the Lowry area have been disturbed by later occupations or modern agricultural practices (Kendrick 1998). Even though pit structures may remain intact, surface manifestations are usually heavily disturbed.

Basketmaker III–Pueblo I sites are widely dispersed throughout the survey area (Fig. 9.3) and are often located on deep, arable soils. Unfortunately, of the 31 sites recorded, only 2 are not in modern agricultural fields or do not comprise later occupations. Although no formal estimates have been attempted, population density during this interval seems to have been low in the immediate Lowry area. Residential aggregation, however, occurred late in the Pueblo I period approximately 10 km (6 miles) northeast of the Lowry Ruin (Martin 1938).

During the early Pueblo II period (about A.D. 900–930 to 1050), the Lowry area comprised widely dispersed and generally undifferentiated households (Fig. 9.4). Most early Pueblo II period residences were positioned on upland mesas with deep arable soils, but occupation within canyons also occurred. Twenty-year momentary population calculations based on habitation (household) lifespans of 20 years provide an estimated population density of 5.5 persons per square kilometer (Kendrick and Judge 1996). That is, we would expect only 5 or 6 persons per square kilometer to be living in the survey area during any given 20-year interval. To compare population estimates with recent surveys, this estimate is based on 1.5 persons per estimated room (following Adler 1990). Assuming an average habitation lifespan of 50 years, population density would be estimated at approximately 14 persons per square kilometer

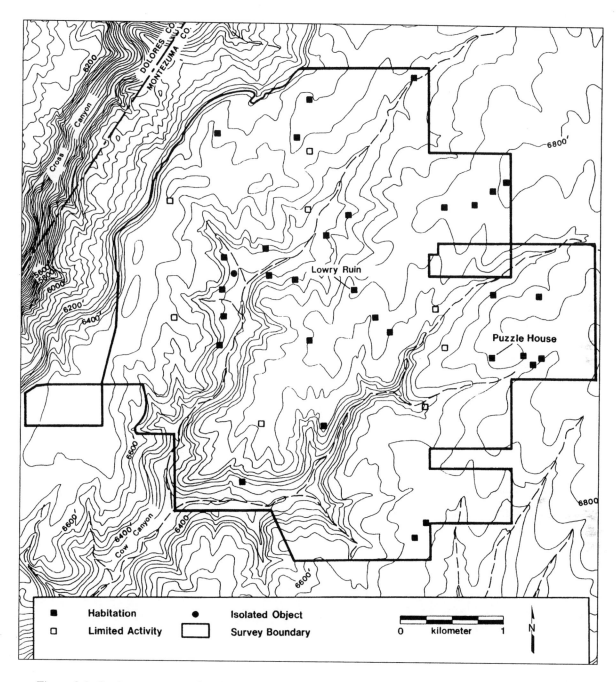

Figure 9.3. Settlement pattern for the Basketmaker III–Pueblo I period (A.D. 450–930) in the survey area.

during any given 50-year interval within the Early Pueblo II period. Both of these estimates are similar to those recorded by Adler (1990) for the Sand Canyon area for the early Pueblo II period.

Puzzle House

The location of Puzzle House (Fig. 9.3), on a gentle, south-facing slope 100 m north of a small drainage,

may be key to understanding the extended length of time it was occupied (intermittently for almost 600 years, from the Basketmaker III to Pueblo III periods). It was a good place for dry farming, and it was near a diversity of woodland resources. Immediate topography is suitable for check dam farming (though modern plowing may have obliterated evidence of it).

Evidence of the Basketmaker III period occupation came from a single pit structure (Fig. 9.5) comprising a

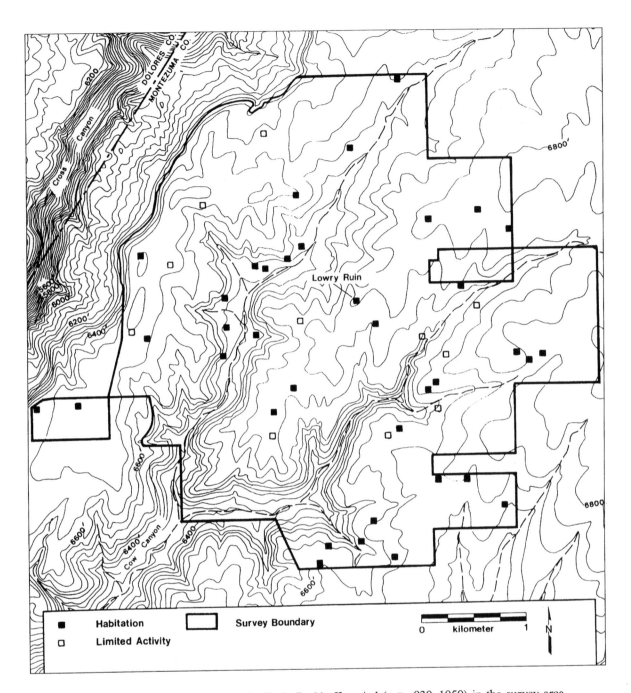

Figure 9.4. Settlement pattern for the Early Pueblo II period (A.D. 930–1050) in the survey area.

main chamber (with an area of 24.5 square meters) and a large antechamber (12.6 square meters) that served as the entrance to the structure. The main chamber had a hearth, deflector, and two wing-walls of vertical sandstone slabs. The partitioned areas formed by the wing-walls typically were used for storage or food preparation functions in pit houses of this time period.

None of the 36 dendrochronological samples taken from the pit house excavations yielded a cutting date.

The hearth was sampled for archaeomagnetic dating and provided a date of A.D. 600 to 675, precisely the range one would expect from a structure of this type.

There was no evidence for occupation of Puzzle House during the Pueblo I or early Pueblo II periods. Artifact collections from the surface and within room fill contained low frequencies of Piedra Black-on-white and Cortez Black-on-white ceramics. No conclusive architectural features, however, dated to these periods.

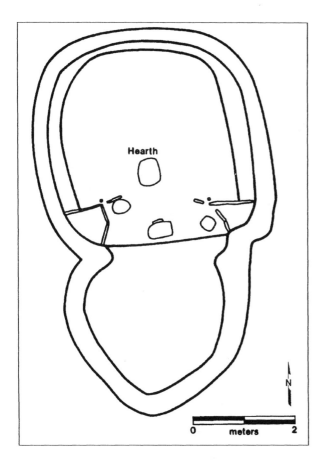

Figure 9.5. Plan of the Basketmaker III pit structure at Puzzle House.

The Lowry Ruin

Pit houses discovered below Room 8 at the Lowry Ruin (Martin 1936) were not fully excavated. In a reanalysis of ceramic artifacts, Kendrick (1996) found both Chapin Black-on-white and Piedra Black-on-white ceramics in Room 8 subfloor contexts, indicating occupation of this locality during the Basketmaker III–Pueblo I periods. An early Pueblo II (about A.D. 900–930 to 1050) occupation of the Lowry Ruin is substantiated by a cutting date from tree-ring samples (Ahlstrom and others 1985) recovered from a room in Martin's north trench (on the eastern slope of the Lowry Ruin) and by the presence of Cortez Black-on-white pottery. Clearly, the locality on which the great house was later built had been occupied for centuries. From our perspective, households occupied the location as early as Basketmaker III times and controlled resources within the immediate area during a long period of time. These local households must have been responsible for initiating the great house construction during the Chaco era.

Chaco Era, Late Pueblo II (A.D. 1050–1150)

Community

Dramatic changes in the settlement pattern occurred during the Late Pueblo II period (A.D. 1050–1150; Fig. 9.6). The once dispersed pattern of settlement changed to distinct clustering. The average number of rooms per site (not including the great houses) increased to approximately 15, a number that may seem high but in some cases several unit pueblos comprised a single site. This increase is a prelude to almost complete residential aggregation during the Late Pueblo III period. The number of habitations expanded from 37 to 65, which undoubtedly indicates population growth.

We see an increase in the variety of site types occurring during this period. A great house complex was built that comprised multiple great houses and a great kiva from which three roads radiated (Fig. 9.7). Other new features appeared that provide insight into the changes the community was experiencing. These additions to the community landscape included reservoirs, nonresidential storage, specialized ceremonial sites, and shrines. Reservoirs built during the Chaco era indicate a need for increased water management. Interestingly, all of the reservoirs recorded were located away from the great house complex on the upland mesas.

Two specialized ceremonial sites discovered during the survey had been positioned away from the great house complex, each below a canyon rim. Based on surface ceramics, one of them apparently dates to the Late Pueblo II period. The other site dates to the Pueblo III period, but it may also have had a Late Pueblo II component. Each of these sites comprised two kivas surrounded by a retaining wall and was associated with rock art. These sites contain no surface rooms and do not appear to be habitations.

A number of small features within the community were probably shrines, reflecting a growing formalization of ideology of the times. Their varied forms included U-shaped, circular, rectangular, and slab-alcove arrangements. The shrines tended to be located near reservoirs, storage facilities, or overlooking canyons. These features are similar in form and setting to shrines used by contemporary Pueblos. Additionally, there is evidence of limited activity sites, field houses, and storage facilities (or granaries).

The survey data indicate that a rapid increase in population occurred during the Chaco era (Table 9.1). When compared to estimates by Van West (1990) of carrying capacity during this period (26 persons per square

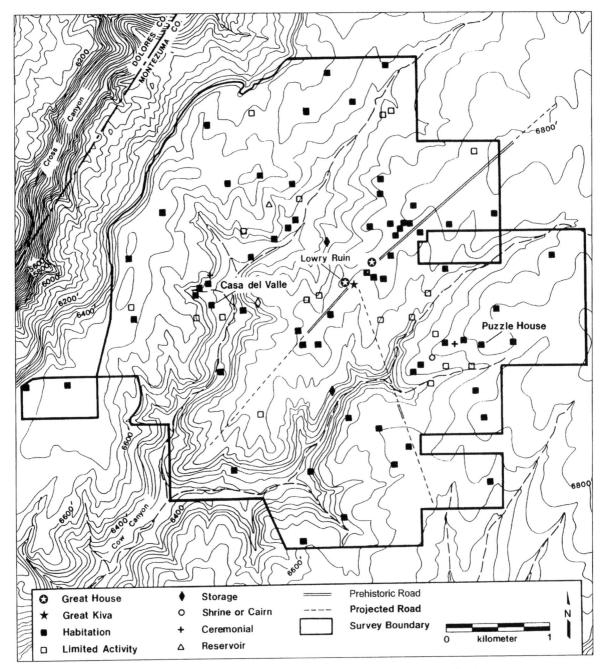

⊛	Great House	◆	Storage	═══ Prehistoric Road
★	Great Kiva	○	Shrine or Cairn	- - - Projected Road
■	Habitation	+	Ceremonial	▭ Survey Boundary
◻	Limited Activity	△	Reservoir	

Figure 9.6. Settlement pattern for the Late Pueblo II period (A.D. 1050–1150) in the survey area.

kilometer for the period between A.D. 1080 and 1120), the Lowry community was pushing the limits of the critical carrying capacity of the area. We believe this predicament created the need for increased resource management, which is consistent with the construction of reservoirs, field houses, and granaries throughout the community.

Puzzle House

The location of Puzzle House, a unit pueblo occupied during the Late Pueblo II period, is relevant to interpret-

ing the distribution of similar pueblos in the community. Of particular importance is the relatively short duration of occupation in these pueblos, which suggests a high degree of residential mobility within the community during this period (Varien and others 1996).

Judge (1991, 1998) proposed that Chacoan communities at this time were ritually integrated, but otherwise relatively independent, an idea supported by the architecture of Puzzle House during its Late Pueblo II period occupation. Though no midden areas can definitely be assigned to this time period (the site perimeter was plowed for farming), the structures appear to have

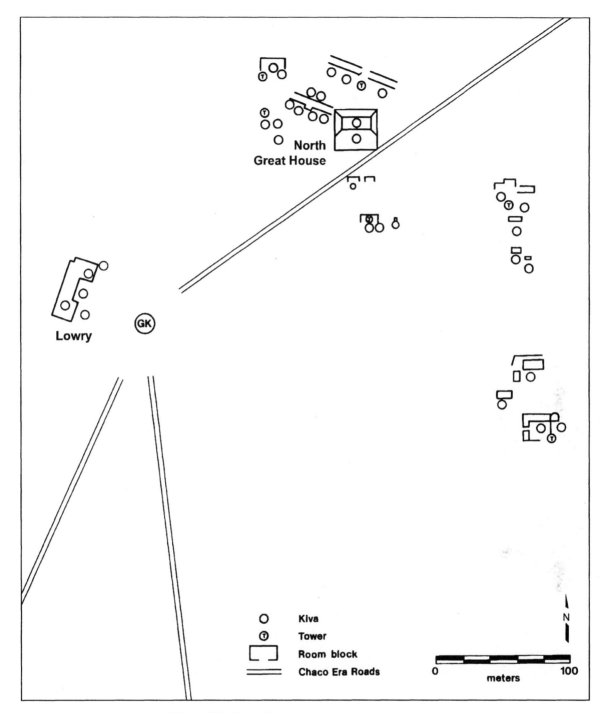

Figure 9.7. Plan of the Lowry great house complex.

been predominantly ritual. One large (Chaco-style) surface room faced a deep, masonry kiva, and to the east and slightly south of the kiva was a square, subterranean masonry room with a tunnel leading from it to the kiva (Fig. 9.8). If this room was used to prepare for a concealed entry to the kiva, then undoubtedly its primary function was ritual, linking it closely with similar features located elsewhere in the Chacoan "system" (for example, Casa Rinconada in Chaco Canyon). A ritual interpretation of square, subterranean rooms in south-

west Colorado sites has been suggested recently by Mobley-Tanaka (1997).

Because it is below other masonry structures at the site, only a portion of the deep kiva could be excavated. The excavated portion revealed a niche and a slightly-burned hearth. The architecture indicates a more ritual than domestic focus, and the poorly-fired hearth and generally low frequencies of Mancos Black-on-white pottery denote a short-lived Late Pueblo II period occupation, with construction tentatively dated in the A.D.

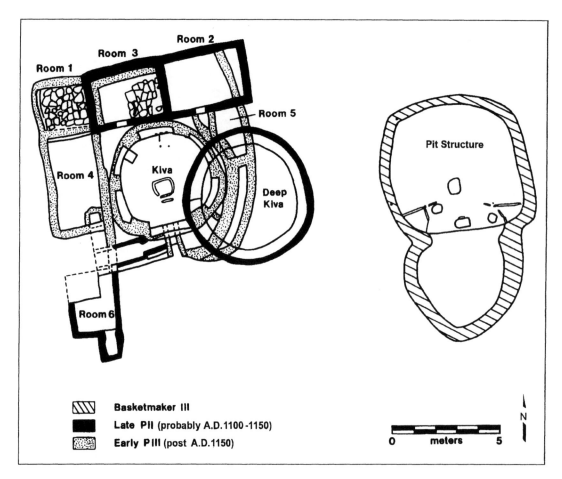

Figure 9.8. Plan of Puzzle House.

Table 9.1. Population Estimates for the Lowry Community during the Early and Late Pueblo II Periods

	Early P II	Late P II Chaco Era[1]	Late P II Chaco Era[2]
Number of habitation sites	37	62	65
Average habitation size (rooms)	8.50	15.40	19.80
20-year average momentary number of habitations	6.25	12.40	12.99
Average 20-year momentary population[3]	79.70	286.44	385.80
Average 20-year momentary population density[4]	5.50	19.80	26.60

1. Estimates do not include Lowry Ruin, North Great House, or Casa del Valle.
2. Estimates include Lowry Ruin, North Great House, and Casa del Valle.
3. Estimate based on 1.5 persons per 10 square meters of rubble area.
4. Based on 14.5–square–kilometer area of the Lowry Community Pattern Survey.

1040–1075 range. No hearths were found in the other structures.

Midden material was not sufficient to verify local economic autonomy at Puzzle House for this time period. It is probable, though, that its occupants exhibited a high degree of economic autonomy locally, as well as within the Lowry community and region as a whole, while at the same time maintaining affinity to a pan-regional ritual expression that had its ultimate origin in Chaco. Such things as land tenure, wild plant and animal procurement, and subsistence storage were probably controlled locally. As population increased, climate deteriorated, and the resource based dwindled in the latter part of the 12th century, a shift toward increased community control of these components took place at the expense of continued allegiance to the regional (Chaco) ritual base.

The Lowry Ruin

The earliest evidence of great house architecture at the Lowry Ruin is the construction of a set of four rooms (Rooms 10, 15, 19, and 21) of multiple stories

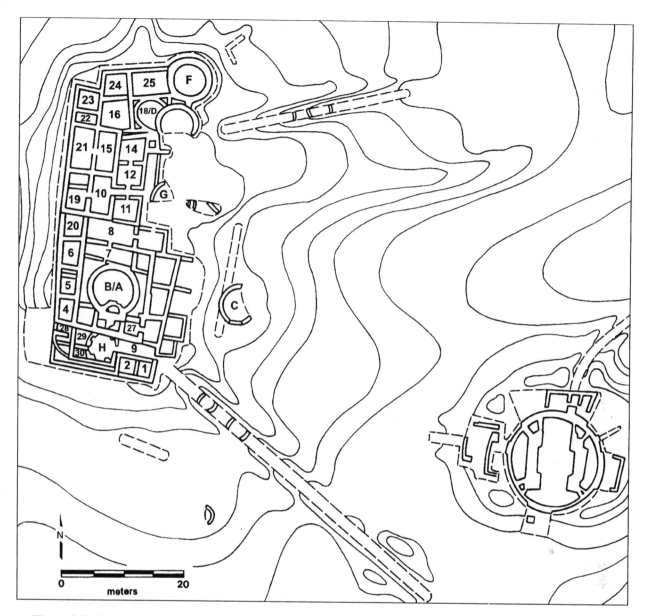

Figure 9.9. Plan of the Lowry Ruin (after Martin 1936), showing kivas (with letters) and rooms (with numbers)..

and Chaco-style masonry and wall construction (Fig. 9.9). These rooms were the largest in the entire pueblo. Tree-ring dates from the nucleus indicate construction between A.D. 1085 and 1090. Martin believed Room 18, Kiva F, and the great kiva were also built at this time, an idea corroborated by Roys' (1936) masonry analysis and tree-ring dates from the great kiva showing construction at 1086. Following this initial construction, numerous building episodes took place during the next three decades.

Martin (1936) identified and described in detail at least six major renovations or additions to Lowry. Next we examine the nature and scale of these building events and interpret them in the context of great house models. The first and second additions consisted of con-

struction of two enclosed kivas (Kiva B and Kiva D) and adjoining rooms, and a row of rooms in front of the original nucleus. It is difficult to assess the scale of the first addition, because much of it was razed for later construction. All that remains of the first addition is the enclosing wall around Kiva B. This wall, however, exhibits Chaco-style masonry. Tree-ring analysis of the lintel of the doorway to Room 27 indicates this portion of the pueblo was constructed in approximately A.D. 1103 (Ahlstrom and others 1985: 40).

The second addition comprised Kivas B and D, their adjoining rooms, and the row of rooms fronting the nucleus. Kiva B contained thin, tabular Chaco-style masonry, and Kiva D exhibited similar style masonry (Roys 1936: 137), along with similar internal features (such as interpilaster shelves). Problematic in Martin's second addition are the rooms adjoining Kiva B (Rooms 4, 5, 6, and 20) and Kiva D (Rooms 16, 22, 23, 24, and 25) and the row of three rooms fronting the nucleus (Rooms 11, 12, and 14). Rooms 4, 5, 6, and 20 had blocky, McElmo-style masonry, which typically postdates Chaco-style masonry. Roys (1936: 137) described the architecture of Room 16 as having many "Chaco-like characteristics although in general appearance it is not entirely Chaco-like." He believed this section of the pueblo dated closer to the time period of the first addition. Rooms 11, 12, and 14 also had McElmo-style masonry, postdating Kivas B and D. Tree-ring analysis from Room 11 suggests this section was constructed around 1120 or later (as the sample was not a cutting date; Ahlstrom and others 1985). Room 8 seems to have been constructed during this second addition, as its northern wall formed the southern wall of Room 11.

The third addition to the Lowry great house included Kiva A and adjoining rooms to the east. Based on tree-ring analysis of a rear wall support, Kiva A was likely constructed around A.D. 1120 (Ahlstrom and others 1985). This building phase has important implications for great house models. The construction of Kiva A required the underlying Kiva B and adjoining rooms to be filled. In addition, both stories of Rooms 5, 6, 7, and 27 were filled to make Kiva A seem subterranean. The effect was a kiva elevated to at least two and possibly three stories above the surrounding landscape.

The fourth addition consisted of Rooms 28, 29, and 30 and possibly construction in the area of Rooms 1, 2, and 9 (which are later; Martin 1936: 200). The fifth addition was the last major renovation of Lowry, consisting of Rooms 1, 2, and 9 and Kiva H. During this building phase, Rooms 9, 29, and 30 were intentionally filled with refuse to give Kiva H the appearance of being subterranean. Martin confessed to not knowing when Kivas C and G were constructed; they were located outside the main structure.

Interestingly, storage bins were placed within 10 rooms (Rooms 5, 8, 10, 11, 12, 14, 15, 19, 21, and 28) following the final building phase. Although Martin provided no time frame for when these features were used, they were most likely built at the end of the Chaco era or during the following phase. At approximately the same time, small pueblos such as Puzzle House were experiencing similar changes in function.

The Lowry great house was built through a period of time with a series of building episodes. No formal planning, other than what it took to build certain additions, guided new construction. Apparently no large group of

people from Chaco, nor even masons or priests, had anything to do with building the great house. More likely, a local household or lineage constructed the great house during the course of several decades. The possibility exists that persons from other households or lineages cooperated in these construction events, but the initiation of any particular building episode was probably directed by a single group. It is unlikely that multiple groups spontaneously decided to initiate new construction simultaneously. This great house, then, was probably not a public building and should not be considered as such when debating models of great house communities.

Post-Chaco Era, Pueblo III (A.D. 1050–1300)

Community

Settlement patterns during the Pueblo III period focused primarily on the canyon heads and drainages (Fig. 9.10). Use of the great house complex and many mesa-top habitations continued into the latter half of the 12th and early 13th centuries. Residential aggregation into a few large pueblos with kiva-dominated room blocks occurred in the late Pueblo III period (A.D. 1225–1300), consistent with other areas of the Montezuma Valley and general Mesa Verde region. Reservoirs continued to be constructed, but now they were built near the aggregated settlements. By the final decade of the 13th century, the Lowry community area had been abandoned, along with all of the other Puebloan community areas throughout the region.

Puzzle House

Major changes took place during the final (Early Pueblo III period) occupation of Puzzle House, changes that suggest its transition from an autonomous unit pueblo to a seasonal field facility and ultimately to a temporary storage location. Beginning in the mid-1100s, the pueblo was reoccupied and largely rebuilt. The large Chaco-style room was subdivided and a small storage room was added to its west wall. The subterranean room was filled in and a new entrance was constructed to the tunnel. A new kiva was built above and to the west of the original kiva, overlapping about one-third of the initial structure. This upper kiva was "squeezed" into the space between the surface room and the tunnel. We think that this, the final construction phase at Puzzle House, can best be described as expedient.

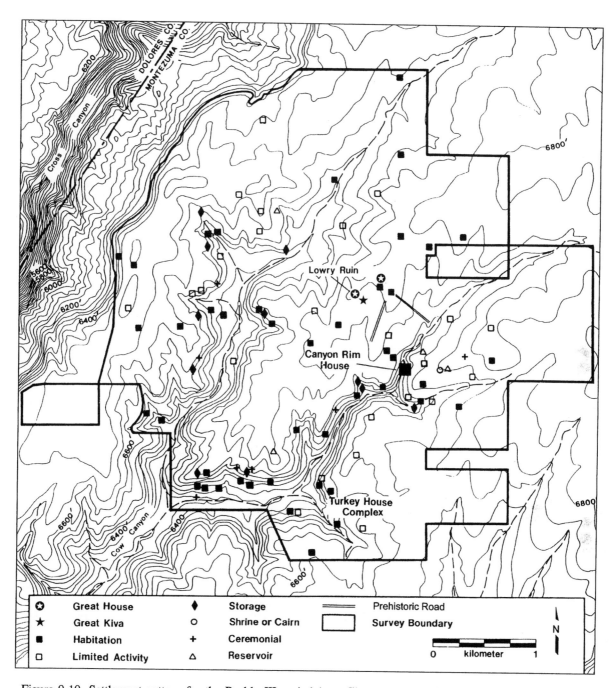

Figure 9.10. Settlement pattern for the Pueblo III period (post-Chaco era, A.D. 1150–1300) in the survey area.

Architecturally, ritual components were altered during this initial reoccupation. The size of the tunnel was considerably reduced to a small passageway through which objects might have been passed into the upper kiva. Though certainly not devoid of ritual at this time, the reoccupational architecture revealed a significant shift away from the original ritual focus.

The new (upper) kiva was used primarily for habitation, and two of the new surface rooms were used for storage. These functions, plus an analysis of the midden deposits associated with this occupation, indicate initial reoccupation as an autonomous unit pueblo, albeit with a more domestic than ritual focus. This focus soon changed, however, when the tunnel was sealed and a new room was built over the tunnel's surface entrance to the west of the upper kiva. Though the kiva continued to serve as a residence, the original surface rooms were filled with trash.

Toward the end of this period (about A.D. 1225), the pueblo had increasingly less domestic storage, with trash deposits occurring in all of the surface rooms. The latest deposits revealed a much less substantial occupation than initially, and perhaps at its end Puzzle House was used only as a temporary field house, with subsistence storage and residential activities taking place elsewhere.

At this time, it is likely that economic control of both Puzzle House and its surrounding fields was located at another pueblo. One interpretation could be that Puzzle House served as a field facility peripheral to, but allied with, a larger residential area in the Lowry community. The Lowry Community Pattern Survey located several contemporaneous sites larger than Puzzle House some 600 m west of it. This distance is not necessarily great enough to mean that Puzzle House served as an independent field house, but it does suggest that its primary function may have been as a resource storage facility. The need to protect resources by residing at least temporarily at the storage location yields important information for understanding the social dynamics and stress induced by population increase in the changing Lowry community of the time.

The Lowry Ruin

The function of the Lowry great house changed at some point during the Pueblo III period. The great house was abandoned as a residence, but continued use of the structure is demonstrated by the fill in Room 8, which comprised an estimated 70.79 cubic meters of ash and "thousands of potsherds" (Martin 1936: 39). The presence of Mesa Verde Black-on-white pottery within this fill indicates that it likely was deposited sometime in the A.D. 1200s. B. Bradley (1993) has observed the late Pueblo III period use of other great houses, such as the one at the Wallace Ruin, and he attributed this use to a possible Chacoan revival movement. We offer no such explanations here, but the abandonment of the great house is no different than the abandonment of other households throughout the community. It is, however, consistent with the loss of economic autonomy at the household level throughout the community.

ECONOMIC PRODUCTION
AND INTEGRATION

The organization of both households and communities underwent significant changes in the Lowry area between the Basketmaker III and the late Pueblo III

periods. We believe these changes reflect a relative loss of autonomy (or control) over economic production at the household level by the end of the 13th century. Autonomy over economic production, though relative in nature and most certainly still within a community structure, allowed and may have even created an economic environment in which households competed against one another. Increased population during the Chaco era may have intensified competition for resources (such as access to productive agricultural land) between households. During the Chaco era, this competition may have been expressed by the incorporation of great house architecture by some households (Kantner 1996a, Sebastian 1992). By the late 13th century, households were aggregated into a few large settlements, the largest of which comprised hundreds of rooms and dozens of pit structures. We believe that it was during this later period when the community made decisions regarding the economic pursuits of households, particularly access to important resources (Adler 1990).

The interplay between population and resource access rights is important. Population density of the Lowry community was low (less than 6 persons per square kilometer during any given 20-year interval prior to the Chaco era). During the Chaco era, however, population density in the Lowry area increased dramatically (rising to an estimated 26 persons per square kilometer during any given 20-year interval in the Chaco era). Additionally, settlement patterns of households shifted from dispersed to clustered. If we compare these population figures with Van West's (1990: 290) estimates for the carrying capacity of the Lowry area between A.D. 1086 and 1120 (26 persons per square kilometer), we note that the Lowry community had reached the limits of the area's critical carrying capacity and there must have been population pressure on the local environment.

Pressure on the environment would have intensified competition between households for access to resources, such as water and productive and predictable agricultural land. Competition for traditionally productive locations probably increased stress levels considerably at places such as Puzzle House. Increased population would have decreased household mobility, essentially locking in resource access rights. Spatial clustering of residences during the Chaco era may reflect attempts by related households (and possibly lineages) to control access rights to agricultural lands. Spatial proximity of related households would have pooled additional labor and possibly fostered greater control of resources, creating competitive advantages over other households or lineages. We believe this time marks the beginning of larger corporate units within the community and the initial loss of household autonomy over economic production.

With this scenario, the question then becomes: why did some households incorporate Chaco-style elements into new residential construction? Traditionally, Chaco-style elements have been interpreted as signifying affiliation in some form with the population at Chaco Canyon. From our perspective, great house construction at the Lowry Ruin, North Great House, and possibly Casa del Valle may be interpreted as precocious attempts by households or lineages to pool labor in order to gain competitive advantages over resources vis-à-vis other lineages (Damp and Kendrick 1998). We believe local households used Chaco-style architecture and landscape settings to attract (or pull) related members and thus control more producers (Damp and Kendrick 1998). This view is consistent with the wide variation noted in great houses throughout the Montezuma Valley (Powers and others 1983).

Great houses such as the Lowry Ruin, then, may not represent communal public buildings. In fact, interpreting great houses as public buildings biases models toward community and regional perspectives. By stating this idea we are not implying that communally integrative activities, such as religious ceremonies, did not take place at or within great houses. Integrative activities were likely conducted throughout the community, at shrines, open spaces, and small houses and great houses alike. Indeed, integrative activities would have been necessary to structure negotiation of resource access rights between different kin groups.

Negotiation among and between households or larger corporate groups for access to resources must have been a constant, on-going process. Great house complexes, though, may have also facilitated negotiation by fostering intracommunity interaction. Great kivas were most likely the venue for formal community integrative activities (Adler and Wilshusen 1990). The mechanism by which great houses may have promoted integration was through construction and maintenance of great kivas (Kantner 1996a).

We know by the recovery of nonlocal ceramics (Martin 1936) that as changes were occurring in economic production and labor organization at the local level, components of the Lowry community were also engaged in interaction on a regional scale. Our focus on economic autonomy does not preclude regional interaction by households or by organized communities. In fact, intercommunity (or even interhousehold) interaction would have provided the opportunity for access

to resources beyond local boundaries. Judge (1989) has suggested that regional interaction during the Chaco era was likely conducted through ritual metaphor. The use of certain Chaco-style architectural features (such as great kivas) and landscaping (such as roads, *nazhas,*) may have provided a grammar for the nature of this interaction. Thus, intercommunity interaction was likely facilitated by ritual integration for the purpose of gaining access to resources beyond local boundaries. These resources may not necessarily have been just for subsistence, but may also have been for ceremonial purposes. Such resources might have included turquoise, pottery, or even esoteric ritual knowledge.

The climatic downturn of the middle A.D. 1100s (Dean and others 1985; Grissino-Mayer and others 1997) and the increased population density created additional pressure on the local environment and hampered the community's economic sustainability. This pressure is demonstrated by the continued residential aggregation and by the changes in function discussed for Puzzle House. We believe these changes in settlement strategy reflect increasing formality of community economic integration, at the expense of the household autonomy over land tenure and the resource control enjoyed earlier. As community-based land tenure systems evolved, residential aggregation emerged as the successful adaptation, resulting in fully developed aggregation and community-controlled economies by the middle A.D. 1200s.

These changes in economic integration at the community level may well have conditioned the nature of the later depopulation of the area in the late A.D. 1200s. That is, more formal economic integration of larger (suprahousehold) corporate units constrained the response to climatic deterioration to full community relocation, rather than to specific household mobility common during earlier periods.

HOUSEHOLD ECONOMIC AUTONOMY

Archaeological investigations have been conducted in the Lowry area of southwestern Colorado since the late 1920s (Martin 1929, 1930). Our recent research has complemented Paul Martin's excavation of the Lowry Ruin (Martin 1936) by providing information on both the individual household and the wider community. We have examined three scales of organization within the Lowry community: the household, the great house and great house complex, and the community. By emphasizing aspects of economic production and resource access rights (Adler 1990) at these scales, we are able to integrate both local and regional processes to propose a tentative model for the development of outlying Chaco-style great houses.

A Tentative Model

This model is based on what we have called household economic autonomy. We define economic autonomy as control over basic aspects of economic production, for example, control over agricultural production. We believe that control, or autonomy, over such pursuits was vested in the domain of the household (Damp and Kendrick 1998) prior to the Pueblo III period (post A.D. 1150). Autonomy over production was manifested in several ways, many of which were exhibited at Puzzle House, in community-wide settlement patterns, and in the development of great houses.

The dispersed spatial distribution of households prior to the Chaco era suggests that individual households controlled access rights to resources within their immediate surroundings. This pattern is well illustrated by early Pueblo II period settlement strategies, which focused on upland mesas that were typified by deep arable soils. Spatial clustering of households during later periods likely reflected attempts to retain access to such resources.

At Puzzle House, economic autonomy was reflected in its multiple occupations but different functions during nearly 600 years of occupation or use. Based on the artifact-ecofact assemblage, the occupants of Puzzle House did not appear to have benefited materially from the great houses during the Chaco era. Few nonlocal ceramics, other than red wares, were recovered during our excavations (Judge 1998).

The recovery of several raw clay samples, polishing stones, and worked sherds (Judge 1998) indicate that ceramic production occurred at Puzzle House. Cores, debitage, and formal tools like projectile points, knives, scrapers, and denticulates reflect flaked stone production. Worked bone and bone tools such as awls reveal other aspects of domestic production.

More direct evidence of control, or lack thereof, over resources appeared in the architectural record of Puzzle House. The structure functioned briefly as a permanent habitation during the late Pueblo II period. In early Pueblo III times, the surface rooms were used for either storage or trash deposition and not for residential purposes. The ritually focused architecture of the late Pueblo II occupation (as indicated by the subterranean room connected to the kiva by a tunnel) was minimized,

then abandoned during the early Pueblo III period, when the function of Puzzle House seemingly was as a peripheral field facility and not as a permanent residence.

The development of the Lowry Ruin great house is informative regarding the dynamics of household economic autonomy. Lowry was probably occupied from Basketmaker III to Pueblo III times. Although it is unclear, apparently the pueblo only became differentiated from nearby contemporaneous households during the late Pueblo II period, when Chaco-style architectural elements like banded masonry and enclosed and elevated kivas were incorporated into new construction efforts. In contrast to small habitations such as Puzzle House, where only one kiva was occupied at any one time, multiple kivas at the Lowry Ruin suggest the incorporation of additional kin groups or related households. This pattern existed later in greater degrees of residential aggregation during the Pueblo III period. Great houses, then, represent the beginning of reduced household economic autonomy, as the primary access group (Adler 1990) became the lineage rather than the individual household.

Our model focuses on the changing nature of the basic economic aspects of production and control of or access to critical resources. Through time in the Lowry area, individual households sacrificed dispersed settlement and relative economic autonomy for residential aggregation and a community-controlled economy. Increased population density, and possibly population pressure, resulted in increased competition among households during late Pueblo II and Pueblo III periods. In response, certain households incorporated Chaco-style architectural and landscaping elements to pull together the settlement of related households. The result was to pool more labor and thus provide competitive advantages over other segments of the community. These larger labor groups may have fostered intra- and intercommunity interaction by sponsoring the construction and maintenance of great kivas.

Environmental degradation during the middle 1100s, the collapse of the Chaco "system," and a continuation of population pressure at the local level accentuated the need for residential aggregation and increased labor, as more intensive strategies were required. These factors led to a more community-controlled economy during the last part of the Pueblo III period. That is, the community as a whole now controlled the allocation and use of critical resources, rather than the individual household. The structure of the Pueblo III community decision-making, however, is not fully understood at this time.

The Implication for Great House Models

The changes we describe in household, great house, and community development in the Lowry area have important implications for our understanding of Chaco-style great houses and ancestral puebloan communities in the Montezuma Valley. The social and economic dynamics described imply that the development of great houses and great house complexes can be attributable in large part to local processes. The presence of pit structures below or in the immediate vicinity of the Lowry Ruin prior to the Chaco era, and the building's incremental growth through time, strongly indicate a local household or lineage was responsible for its construction. Indeed, Chaco-style architecture was incorporated into the pueblo during a brief interval of approximately 30 years between A.D. 1086 and 1120. Occupation and use of the Lowry Ruin, however, spanned more than 500 years. Although nonlocal ceramics were present, there is no evidence that indicates nonlocal persons constructed the great house.

Examined from this perspective, great houses would not be interpreted as public buildings (communally owned and operated). Research in the Lowry area indicated (at least to us) that great houses developed from and were built by local households. As changes in economic production and labor organization were taking place in the late A.D. 1000s and early 1100s, these households incorporated Chaco-style architectural elements into new construction. Chaco-style architecture may have been chosen for several reasons, one of which may have been to attract kin for pooling and controlling more labor. Great kivas, on the other hand, were the likely venue for housing public forums. The roads at Lowry, which radiated from the great kiva and not the great house, provide additional supporting evidence.

At the beginning of this discussion we divided great house models into two basic categories: colonization models and local development models, and information from the Lowry area indicates local processes were more likely responsible for the development of great houses. Many of the colonization models cannot be tested with data obtained from the archaeological record. Priests (Eddy 1972), missionaries (B. Bradley 1993), and armies (Wilcox 1993) may have been part of the social environment of the San Juan Basin and its peripheries during the Chaco era, but we seriously doubt that these models can be adequately tested. The movement of people into the Lowry area is supported by evidence of a population increase during the Chaco era. Unfortunately, without more settlement pattern and household data from across Montezuma Valley, we will not know if this population came from areas just outside our survey boundaries or from greater distances. Recent investigations in the Montezuma Valley indicate population decreases in certain areas during the Chaco era, such as the Ute Mountain area (Huckleberry and Billman 1998) and Mockingbird Mesa (Fetterman and Honeycutt 1987). These "local" population dynamics could have resulted in the increased population observed for the Lowry area, rather than movement by groups from Chaco Canyon. Incorporation of local population is also consistent with the model of increasing economic integration, when kin relations were attracted to larger corporate groups.

Our model of increasing integration of economic production above the household level potentially identifies the underlying mechanisms for the development of outlying Chaco-style great houses. Traditionally, local development models have focused on community elites (Powers and others 1983), political competition (Kantner 1996a; Sebastian 1992), or social integration (Varien and others 1996). All of the factors or processes described in these models can be included in our model. We think, however, that the basic and underlying factors that may have precipitated local elites, or political competition, or the need for formal social integrative mechanisms and facilities, involved changes in household control over economic production.

Acknowledgments

Investigations in the Lowry area were partially funded by the Wenner-Gren Foundation for Anthropological Research (GR 5734), the Colorado Historical Society (Project #95–01–87), and Fort Lewis College in Durango, Colorado. We are indebted to the dedicated staff of the Anasazi Heritage Center for their support throughout the entire project. Numerous individuals (far too many to name here) have contributed to the fieldwork summarized in this chapter, and we gratefully thank everyone who has been a part of the project. We express appreciation to John Kantner and Nancy Mahoney for asking us to participate in the symposium and for their comments on our chapter. Jonathan Damp and Mike Adler provided substantive comments on household economy and community organization. Any errors are strictly our own.

CHAPTER TEN

Interaction Among Great House Communities
An Elemental Analysis of Cibolan Ceramics

John Kantner, Nathan Bower, Jeffrey Ladwig,
Jacob Perlitz, Steve Hata, and Darren Greve

Theories on the development of the Chaco socio-cultural tradition have always paid attention to the topic of economic exchange. Many early researchers investigating Chaco Canyon noted the presence of copper bells, turquoise, marine shell, macaws, and other exotic materials, often regarding them as clear evidence of a far-ranging exchange network that must have shaped Chacoan development (Brand and others 1937; Dutton 1938: 71–72; Pepper 1920). Similarly, scholars such as Neil Judd examined the distribution of imported pottery in Pueblo Bonito and considered ceramic exchange across long distances in their discussions of the origins and demise of Chacoan society (Judd 1954: 29–36, 181–182, 234–235). More recently, with the identification of numerous great house communities located outside of Chaco Canyon, attention has turned to local exchange networks within the San Juan Basin. This emphasis has stimulated a number of models in which critical resources are argued to have moved from outlying communities to Chaco Canyon for redistribution to people experiencing subsistence stress. Current discussion of Chacoan cultural change continues to emphasize the importance of trade between great house communities, especially focusing on the role of reciprocal exchange in the development of sociopolitical asymmetries (Kantner 1996a; Saitta 1997; Sebastian 1992).

The majority of research on Chacoan economic exchange has focused on materials imported into Chaco Canyon. Such study has been critical for reconstructing the complicated patterns of exchange that occurred there, and it has made important contributions to the evaluation of models of Chacoan economic evolution. However, few scholars have yet attempted to reconstruct patterns of exchange among the numerous communities located outside of Chaco Canyon. An understanding of how these communities interacted both with one another and with Chaco Canyon is crucial for eval-

uating the many models of Chacoan development, most of which include explicit or implicit expectations of intercommunity exchange. This chapter contributes to this research by reporting the results of elemental analyses of ceramics from five communities located in the southern part of the San Juan Basin. These analyses provide insights into both the production of pottery and the distribution of this pottery among neighboring communities. The results add more detail to our reconstruction of Chacoan economy and assist in our continuing evaluation of various models of the development of this sociocultural tradition.

RESEARCH ON GREAT HOUSE COMMUNITY EXCHANGE

With the exception of the long-distance exchange of exotic items, a topic not considered in this chapter, the discussion of exchange among Chaco groups has most often focused on the interaction between outlying communities and Chaco Canyon. This interest was first stimulated by the redistribution models of the 1970s and 1980s, which proposed that Chaco Canyon was the center of a complex redistributive economy. According to the general scenario, archaeologists thought that prehistoric groups living within the greater San Juan Basin took advantage of environmental spatial variability by pooling resources and redistributing them to people experiencing subsistence stress (Judge 1979, 1984, 1989; Judge and others 1981). These redistribution models stimulated important research on the Chaco sociocultural tradition, including regional surveys that have been major influences on our understanding of the extent and function of the hypothesized Chaco "system" (Marshall and others 1979; Powers and others 1983). Most of this research focused on identifying the major characteristics of the Chaco tradition, especially architecture and community structure. However, many authors of these studies also hypothesized about the structure of regional economic interactions (Irwin-Williams 1977; Neitzel 1989; Schelberg 1984). An especially important result of this work was the identification of the famous Chacoan roadways, which illustrated the intensity of economic interaction between outlying communities and Chaco Canyon (Ebert and Hitchcock 1980; Powers 1984).

Although many of the projects investigating the Chacoans have focused on settlement patterns, several studies have also attempted to identify artifactual evidence of the proposed systems of exchange. Research on ceramics has been especially important, for scholars assume that the proposed redistribution of foods and associated exchange activities would have relied on ceramic containers for transporting materials across the region. Toll's examination of pottery from Chaco Canyon is particularly enlightening in this regard, because his study shows that large quantities of ceramics were produced in outlying areas and then brought into Chaco Canyon (Toll 1985, 1991; see also Blinman and Wilson 1993; Mathien 1993). Toll also determined that the origins of these ceramics varied through time, with almost all imports coming from the south during the A.D. 900s, from the west during the 1000s, and from the north in the 1100s (Toll 1991: 97–98). Other studies demonstrate that this pattern of shifting exchange was mirrored in other materials, such as lithics (Cameron 1984; Jacobson 1984) and faunal remains (Akins 1985). Researchers are also finding, however, that materials flowing into Chaco Canyon were not being exported back to outlying communities (Mathien 1993; Toll 1985, 1991). Research in outlying great house communities supports this conclusion, and archaeologists are discovering that ceramic materials in these areas were homogeneous and tempered with local materials; apparently little of the pottery was being imported from distant parts of the Chaco world (Eddy 1977; Pippin 1987). For example, a recent study of ceramics in the Red Mesa Valley south of Chaco Canyon convincingly confirms how infrequently materials from Chaco Canyon or other distant parts of the San Juan Basin were imported into outlying great house communities (Van Dyke 1997a). All of these patterns undermine models that regard the development of the Chaco sociocultural tradition as having been closely tied to the emergence of a well-integrated regional economy.

Most studies of Chacoan exchange have relied on macro- or microscopic analyses to distinguish between the sources of prehistoric ceramics. In recent years, however, elemental approaches have been used to supplement the traditional methods of compositional analysis. In their study of Dogoszhi-style ceramics in both Chaco Canyon and outlying areas, Neitzel and Bishop (1990) utilize an elemental compositional analysis to determine that vessels recovered from Chaco Canyon differ significantly from those found in the Allentown great house community located on the Rio Puerco of the West in Arizona. They also report that Allentown ceramics were more variable than those in Chaco Canyon, suggesting that vessels in Allentown were produced from a variety of sources, that the Chaco Canyon vessels came from a single source, or a combination of both conclusions.

Despite a growing understanding of ceramic exchange between Chaco Canyon and outlying communities, comparatively few studies have investigated the localized exchange of materials among or within great house communities. Exceptions include the summary of evidence from the northern San Juan Basin by Blinman and Wilson (1993: 79–81), which notes the high frequency of ceramic exchange within local areas. Their conclusions are augmented by a recent study summarizing elemental analyses from this region (Glowacki and others 1997). Although the results are preliminary, researchers identify evidence of vessel movement between the Mesa Verde area and the Lowry great house community as well as exchange between Lowry and unidentified settlements near Chaco Canyon. Another intriguing study uses elemental analysis to reconstruct the dynamics of exchange between a local great house and surrounding habitations (Duff 1994a, 1994b; Kintigh and others 1996). This research, which focuses on the post-Chaco Hinkson great house near Zuni, has shown that all of the residential areas interacted extensively with one another, but that locally made vessels were apparently brought to the great house at a rate greater than the movement of ceramics away from the structure. An extension of this analysis to the earlier Chacoan occupation in the same area has identified similar patterns (Huntley and others 1998).

Two patterns have emerged from the research on Chacoan exchange. First, evidence indicates that the exchange of pottery with Chaco Canyon appears to have been one-way, with locally made vessels moving from outlying areas into the canyon but no pottery of any type moving back out to distant communities. Duff's study offers the intriguing but still untested possibility that this pattern was emulated at a smaller scale between habitations and their local great houses. The second pattern is that most communities appear to have produced their own pottery; researchers have not found evidence for extensive specialization in puebloan communities (Deutchman 1980; Hegmon and others 1995; Kojo 1996) and, as Wilson and Blinman (1995: 74) note, "the level of specialization is low, with many pottery-producing households for each nonproducing household." Accordingly, the distribution of pottery in most areas (with the obvious exception of Chaco Canyon) indicates that few ceramics were consistently exchanged across long distances but that locally produced pottery was frequently exchanged with other communities located nearby (Blinman and Wilson 1993: 78–82; Duff 1994a; Franklin 1982: 925; Kojo 1996). However, despite the promising convergence of microscopic and elemental techniques to reconstruct patterns of Chacoan exchange, we do not yet have a clear idea of how this exchange among communities was patterned, and this important topic deserves further attention.

CERAMIC EXCHANGE IN THE SOUTHERN SAN JUAN BASIN

The research reported here addresses one of the most important aspects of Chacoan economy through the detailed reconstruction of ceramic production and exchange within a region located outside of Chaco Canyon. These analyses are part of a larger study, the Lobo Mesa Archaeological Project, that has focused on a 2,500 square-kilometer (965 square-mile) study area located south of Chaco Canyon and centered on Hosta Butte (Fig. 10.1). The analyses were initiated to contribute to the project's ongoing attempt to reconstruct sociopolitical interactions within and among neighboring great house communities (Kantner 1996a, 1997, 1999), with the ultimate goal of understanding how changes in outlying regions of the greater San Juan Basin were associated with developments in Chaco Canyon. The underlying assumption is that the important yet poorly understood relationship between outlying great house communities and the central canyon is reflected in patterns of interaction among neighboring communities located in peripheral areas. This chapter complements others in this volume that consider how patterns of intercommunity exchange can be used to better understand the development of the Chaco sociocultural tradition.

Ceramic Compositional Analysis

Archaeologists use a wide variety of methods for reconstructing patterns of production and exchange from ceramic materials (Rice 1987: 177–204, 413–426). The simplest method is the macroscopic examination of sty-

listic characteristics, which can be successfully used to distinguish among ceramics produced in markedly different areas. However, this method can be problematic for distinguishing between areas where potters used similar designs on their vessels, as in the case of many of the ceramics produced in different regions of the northern Southwest. In these situations, microscopic compositional analysis and refiring can be used to examine clays and tempers. These approaches have been effective in distinguishing major areas of production, such as Chuska and Cibola (Goetze and Mills 1993; Toll and others 1980).

When clays and tempers are similar in appearance, neither macroscopic nor microscopic techniques are adequate. In these situations, elemental analysis is especially useful, because it can distinguish between production areas that produce visually similar ceramics (Bishop and Neff 1989; Crown 1994; Gilman and others 1994; Neff 1992; Thomas and others 1992:26). This approach is less affected by operator bias than are methods that require the consistent visual identification of ceramic components. Because the ceramics in this study are from neighboring communities with ceramics that are both macroscopically and microscopically similar, we chose elemental analysis as the primary method for identifying areas of production.

Many different kinds of elemental analysis have been used by archaeologists, and each has its strengths and weaknesses (Pollard and Heron 1996). In the Americas, the most common technique has been instrumental neutron activation analysis (INAA), which is capable of detecting very low amounts of a wide variety of elements. Because the method requires access to a nuclear reactor, it is the most expensive and perhaps least environmentally sensitive technique. Another method, inductively coupled plasma emission (ICP), is probably the least expensive and most readily available approach, but variations in the extractability of the complex ceramic body may compromise its accuracy (Neff and others 1996). X-ray fluorescence (XRF) is a good compromise, because it offers superior precision and accuracy for major components while also providing enough sensitivity to identify many of the trace elements, all at a relatively low cost (Thomas and others 1992: 26).

Methods

For this study, we randomly selected 214 sherds from the trash areas of habitation sites within five great house communities south of Chaco Canyon (Fig. 10.1, Table 10.1). Muddy Water and Kin Ya'a are in drainages that

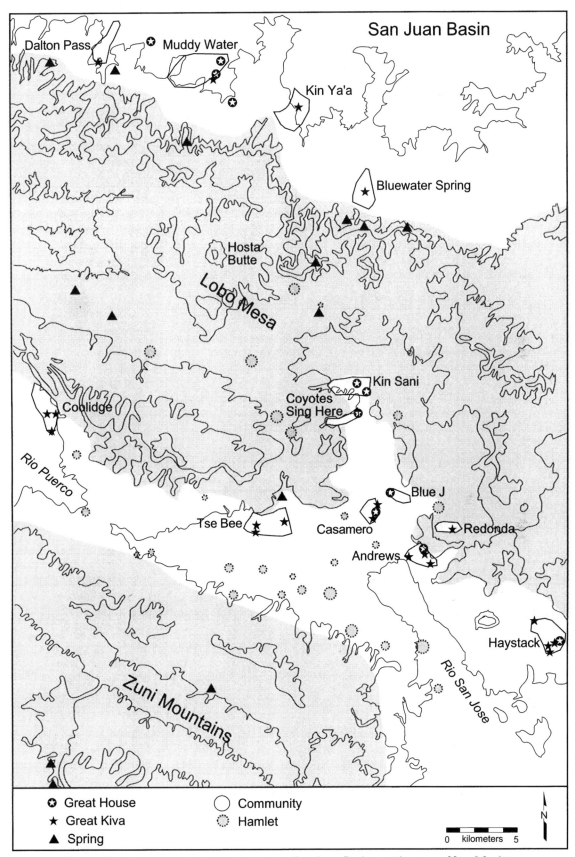

Figure 10.1. Location of sites studied in the San Juan Basin, northwestern New Mexico.

Table 10.1. Description of Analyzed Sherd Samples

Community	Site No.	Site type	Mean ceramic date	Ceramic date range	Geological context	No. of samples
Muddy Water	LA 2987	Habitation middens	A.D. 1065	A.D. 1001–1129	Mancos shales; Gibson Coal Member; Point Lookout Sandstone	38
Kin Ya'a	LA 2985	Habitation middens	A.D. 1067	A.D. 1003–1130	Dalton Sandstone; Gibson Coal Member	40
Haystack	LA 68896	Great house middens	A.D. 1073	A.D. 1004–1143	Entrada Sandstone; Todilto Limestone	29
	LA 12574	Habitation middens	A.D. 1070	A.D. 1002–1138	Entrada Sandstone; Todilto Limestone	17
Blue J	TNE–1	Habitation middens	A.D. 1063	A.D. 1004–1122	Summerville Formation; Bluff Sandstone; Todilto Limestone	37
Casamero	LA 8779	Great house trash fill	A.D. 1060	A.D. 987–1137	Entrada Sandstone; Wingate Sandstone; Todilto Limestone	40

NOTE: The numbers of samples do not include the 13 sherds that were removed during sample preparation.

descend along the northern edge of Lobo Mesa (also known as the Dutton Plateau), and Blue J, Casamero, and Haystack are in the Rio San José Valley (often referred to as the Red Mesa Valley) between Lobo Mesa and the Zuni Mountains. The samples were collected from the expansive midden areas surrounding one or two structures in each community. The operating assumption was that the sample of sherds around each structure was generally representative of the ceramics distributed throughout the entire community, an assumption that was supported by the close spacing between unit pueblos in communities in this part of the San Juan Basin (Gilpin and Purcell, this volume; Kantner 1996a). The habitation densities in these communities suggested a substantial degree of interaction among neighboring unit pueblos. The assumption was also supported by the comparable results produced by the multistructure samples from Haystack, as discussed below.

All five of the sampled communities appear to have been occupied contemporaneously, but to further minimize compositional variability not attributable to location, we selected only mineral-painted sherds exhibiting Dogoszhi-style straight hachure designs. Standard stylistic identifications as defined by Goetze and Mills (1993) indicate that the sample is dominated by Gallup Black-on-white (87%), with smaller quantities of sherds that are stylistically defined as Chaco Black-on-white (9%) and Reserve Black-on-white (4%). A few sherds

could not be confidently classified because of insufficient design.

For each sherd, we first recorded data on paste and temper using a binocular microscope. Each sherd was carefully cleaned with distilled water and dried, and a small portion of the sherd free of mineral paint was broken off for elemental analysis. Each sample was then pulverized, mixed with lithium tetraborate flux (Spex), and fired to 1050°C. The molten material was poured into a mold. We analyzed the resulting glass disk using K_α lines on a Rigaku model 3070 WDXRF, which measured 10 major and 10 minor components (Table 10.2). At various stages of this process, 10 sherds were removed from the analysis, either due to preparation errors or because the samples were too small.

We used Minitab and SPSS statistical packages to analyze the resulting data set for the remaining 204 sherds. The data were first examined for samples whose total elemental composition was significantly less than 100 percent. This low percent can occur if a sherd still has water in it even after thorough drying or if there is residual carbonate (either from low-temperature firing of the original clay or from groundwater deposits) that burns out of the sample during preparation of the glass disk. Depending on the circumstances, the samples were then either removed from subsequent analyses or the data were adjusted so that the elements added up to 100 percent. In this case, three sherds were removed and two

Table 10.2. Elements Examined by the X-ray Fluorescence

Major Components	Minor Components
Sodium (Na)	Vanadium (V)
Magnesium (Mg)	Chromium (Cr)
Aluminum (Al)	Cobalt (Co)
Silicon (Si)	Zinc (Zn)
Phosphorus (P)	Rubidium (Rb)
Potassium (K)	Strontium (Sr)
Calcium (Ca)	Yttrium (Y)
Titanium (Ti)	Zirconium (Zr)
Manganese (Mn)	Niobium (Nb)
Iron (Fe)	Barium (Ba)

that appeared to have water contamination were adjusted. The data were then normalized using z-scores so that elements with high concentrations would not dominate subsequent data processing.

Next we submitted the data set to a cluster analysis to identify groups of compositionally similar sherds. Experience has demonstrated that Ward's method of hierarchical cluster analysis on squared Euclidean distances works best for ceramic elemental data (Thomas and others 1992: 26). The cluster analysis produced a dendrogram illustrating similarities among all of the samples, as well as an agglomeration schedule that we used to identify the most substantial jump in the clustering process. We evaluated this cluster solution in two ways. First, each cluster was correlated with microscopic compositional characteristics of its member sherds. Because these visual attributes were independent of the cluster analysis, consistencies within clusters and differences between clusters validated the clustering solution. Second, we generated probabilities of group membership for each case in order to identify problematic sherds that could have potentially belonged to more than one cluster or that had low probabilities of belonging to any of the clusters. Both methods provided insight into the success of the cluster analysis in identifying meaningful groups in the data.

Once the sherd clusters were defined and evaluated, each was examined for dominance by sherds recovered from a single community. This process facilitated the identification of probable sources for the ceramics, assuming that a cluster dominated by sherds recovered from one community represented pottery produced in that community. To assist in this evaluation, we collected at least one raw clay sample from the area surrounding each of the communities and analyzed it in the same manner as the sherds. The resulting elemental data from the clay samples (Table 10.3) was compared with the data from the sherd clusters to evaluate the validity

Table 10.3. Elemental Compositions of Clay Samples

	Muddy Water 1	Muddy Water 2	Kin Ya'a	Casamero	Blue J	Haystack
Na_2O	1.176	1.626	0.985	0.840	0.563	0.168
MgO	0.741	0.937	0.162	2.899	0.509	0.395
Al_2O_3	12.425	12.814	6.711	14.127	4.388	2.038
SiO_2	72.184	66.975	86.550	58.728	89.425	44.838
P_2O_5	0.075	0.109	0.026	0.096	0.023	0.112
K_2O	2.594	2.697	1.654	1.658	1.663	0.700
CaO	0.779	4.193	0.736	2.841	1.971	23.523
TiO_2	0.683	0.587	0.235	0.694	0.112	0.061
MnO	0.020	0.014	0.004	0.061	0.028	0.086
Fe_2O_3	1.856	0.868	0.755	3.025	0.300	0.000
V	73.000	60.000	20.000	89.000	7.000	8.000
Cr	71.000	85.000	64.000	56.000	122.000	23.000
Co	11.000	7.000	2.000	15.000	7.000	3.000
Sr	127.000	283.000	160.000	275.000	97.000	196.000
Zn	68.000	60.000	32.000	65.000	19.000	15.000
Y	42.000	53.000	39.000	35.000	71.000	44.000
Zr	469.000	311.000	206.000	196.000	207.000	109.000
Nb	17.000	16.000	12.000	14.000	13.000	9.000
Rb	103.000	90.000	64.000	88.000	49.000	25.000

of identifying specific clusters with particular communities. However, because the clay samples were devoid of the tempers present in the sherds, because at least one clay sample was of dubious quality (Kin Ya'a), and because there were so few clay samples, we were able to conduct only a general comparison between the clays and the sherds.

X-ray Fluorescence Analyses

The dendrogram produced by the cluster analysis (Fig. 10.2) illustrates how similar samples are to one another. Sherds paired with one another on the left side of the dendrogram have extremely similar compositions, but as you move to the right, the sherds become more and more dissimilar. For example, all of the sherds in Cluster 1 are more similar to one another than any of them are to the sherds from the two sites in Cluster 2. Sherds in Clusters 1 and 2 are more similar to one another than to sherds in Cluster 3. By extending this logic to the entire sample, the result is a "tree" that starts on the right with total dissimilarity and branches out to the left to illustrate greater and greater levels of similarity. Longer "branches" in the dendrogram indicate that the members of that branch are especially dissimilar from either of the neighboring branches.

The analysis clearly divides the sherd samples into three major branches. The distinctive branch at the top of the dendrogram is dominated by sherds from Kin Ya'a and Muddy Water, both of which are located north of Lobo Mesa (Fig. 10.1). The next two major branches consist primarily of sherds from sites in the Rio San José Valley south of Lobo Mesa: the branch at the bottom is dominated by samples from Hay-

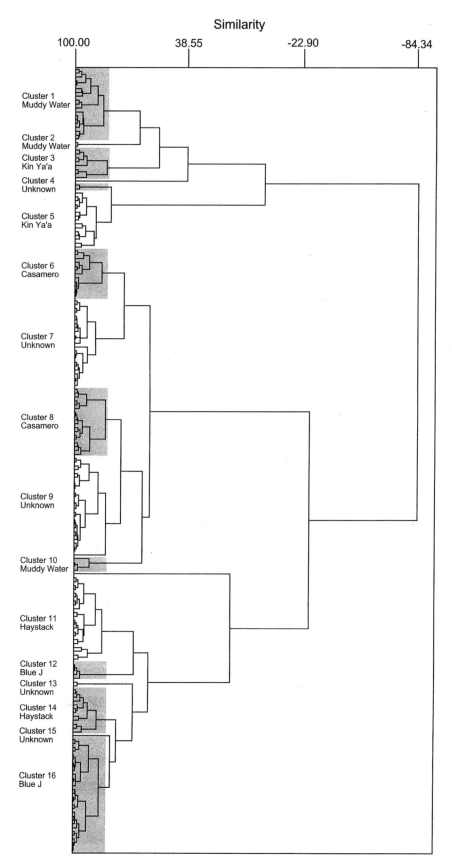

Figure 10.2. Dendrogram illustrating clusters of compositionally related sherds.

stack and Blue J, and the middle branch is more mixed but includes most of the sherds from Casamero. These major divisions appear to reflect the distinctive geological contexts in which the sampled communities are located (Fig. 10.1), with communities north of Lobo Mesa clearly situated in the upper layers of an Upper Cretaceous geological environment and those in the San José River Valley placed completely in Jurassic and Triassic deposits. The separation of Casamero into the middle branch of the dendrogram may be attributed to the fact that it is the only community represented in the elemental analysis associated with Upper Triassic deposits.

The geology represented within the major ceramic zones identified in the dendrogram is so varied that even the communities of Blue J and Casamero, located only a few kilometers apart, are in distinctive geological environments. Accordingly, perhaps the most interesting distinctions occur at the next level of the dendrogram (Fig. 10.2). The agglomeration schedule for the cluster analysis indicates that a large jump in the similarity measure occurs at the 16-cluster solution (that is, the point where the samples are divided into 16 "branches"), which is relatively stable even when the parameters of the cluster analysis are changed or if cases are removed; in fact, the general patterns of this solution were anticipated in a preliminary study that was conducted on a smaller set of approximately 50 sherds. The 16-cluster solution is also confirmed by correlations of each cluster with compositional characteristics identified using the binocular microscope (Table 10.4); each of the groups exhibits consistent visual characteristics that tend to distinguish the clusters from one another.

Table 10.5 summarizes the elemental data for each of the 16 clusters. We conducted a factor analysis on the elemental data to evaluate the elements that contributed most to distinguishing among clusters. Table 10.6 lists the rotated factor loadings for 6 factors with eigenvalues greater than 1.0, which together account for 72.7 percent of the variation in the original 20 variables. The table also indicates the geological components that may be represented by each factor, as suggested by a comparison of the element loadings for each factor with National Institute of Science and Technology (NIST) standards for various rock and mineral types (Bower and others 1992). Using this information, some insight can be gained as to the geological components that may be contributing most directly to the distinctions among clusters, especially when the factors are plotted two at a time. For exam-

Table 10.4. Characteristics of Sherds According to Cluster

Cluster	N	Paste Color	Firing Core	Inclusion Size	Inclusion Density	Sorting	Slip Thickness	Major Inclusions
1	19	gray–dk. gray	absent–moderate	average	10%	average	moderate	sherd, sand, crushed quartz, "calcite"
2	2	dk. gray–black	narrow–moderate	average	5–20%	poor–average	moderate	sherd, sand, limonite
3	8	lt. gray–gray	none	average	5–10%	poor–average	thin–mod.	sherd, crushed quartz, vesicular igneous
4	2	lt. gray–dk. gray	thick	small	20–30%	poor–average	none–mod.	sherd, sand, crushed quartz, vesicular igneous, "calcite"
5	15	lt. gray–gray	none	average	10%	poor–average	thin	sherd, crushed quartz, vesicular igneous
6	13	gray	narrow–moderate	average	5–10%	poor–average	none	sherd, crushed sandstone
7	23	lt. gray–black	none–thick	average	5–20%	poor–average	none–mod.	sherd, sand, crushed quartz, limestone, clay nodules
8	18	gray–dk. gray	narrow–moderate	average	10%	average	thin	sherd, sand, crushed quartz, "calcite"
9	25	gray	none–narrow	average	10–20%	poor–average	none–thick	sherd, sand, crushed quartz
10	4	white	none	average	5–10%	average	thin	sherd, crushed quartz
11	22	gray	thick–moderate	average	5–20%	poor	thin–mod.	sherd, crushed quartz, clay nodules
12	5	dk. gray	moderate–thick	large	20%	very poor–poor	moderate	sand, limestone, limonite, "calcite"
13	2	dk. gray–black	moderate–thick	ave.–large	10–20%	poor–average	moderate	sherd, crushed quartz
14	12	black	thick	ave.–large	10%	poor	none–thin	sherd, sand
15	1	black	narrow	average	20%	well	thin	sand
16	30	dk. gray–black	moderate–thick	average	10%	poor–average	thin–mod.	sherd, sand, crushed quartz, crushed shale?

Table 10.5. Elemental Compositions for the 16 Clusters

	CLUSTER 1		CLUSTER 2		CLUSTER 3		CLUSTER 4		CLUSTER 5		CLUSTER 6		CLUSTER 7		CLUSTER 8	
	Mean	StDev	Mean	StDev	Mean	StDev	Mean	StDev	Mean	StDev	Mean	StDev	Mean	StDev	Mean	StDev
Na_2O	0.528	0.207	2.752	0.242	0.603	0.265	0.894	0.358	0.583	0.321	0.620	0.453	0.238	0.163	0.293	0.197
MgO	1.601	0.228	1.532	0.007	1.686	0.198	1.294	0.167	1.801	0.280	1.018	0.173	1.253	0.245	1.248	0.228
Al_2O_3	20.923	1.281	20.507	1.526	22.855	1.761	24.165	0.696	22.082	1.131	21.269	1.962	22.289	2.171	22.949	1.798
SiO_2	68.342	0.841	67.559	0.674	65.950	0.743	66.744	0.594	67.890	1.341	69.556	1.676	68.576	1.963	67.347	2.295
P_2O_5	0.117	0.043	0.096	0.003	0.162	0.061	0.081	0.001	0.070	0.013	0.064	0.016	0.067	0.017	0.128	0.038
K_2O	2.645	0.408	2.744	0.074	3.403	0.310	2.285	0.232	2.935	0.544	2.693	0.540	2.307	0.349	2.765	0.364
CaO	1.256	0.569	1.338	0.389	1.225	0.688	1.246	0.073	0.603	0.215	1.152	0.581	1.027	0.303	1.223	0.541
TiO_2	0.890	0.062	0.862	0.097	0.956	0.094	0.851	0.046	0.906	0.094	0.953	0.134	0.956	0.069	0.943	0.078
MnO	0.027	0.011	0.015	0.004	0.012	0.004	0.010	0.002	0.014	0.007	0.010	0.004	0.011	0.004	0.010	0.006
Fe_2O_3	3.185	0.602	2.596	0.244	3.225	0.821	2.432	0.258	2.977	0.267	2.380	0.272	2.610	0.380	2.713	0.336
V	111.500	16.298	109.544	14.519	123.787	13.101	109.279	8.549	118.179	17.129	79.021	17.138	114.789	15.129	110.422	14.227
Cr	126.053	32.947	92.571	9.484	148.384	43.931	160.895	58.724	203.176	54.146	111.264	18.594	113.092	20.697	142.971	36.335
Co	15.623	5.632	16.922	1.340	9.365	3.193	6.071	0.002	11.914	4.802	7.245	4.416	7.879	2.579	6.134	2.935
Sr	194.784	34.782	212.553	2.667	347.760	81.460	177.573	46.447	159.387	31.767	146.013	29.362	158.287	44.368	205.998	46.702
Zn	118.430	36.181	111.022	6.781	92.290	24.422	61.219	10.753	88.378	19.019	44.287	13.312	87.277	35.858	59.370	12.160
Y	141.117	66.512	266.992	86.958	249.577	128.345	839.842	21.747	456.303	125.471	127.585	29.021	97.967	36.788	190.759	127.589
Zr	232.651	23.077	257.296	32.055	271.489	53.932	228.675	24.250	226.471	27.792	318.711	36.641	235.744	26.934	248.415	29.807
Nb	33.685	7.379	48.305	9.346	48.379	16.743	119.905	2.187	72.425	14.632	36.977	4.595	29.929	4.175	42.198	15.883
Rb	111.509	32.758	120.981	8.229	140.413	17.575	109.277	19.997	130.379	16.326	107.090	21.171	107.619	14.577	121.110	15.310

	CLUSTER 9		CLUSTER 10		CLUSTER 11		CLUSTER 12		CLUSTER 13		CLUSTER 14		CLUSTER 15		CLUSTER 16	
	Mean	StDev	Mean	StDev	Mean	StDev	Mean	StDev	Mean	StDev	Mean	StDev	Mean	StDev	Mean	StDev
Na_2O	0.424	0.317	0.322	0.183	0.274	0.202	0.344	0.166	0.171	•	0.209	0.144	0.309	•	0.221	0.093
MgO	1.536	0.269	1.256	0.472	1.397	0.157	1.225	0.037	1.204		1.188	0.200	0.527		1.234	0.180
Al_2O_3	23.872	2.569	21.319	0.767	25.814	2.153	21.511	0.227	28.831		28.926	2.161	25.713		25.947	2.091
SiO_2	65.600	2.561	70.541	2.341	64.825	1.824	68.970	0.588	63.427		61.713	2.747	68.200		65.234	2.316
P_2O_5	0.083	0.024	0.053	0.013	0.064	0.015	0.083	0.006	0.068		0.073	0.017	0.043		0.070	0.018
K_2O	3.117	0.320	2.642	0.353	2.091	0.501	2.228	0.031	1.638		1.716	0.464	0.816		2.090	0.292
CaO	0.900	0.423	0.868	0.440	1.192	0.361	0.773	0.040	1.396		1.573	0.577	1.214		1.298	0.381
TiO_2	0.994	0.130	0.949	0.029	1.019	0.064	0.773	0.009	1.032		1.115	0.112	1.206		0.980	0.081
MnO	0.011	0.005	0.010	0.004	0.010	0.005	0.008	0.001	0.067		0.007	0.004	0.009		0.008	0.003
Fe_2O_3	3.032	0.668	2.544	0.453	3.213	0.573	5.484	0.123	2.167		2.856	0.999	1.644		2.627	0.388
V	123.877	21.169	109.000	20.704	123.476	30.080	72.600	7.335	92.921		122.541	19.204	87.000		80.269	12.611
Cr	133.706	28.974	115.250	3.862	162.102	34.034	127.800	39.124	137.361		98.779	27.568	281.000		121.755	34.891
Co	8.843	3.098	7.000	2.943	10.273	3.211	7.200	6.221	0.000		7.317	3.097	7.000		6.583	3.557
Sr	164.359	36.824	145.250	52.468	177.425	47.906	129.000	3.937	190.892		163.388	101.705	107.000		158.011	29.025
Zn	79.751	13.647	76.649	36.877	67.712	19.827	80.154	0.000	45.450		54.814	19.065	24.066		44.626	12.409
Y	116.394	38.965	71.000	43.451	207.364	103.222	168.000	26.029	200.992		107.268	37.006	345.000		210.150	114.468
Zr	255.115	36.056	260.750	78.215	280.743	56.574	325.800	4.025	331.283		334.446	24.995	572.000		346.033	34.149
Nb	32.977	4.880	29.750	9.032	46.563	13.524	39.000	3.937	52.521		41.152	4.655	79.000		49.728	13.528
Rb	136.052	10.893	271.000	2.944	96.667	19.464	81.200	2.588	73.731	•	69.130	16.398	30.000	•	85.201	9.634

Table 10.6. Results of the Factor Analysis of Ceramic Elemental Data

	Factor 1	Factor 2	Factor 3	Factor 4	Factor 5	Factor 6
Eigenvalue	5.09433	2.80515	2.0819	1.41714	1.35324	1.06357
% Variance	26.8	14.8	11.0	7.5	7.1	5.6
Na_2O	0.33009	0.06539	-0.27417	-0.04026	0.14522	0.74436
MgO	0.58554	0.40810	-0.08706	0.09928	0.35337	-0.11917
Al_2O_3	-0.35871	0.09073	0.70124	-0.45408	-0.05478	-0.12648
SiO_2	0.15838	-0.10576	-0.65270	0.51906	-0.21023	0.14069
P_2O_5	0.25752	-0.18595	-0.20413	0.03666	0.73775	-0.07307
K_2O	0.19008	0.12763	-0.27880	0.68867	0.35368	0.08282
CaO	-0.06891	-0.27455	0.05533	-0.57073	0.46774	0.07585
TiO_2	-0.16093	-0.14151	0.78254	-0.10943	-0.17232	0.08871
MnO	0.69126	-0.11587	-0.32185	-0.00166	0.13024	-0.02877
Fe_2O_3	0.35932	0.06033	-0.35509	-0.23200	0.08822	-0.63127
V	0.50275	0.19555	0.56448	0.18948	0.22745	-0.06937
Cr	0.13314	0.73039	0.04540	0.19767	-0.02840	-0.22867
Co	0.75607	-0.05703	0.03787	0.09826	-0.19913	0.18474
Sr	0.04277	0.07116	0.11317	0.16295	0.77583	0.10065
Zn	0.82131	0.01945	-0.12821	0.16983	0.15324	-0.02636
Y	0.03793	0.95881	-0.07331	0.04710	-0.01237	0.10632
Zr	-0.61088	-0.18811	0.10807	-0.37994	-0.25669	-0.02510
Nb	-0.10906	0.94329	0.06811	-0.03956	-0.07312	0.11232
Rb	0.14319	0.02735	-0.06025	0.82433	0.14056	0.03227
Associated Rock Type?	Mafic	Alkaline? Syenite?	Clay	Feldspar/ Quartz	Phosphate	Unknown

NOTE: Gray cells indicate those elements that have relatively high loadings for each factor.

ple, Figure 10.3 illustrates that Factors 1 and 4 are most responsible for the distinction between communities north of Lobo Mesa and those to the south. Based on comparisons between the NIST standards and the element loadings for these factors, the pattern in Figure 10.3 may represent the separation of the groups based on the amount of mafic and feldspar–quartz components in the sherds. Similarly, what may be mafics and felsics appear to contribute most to the distinctions among northern communities (Fig. 10.4), whereas clays and calcic–phosphate rocks help to distinguish the southern communities (Fig. 10.5). However, the factor loadings also indicate that any two factors are not adequate for distinguishing between the clusters, a conclusion confirmed by the overlap between cluster confidence intervals (represented by the ellipses in the figures) when the factor scores are plotted two at a time.

An inspection of the probabilities of group membership for each sample derived through discriminant analysis further confirms that the clusters are significantly distinct. Cluster identification and discriminant analysis group identity match 100 percent for samples in all but four of the clusters, with an overall correspondence of 94.1 percent: the exceptions were Cluster 7 (95.7%), Cluster 9 (88.5%), Cluster 11 (68.2%), and Cluster 16

(96.7%). Only 12 sherds had higher probabilities of belonging to a group different from the one in which the cluster analysis placed them, and in these cases group identities were adjusted accordingly. However, the discriminant analysis also indicated that 29 sherds had low probabilities of belonging to any of the clusters. These sherds likely represent pottery sources that were rarely used by people living in these communities; the sherds were therefore removed from subsequent analyses.

The distribution of the remaining sherds among the 16 clusters is used to identify the sources represented by each group. Table 10.7 shows the numbers of sherds from each community in each cluster; gray cells indicate the communities that dominate sherd frequencies in each cluster. Because the evidence shows that each community produced its own pottery, the frequency of samples in each cluster most likely indicates the sources for its member sherds. For example, Table 10.7 shows that of the 12 sherds in Cluster 11, half were recovered from the Haystack sites; many fewer sherds in Cluster 11 were found in the remaining communities. In contrast, sherds in Cluster 9 are evenly distributed among most of the communities, suggesting that the sherds in this group were not locally produced. These kinds of patterns, further correlated with visual temper charac-

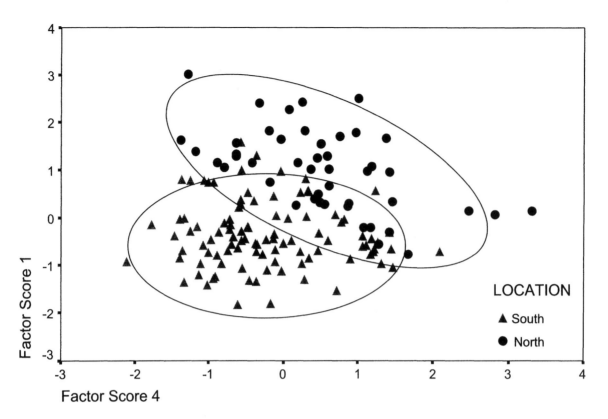

Figure 10.3. Scatterplot of factor scores 1 and 4, illustrating differences between communities north and south of Lobo Mesa.

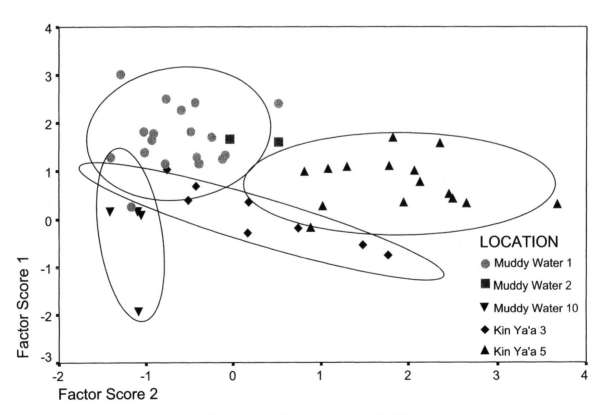

Figure 10.4. Scatterplot of factor scores 1 and 2, illustrating differences among the communities north of Lobo Mesa.

[140]

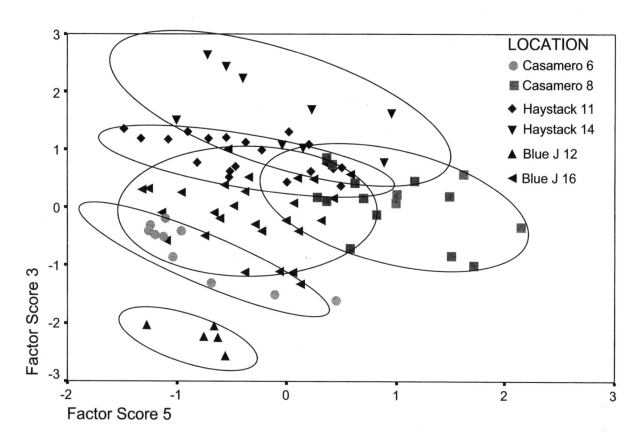

Figure 10.5. Scatterplot of factor scores 3 and 5, illustrating differences among the communities south of Lobo Mesa.

Table 10.7. Distribution of Samples Among the 16 Clusters

	Community where sherds were found				
Clusters	Muddy Water	Kin Ya'a	Haystack	Blue J	Casamero
1	10	4	2	0	1
2	2	0	0	0	0
3	0	7	0	1	0
4	1	0	1	0	0
5	2	10	1	0	0
6	3	1	1	2	5
7	7	6	5	2	3
8	0	2	2	1	9
9	6	4	6	0	6
10	4	0	0	0	0
11	1	0	7	2	2
12	0	0	0	4	0
13	0	0	1	0	1
14	0	0	5	3	3
15	0	0	0	1	0
16	0	2	7	12	4
Total	36	36	38	28	34

NOTE: For each cluster, the gray cell indicates the community with the highest frequency of analyzed sherds.

teristics and clay samples from each community, can be used to reconstruct both the production of pottery in the study area and the manner in which the vessels moved among communities.

RECONSTRUCTION OF CERAMIC PRODUCTION

The results of the analyses reveal that each community was using compositionally distinct clays, tempers, or both to produce pottery, as would be expected considering the different geological contexts in which each community was located (Table 10.1). These conclusions are based on cluster dominance by sherds recovered from each community (Table 10.7) and further corroborated by comparing the elemental characteristics of each cluster both with geological components identified with a microscope (Table 10.4) and with the elemental qualities of the clay samples associated with each community (Tables 10.3 and 10.5).

Three of the clusters (1, 2, and 10) appear to be associated with Muddy Water (Table 10.7). Clusters 1 and 2 exhibit similar visual characteristics, with the two sherds in Cluster 2 having darker pastes and perhaps slightly different tempers than the sherds in Cluster 1 (Table 10.4). It is probable that these two clusters represent pottery produced in Muddy Water, as corroborated by the two clay samples taken at that community; both the clays and the sherds exhibit relatively high quantities of sodium, zinc, and cobalt, the last two being important components of mafic rocks. The elemental compositions of the four sherds from Cluster 10, however, do not correlate well with the clay samples and those vessels may have actually originated elsewhere.

Sherds from two of the clusters (3 and 5) came primarily from Kin Ya'a (Table 10.7). Sherds from these clusters exhibit similar compositions, and visual inspection under a polarizing microscope indicates that many of these samples contain small inclusions of a vesicular igneous rock identified as pumice (Table 10.4). The clusters are distinguished from one another primarily by the slightly higher inclusion density of Cluster 5 and the thicker slip on Cluster 3 sherds; many Cluster 5 sherds have no slip at all. Unfortunately, the clay sample collected from Kin Ya'a does not help to confirm the identification of these clusters with that community. There were difficulties in gaining access to most parts of the area where this community was located; the sample is of poor quality and probably does not adequately represent clays available to the inhabitants of Kin Ya'a.

Sherds recovered from Casamero dominate Clusters 6 and 8 (Table 10.7). Cluster 6 consists of sherds with a gray paste and relatively large-size inclusions, including crushed sandstone with a white or pink opal or chalcedonic cement (Table 10.4). This sandstone is a distinctive component of the Westwater Canyon Member of the Morrison Formation, which is exposed in cliffs farther up the drainage that runs by Casamero. Most of the Cluster 6 sherds are unslipped, and those few that are slipped have a thin white wash. Sherds from Cluster 8 are similar to Cluster 6, but their pastes tend to be darker, they have no sandstone temper, and almost all of them have a thin white slip. Although the raw clay sample associated with Casamero was recovered some distance away from the community itself, the clay shares some characteristics with the sherds in Clusters 6 and 8, including high phosphorus and strontium, both components of calcic or phosphate rocks.

Clusters 11 and 14 are dominated by sherds recovered from the two Haystack structures (Table 10.7), indicating that these ceramics were produced in this community. In contrast with the clusters associated with Kin Ya'a and Muddy Water, sherds in Cluster 11 are more variable, with a greater variety of poorly sorted inclusions (Table 10.4). Perhaps for this reason, the discriminant analysis indicated that this cluster is not as stable as the others. The sherds in Cluster 11 do consistently have thicker slips than those in Cluster 14 (Table 10.4). Another difference is that many of the sherds in Cluster 11 have a high frequency of mica flakes in the slip that appear as if they were purposely added. The clay sample collected from Haystack is most similar to Cluster 14, for both contain relatively low quantities of rubidium, chromium, and potassium, as well as high amounts of calcium. There is no discernible difference between sherds recovered from the great house and those from the habitation in Haystack; both appear to come from the same sources represented by the two clusters.

The sherds in Clusters 12 and 16 represent the Blue J community (Table 10.7) and are fairly easily distinguished from the other clusters. They are characterized by a very dark friable paste with a relatively high percentage of large inclusions (Table 10.4). Most of the sherds are characterized by a heavy sand temper with comparatively little crushed sherd. Cluster 12 differs from Cluster 16 in that the sherds have a thicker slip and the pastes have no sherd temper at all, an attribute that has led some archaeologists working in the area to misidentify these ceramics as Mancos Black-on-white. The friability and size of inclusions in sherds in these two clusters are consistent with the poor quality of the clays that could be identified during a reconnaissance of the surrounding area. The clay sample collected from Blue J is similar to the sherds in Cluster 16 in that it has relatively low quantities of zinc, vanadium, and titanium.

Clusters 4, 7, 9, 13, and 15 could not be clearly identified with specific sources (Table 10.7). These groups exhibit a variety of visual and elemental compositions and likely represent "catch-all" clusters consisting of samples that did not fit into any of the other groups. Whether each of these clusters represents a specific source of pottery is difficult to determine. However, at least in the case of Clusters 7 and 9, there are intriguing patterns that might provide insight into the origins of these sherds.

Clusters 7 and 9 are internally quite similar, a pattern confirmed by the discriminant analysis. In the case of Cluster 9, visual observations of its member sherds indicate that they are dominated by gray pastes and few inclusions besides crushed sherd and sand. Although the elemental compositions of the sherds in this group are similar to one another, no one community dominates the cluster. This evidence may mean that Cluster 9 represents one or two of the other communities in the immediate area that were not sampled in this study. Other patterns support this suggestion. For example, a subgroup of Cluster 9 consists of sherds recovered almost entirely from the great houses in Haystack and Casamero, contexts where exchange likely took place. Another small subgroup of seven sherds recovered from Muddy Water consists entirely of bowl sherds with similar elemental compositions indicative of a single source. In fact, Cluster 9 has an unusually high proportion of bowl sherds compared with the other clusters, again indicating that it represents a source of vessels imported into the sampled communities. Similar patterns are exhibited by Cluster 7.

The dendrogram places both Clusters 7 and 9 with the communities to the south (Fig. 10.2), and their association with the Casamero clusters is intriguing because Casamero is situated in Triassic deposits; other communities that were not sampled for this analysis, in particular Tse Bee Kintsoh and Coolidge, are in similar geologic contexts and may therefore be represented by Clusters 7 and 9. Despite this possibility, the sherds in these clusters conceivably could have come from any of several communities in the area or even from a source outside of the study area. More research on the sherds in these unidentified clusters is needed before they can be interpreted with any confidence.

RECONSTRUCTION OF CERAMIC EXCHANGE

Considering the distribution of sherds among the clusters and the subsequent association of those clusters with specific sources, we can offer some ideas regarding the movement of ceramics between the communities. The basic assumption is that ceramics appearing in comparatively small numbers in each cluster are indicative of the exchange of vessels from their sources to the places from which the sherds were actually recovered. For example, most sherds in Cluster 8 came from Casamero, which suggests that all sherds in Cluster 8 came from vessels produced in Casamero. If this is true, then the two sherds in Cluster 8 that were actually recovered from Kin Ya'a must represent vessels that had been imported into Kin Ya'a from Casamero. This pattern provides potential insight into the structure of exchange relationships between these two communities. When this inferential process is extended to all of the communities examined, patterns of exchange throughout the study area can be elucidated.

The exchange of pottery can be considered from two perspectives: examining the *origins* of the ceramics sampled from each community (Table 10.8) and examining the *destinations* of pottery exported from each community (Table 10.9). The data indicate that less than half of the sherds from each community came from vessels actually produced there, with the exception of Blue J. This conclusion is consistent with other studies that have shown that a high proportion of sherds in any given puebloan community represented imported vessels, through either the direct exchange of pottery or the exchange of food or other goods that the pottery contained (Blinman and Wilson 1993: 79–80; Duff 1994a: 15; Franklin 1982: 925; Plog 1995: 274–275; Toll and McKenna 1997: 146–148).

Although each community exhibited a somewhat unique distribution of imported ceramics (Table 10.8), several general patterns are apparent. First, relatively few ceramics were moving across Lobo Mesa; perhaps this prominent feature was a barrier to the exchange of pottery or goods transported in pottery (Fig. 10.6). Second, although Muddy Water and Kin Ya'a were located close to one another, relatively few ceramics moved between them. In fact, only four of the sherds in the sample representing production in Muddy Water were recovered from Kin Ya'a, and only two from Kin Ya'a were in the sample from Muddy Water. In contrast, the communities south of Lobo Mesa were exchanging larger quantities of the Dogoszhi-style ceramics with one another than were the two communities to the north.

Table 10.8. Origins of Ceramics Recovered from Each Community

Where original vessels were produced	Where sherds were actually recovered				
	Muddy Water	Kin Ya'a	Haystack	Blue J	Casamero
Muddy Water	0.44	0.11	0.05	0.00	0.03
Kin Ya'a	0.06	0.47	0.03	0.04	0.00
Haystack	0.03	0.00	0.32	0.18	0.15
Blue J	0.00	0.06	0.18	0.57	0.12
Casamero	0.08	0.08	0.13	0.11	0.41
Cluster 4	0.03	0.00	0.03	0.00	0.00
Cluster 7	0.19	0.17	0.13	0.07	0.09
Cluster 9	0.17	0.11	0.16	0.00	0.18
Cluster 13	0.00	0.00	0.03	0.00	0.03
Cluster 15	0.00	0.00	0.00	0.04	0.00

NOTE: Gray cells indicate the frequencies of analyzed sherds recovered from each community that represent vessels produced in that community.

Table 10.9. Destinations of Ceramics Produced in Each Community

Where the sherds were actually recovered	Where the original vessels were produced				
	Muddy Water	Kin Ya'a	Haystack	Blue J	Casamero
Muddy Water	0.70	0.10	0.04	0.00	0.12
Kin Ya'a	0.17	0.81	0.00	0.07	0.12
Haystack	0.09	0.05	0.52	0.24	0.12
Blue J	0.00	0.05	0.22	0.55	0.12
Casamero	0.04	0.00	0.22	0.14	0.54

NOTE: Gray cells indicate the frequencies of analyzed sherds originating in each community that represent vessels used in that community.

When examining the destinations of pottery exported from each community (Table 10.9), we find the patterns are generally consistent with those in Table 10.8, such as the evidence that few ceramics were moving across Lobo Mesa. However, additional patterns are also apparent. First, most ceramics produced in Muddy Water and Kin Ya'a were used locally rather than by the other communities considered in this study. In contrast, both Haystack, Blue J, and Casamero were producing ceramics that often ended up in other communities located south of Lobo Mesa. Without a sample of ceramics from all possible trading partners, these patterns are difficult to definitively interpret, but they do illustrate that interaction among communities south of Lobo Mesa was more frequent than was the interaction either between Kin Ya'a and Muddy Water or between northern and southern great house communities.

Despite the intriguing patterns identified in this study, there are three potential problems that we acknowledge.

Compared with many other elemental studies of prehistoric pottery, the number of sherds considered in this study was appreciably high. However, for statistical purposes, the sample size may be problematic, especially since the 201 original samples were reduced after removing low-probability cases and the remaining 177 were divided among several clusters.

Another important issue is that this study could not possibly consider all of the potential exchange relationships in which each community was involved. Although we can determine the proportion of ceramics entering each community that came from elsewhere, we cannot know how many ceramics made in the five communities were being exported to other communities not considered in this study. This means that the proportions in Table 10.9 should be regarded as potentially biased.

Finally, another important issue to consider is that the combination of samples from both great houses and habitations introduces a potential bias since it arguably

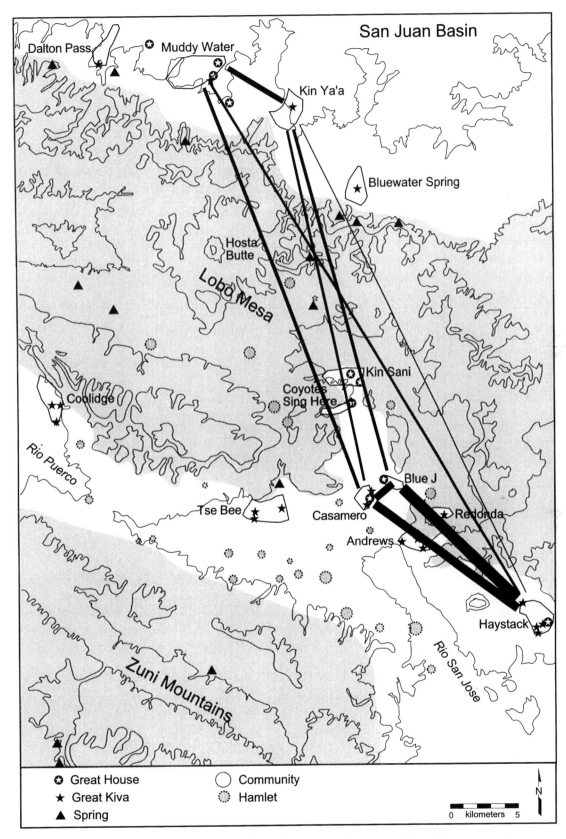

Figure 10.6. Movement of ceramics among the communities. Line
thickness represents relative amount of pottery being moved.

results in the comparison of incommensurate contexts. Fortunately, the samples from Haystack came from both a great house and a nearby habitation, and there were no discernible differences between the ceramics associated with these two structures. When the samples for these features were separated and the figures from Table 10.8 recalculated independently for each one, the results were nearly identical. This observation may mean that the great house and habitation were involved in similar patterns of exchange involving local ceramics. Note, however, that this pattern did not apply to foreign ceramics imported from distant sources, such as carbon-painted or trachyte-tempered pottery, which did occur in higher quantities at the great house (Kantner 1996b; see also Franklin 1982: 927).

COMMUNITY INTERACTION

The X-ray fluorescence elemental analysis of sherd samples from five great house communities in the southern San Juan Basin has identified several patterns. First, each community apparently produced its own ceramics, but large quantities of this local pottery were then being traded to nearby communities (Table 10.9). Similarly, many if not most ceramics recovered from each community were actually imported from nearby sources (Table 10.8). A third important pattern is that few ceramics moved across Lobo Mesa (Table 10.9, Fig. 10.6). Finally, few if any of the Dogoszhi-style ceramics examined in this study appear to have come from especially distant sources. Even the ceramics in the unidentified clusters were compositionally quite similar to those produced in the five communities, and perhaps they were produced in one of the nearby great house communities that was not sampled (Fig. 10.1).

The differences between the communities north of Lobo Mesa and those in the Rio San José Valley to the south are intriguing. They suggest that Kin Ya'a and Muddy Water, despite the short distance between them, did not extensively interact with one another (Fig. 10.6), at least in activities involving the exchange of pottery. Evidence for this conclusion is provided by the relatively low number of ceramics that moved between these two communities (Table 10.8) as well as by the relatively high quantity of ceramics that was produced and consumed within each (Table 10.9). In contrast, the communities south of Lobo Mesa appear to have been exchanging greater quantities of ceramics with one another (Tables 10.8, 10.9). These patterns distinguishing the intensity of intercommunity interaction on either side of Lobo Mesa are consistent with previous research

that concluded that neighboring communities along the northern edge of Lobo Mesa were directly competing with one another, whereas communities south of Lobo Mesa were less centralized, internally more heterogeneous, and involved in less competitive relationships with their neighbors (Kantner 1996a). The ceramic patterns are represented by relatively small numbers of sherds, however, and the proportions representing intercommunity exchange are sensitive to small changes in quantities. These conclusions should therefore be regarded as preliminary until further evidence is available.

The results of this study provide an additional source of data for evaluating models of Chacoan development. In general, this research does not provide evidence to support propositions that the Chaco people participated in a regionally based, well-integrated economy; similar conclusions based on ceramic distributions are presented in Gilpin and Purcell (this volume) and Windes and others (this volume). The elemental analysis instead indicates that the clear majority of ceramics used in each community came from the immediate area and that localized exchange superseded regional exchange, at least for interactions involving pottery. In fact, the evidence indicates that Lobo Mesa was an important physical boundary that substantially restricted economic and perhaps sociopolitical interactions. We further note that patterns of local exchange were more complex than is often acknowledged, with some communities apparently avoiding interactions with their immediate neighbors in favor of more distant exchange partners. Future considerations of Chacoan development will benefit by more carefully considering the effects of physical boundaries on the expansion of Chaco Canyon influence and acknowledging that outlying great house communities were likely engaged in complex relationships with one another that may have been at least as important in shaping their histories as was their relationship with Chaco Canyon.

Acknowledgments

The authors thank Mark Aldenderfer, Nancy Mahoney, Joan Mathien, and Mark Varien for their helpful comments and advice during various stages of this research. All errors in fact, method, or logic are the responsibility of the authors. The X-ray fluorescence analyses were supported by a National Science Foundation Dissertation Improvement Grant and various University of California, Santa Barbara grants awarded to the primary author, who was also supported by a Robert H. Lister Fellowship from the Crow Canyon Archaeological Center.

Part 4

Great House Communities
in the Prehistory of the
American Southwest

Figure Part 4. Computer reconstruction of the Casamero great house positioned on the site in northwestern New Mexico. (Photograph and reconstruction by John Kantner.)

CHAPTER ELEVEN

Communities and the Chacoan Regional System

Mark D. Varien

John Kantner and Nancy Mahoney asked me to provide a final comment on these chapters because my research has focused on communities, primarily communities in the Mesa Verde region (Adler and Varien 1994; Varien 1999). In my own research, I have tried to think about communities in a way that makes sense in terms of social theory and as a unit for archaeological analysis that is both useful and identifiable. This approach closely resembles the position presented by Kolb and Snead (1997) in their discussion of communities.

I begin with a simple definition to touch on the social theory that underscores why communities are important analytical units: communities consist of many households that live in close proximity to one another, have regular face-to-face interaction, develop historically, and share the use of local social and natural resources. This definition emphasizes the geographic, demographic, temporal, and social dimensions of community organization. The geographic dimension means that the territory occupied by a community must be small enough to permit regular, face-to-face interaction. The demographic dimension means that there are lower limits (Gaines and Gaines 1997) and upper limits (Varien 1999: 22) to the population size of communities, especially in prestate sedentary societies. The temporal dimension is both synchronic and diachronic. Synchronically, community members must reside within the community *most* of the time in order to interact on a regular basis. Diachronically, communities develop historically, and this history is fundamental to the social dimension of communities. Finally, for the social dimension community members necessarily share access to local resources because they interact on a regular basis in a geographically limited area and they share a historically derived self-awareness of what it means to be a community member.

Each of these dimensions stresses the importance of interaction. Regular face-to-face interaction has long been a part of our definition of archaeological communities (for example, Murdock 1949) because it provides a link between our definition of communities and the settlement clusters we observe in the archaeological record. But let me emphasize what I consider to be the simple but profound theoretical importance of regular face-to-face interaction. Gidden's jargon for regular face-to-face interaction is "interaction in the context of copresence"; this type of human interaction is the primary mechanism by which society is reproduced and transformed (Giddens 1984: 64–72). From this perspective, the importance of communities as places where people interact on a regular basis, where human agency is expressed and society is created and transformed, cannot be overstated.

In their definition of community, Kolb and Snead identify social reproduction and subsistence production as key attributes of communities, and they add another important element: self identification and social recognition among community members, or a shared identity that produces a sense of place that is linked to community identity (Kolb and Snead 1997:611). I have avoided this property of communities in my previous work because it is difficult to examine with archaeological data, but I agree that a shared identity is a fundamental element of how people constitute their community. I would characterize this shared identity in slightly different terms, however, as a shared historical self-awareness, which is a key element of what has been termed "structure" in the parlance of modern social theory. Thus, communities are people, place, and history. It is through the historic development of a community, however brief or long-lived, that people transform a physical landscape devoid of meaning into a historically constituted cultural landscape thoroughly imbued with meaning. Individuals occupy this cultural landscape from a variety of social positions that include, among others, differences in age, gender, and personal history. These differences mean that the historical self-awareness that is the basis for the shared identity that defines a community *is not* shared *identically* by all community members. Instead, these distinctions are fundamental to the social differentiation that characterizes local communities.

Communities provide a social context critical to the reproduction and transformation of society, a social context characterized by the active interplay of human agency and historically constituted structure. I believe this perspective is important for understanding the Chacoan communities that are the subject of this volume. Understanding communities in these terms does not simply produce a series of individual case studies; instead, it is an undertaking that is fundamental to understanding the social, economic, and political dynamics that characterized the larger Chacoan world. This was the objective of the editors of this book and the authors of the individual chapters, and collectively they have made significant progress toward this understanding.

GEOGRAPHIC AND DEMOGRAPHIC SCALES

There is still much to learn about the organization of ancient southwestern communities and about their boundaries, but I agree with Lekson when he writes, "If the unit house is the fundamental element of Anasazi architecture, the community is the fundamental unit of Anasazi settlement" (Lekson 1991: 42). This observation is exemplified in the Mesa Verde region, where every archaeological survey has shown that residential sites are not isolated or evenly dispersed. Instead, residential sites are typically grouped into settlement clusters (Adler 1990; Fetterman and Honeycutt 1987; Greubel 1991; Hayes 1964; Neily 1983; Rohn 1977; Smith 1987). This pattern is also evident outside of the Mesa Verde region, as documented by several studies in this volume (for example, Mahoney, Gilpin and Purcell, Windes and others). The problem with using settlement clusters as the archaeological correlate for ancient communities is that these clusters occur at a number of inclusive levels, and the questions arise: which cluster represents a community and where do we draw community boundaries? Archaeologists working in the Southwest have drawn widely different boundaries around settlement clusters in their attempts to identify ancient

communities (Adler and Varien 1994; Dykeman and Langenfeld 1987; Eddy 1977; Fetterman and Honeycutt 1987; Neily 1983; Rohn 1977). In this volume, the issue of community scale and boundaries is most explicitly addressed by Nancy Mahoney. Her distinction between residential and sustainable communities is useful because both are analytical units that we can examine empirically. In their chapter, Gilpin and Purcell demonstrate how such an empirical study might proceed.

The sustainable communities Mahoney proposes are much larger than the residential communities that are the focus of most work on Chacoan communities, but the size of these sustainable communities is relatively consistent with the spacing between great houses in the Mesa Verde region (Varien 1999). This spacing averages about 7 km (4.3 miles; Adler 1990: 340), producing community territories that range from about 40 square kilometers to territories more than a hundred square kilometers (15.4–38.6 square miles; Varien 1999: 156). The spacing is variable within the Mesa Verde region (ranging from less than 1 km to more than 20 km; 0.6–12.4 miles) and in other areas where Chacoan communities are identified (Windes and others, this volume, report a 9-km to 13-km, 5.6- to 8.1-mile, spacing for Chaco Canyon communities). The important point is that in almost every case this spacing exceeds the 2–km (1.2–mile) radius proposed by Adler and Varien for the size of residential communities (Adler and Varien 1994; Varien 1999).

The size of these sustainable communities is similar in geographic scale to communities identified elsewhere in the Southwest, including the Hohokam area, where researchers have also used the spacing of public architecture to examine the geographic scale of communities (Fish and Fish 1992). Ballcourts and platform mounds, which served as focal points for communities in successive periods, had an average spacing of 5.5 km and 5 km (3.4 and 3.1 miles) respectively (Fish and Fish 1992: 98). Community territories averaged 40 square kilometers (15.4 square miles) in size in the core areas along the Salt and Gila rivers, but approached 150 square kilometers (58 square miles) in noncore areas (Fish and Fish 1992: 99).

The fact that Hohokam public architecture and Chacoan great houses display similar spacing may be a coincidence, but it merits closer inspection. A quick comparison indicates that demographically the Hohokam communities were much larger, numbering in the thousands of people (Fish and Fish 1992: 99). So similar spacing between public architecture in the Hohokam and Chaco-Puebloan communities does not appear to be driven by the demography of mating networks. Demography and mating networks may be an important part of Chaco-Puebloan sustainable communities, but the Hohokam example suggests that other factors might contribute to the regular spacing of public architecture and the size of community territories. For example, the geographic scale of Hohokam communities may reflect the optimal distance for agricultural travel and day-to-day communication within a single community or between adjacent community centers (Fish and Fish 1992: 98). Regular travel to and from community centers raises the question of the role of these centers and their public buildings in the larger social landscape. In this regard, Mahoney proposes that the appropriate scale for understanding the use of great houses extends beyond their immediate residential community and may include the larger sustaining community.

I conclude this section with a final comment on settlement clustering and the distinction between sustainable and residential communities. Survey data show that there are numerous settlement clusters within the area of a sustainable community. Some of these clusters equate with what Mahoney terms residential communities, but there are even smaller clusters that could represent sequential occupation by a single household or contemporaneous occupation by multiple-household corporate groups (Adler 1990; Fetterman and Honeycutt 1987). We need to unravel the patterns of interaction at each of these inclusive scales if we are going to understand the Chacoan cultural landscape. Most importantly, we should not let whatever we call a community keep us from recognizing and analyzing interaction at each of these different scales.

INTERACTION

The chapters by John Kantner and his colleagues and by Dennis Gilpin and David Purcell examine the scale of interaction most directly. Kantner documents a number of patterns that are worth enumerating again. First, most of the communities he examined engaged in a substantial amount of exchange, but this exchange was dominated by the short-distance movement of pottery among neighboring communities. In all cases, the amount of long-distance exchange was negligible, which supports Mahoney's view that smaller residential communities must have regularly engaged in a wider sphere of interaction in order to create larger sustainable communities. Kantner's research also shows how physiography affects pottery exchange and illustrates how research into exchange can use the new tools that GIS

systems offer to examine how the physical landscape affects travel costs and interaction. Finally, Kantner documents cases where exchange and interaction are *not* a simple function of distance and the cost of travel, perhaps indicating that local politics play a large role in intercommunity dynamics. Elsewhere, Kantner demonstrates that differences in the local context of individual communities, including differences in their social and natural setting, help explain the variation in the patterns of interaction that he has documented (Kantner 1999).

Research in the Peach Springs community by Gilpin and Purcell nicely complements Kantner's work. The methods used by Kantner and his coauthors allow them to discuss exchange among a group of residential communities; the methods used by Gilpin and Purcell examine the exchange patterns of households within a single community. In general, the pattern of interaction as revealed by pottery exchange in the Peach Springs community is similar to the pattern documented in Kantner's study: local production and exchange was much more common than long-distance exchange. Gilpin and Purcell also make another important point, one echoed by many of the papers: exchange linked Peach Springs households to other communities, but not to Chaco Canyon itself. The authors' focus on households provides a final significant insight that is not revealed when interaction is studied at the scale of the entire community: individual households appear to negotiate their own exchange relationships and trade does not appear to be controlled by occupants of the great house.

One type of exchange that may have been controlled by Chaco Canyon and that may have shaped the larger Chacoan world was the exchange of rare and valuable items. A few studies in this volume touch on the issue of long-distance exchange, documenting that these items are present but that they occur in exceptionally low numbers. As Lekson (1999 and this volume) notes, the fact that these items are rare underscores their importance. But the role of these objects in the political economy of the larger Chacoan world will remain an issue that is difficult to resolve because of the inherently small sample size of these items. At issue is whether leaders at Chaco Canyon controlled the distribution of these items, transforming this control into political power by circulating these goods to leaders in far-flung Chacoan communities in return for political favors. Similarly, we need to know if these local leaders controlled the distribution of these goods to legitimize and manipulate their authority. Toll (1991: 80–86) demonstrates three points about exotic items within Chaco Canyon: their quantity is minuscule when compared to other more mundane goods, they are unevenly distributed, and they are present at both great houses and small residences. These observations are a start, but they are not adequate for evaluating the role of exotics in the political economy of Chacoan society, just as the observation that they are rare and exotic is not sufficient for this evaluation. We will only be able to answer this question when someone quantifies this issue as a sampling problem, determining the sampling fraction necessary to evaluate range of variation in the number of these items at sites and documenting whether sampling error could account for this variation and for cases where these items are absent.

VARIATION

The analyses of community scale and interaction illustrate an important point about community boundaries: they were extremely permeable. Individuals, households, and perhaps larger groups almost certainly moved between and among communities, and, of course, the composition of communities changed through time simply as a result of the birth of new community members and the death of others. The form and composition of communities was therefore ever-changing.

Ongoing changes in community form and composition produces variation among communities across space and through time, but what factors structure these ongoing changes? Jalbert and Cameron examine three Chacoan communities and conclude that local factors, rather than control from Chaco Canyon, account for most of the observed variation. They contend that local ecological factors related to agricultural production were of primary importance in structuring this variation, a point also emphasized by Kantner in his expanded research (Kantner 1999). This conclusion strikes me as being right on the mark. These are fundamentally agrarian communities and understanding the agrarian ecology of each is critical to understanding the Chacoan cultural landscape.

Tom Windes and his coauthors focus on the agrarian ecology of the East Community, arguing that this community is located in an optimal setting for agriculture when compared to the rest of the surrounding local environment. He proposes the most dramatic ongoing changes in community form and composition when he argues that many (but not all) of the East Community residences were only occupied during the spring through summer growing season. This inference is based on an exemplary analysis of landform selection, structure orientation, and the skyline, providing an important

example of the information that can be squeezed out of surface remains. It would be interesting to see similar analyses of all Chaco communities where we have survey data.

I find the seasonality arguments compelling, but being the skeptical sort I would like to see the inference of seasonal use expanded through additional studies, many of which would likely require excavation and that were therefore beyond the scope of the study by Windes and his colleagues. I would begin with comparative studies between the seasonally occupied houses and those occupied year-round. Household composition at seasonal versus year-round residences might differ, producing differences in arrangement of space at these settlements. Regardless of household composition, the type and range of activities should differ, producing not only differences in the organization of space but also variation in artifact assemblage composition and in the number and type of structures present. Do seasonal residences have the same number of rooms as the year-round habitations? Do the seasonal settlements have pit structures-kivas (which are absent at most sites classified as seasonally occupied field houses)? It seems to me that a settlement inhabited for a spring-summer growing season does not need a pit structure-kiva. If one is present, what does it say about social organization at the settlement and in the community?

Assume for now that many of the East Community households did practice seasonal residential mobility. Documenting seasonal use is only one dimension of occupational duration. Equally important is determining how long this seasonal residential mobility was sustained; the relative depth of midden deposits or some measure of artifact accumulation could be used to evaluate that duration (Varien and Mills 1997; Varien 1999). The analysis of surface pottery by Windes and his colleagues indicates that seasonal occupation by some of these households was sustained for an exceptionally long time with many residences occupied during successive ceramically defined periods, which also appears to be the case for households that Gilpin and Purcell document in the Peach Springs community. Maintaining the seasonal use of settlements through many human generations is remarkable and something that distinguishes the East Community from other settlement systems characterized by primary residences and seasonally occupied structures associated with agricultural fields. If seasonally occupied areas are being repeatedly reused through decades or centuries as the data suggest, they could be viewed as evidence for intensified agricultural production. Individual households may have occupied multiple habitations during a single growing season, and they may have transmitted ownership of these houses from one generation to the next.

The Rarámuri (Tarahumaran) settlement system is characterized by some households that maintain multiple residences during the growing season. (Graham 1993, 1994; Hard and Merrill 1992). In the Rarámuri case, this residential mobility is driven by two main factors: (1) agricultural production is intensified to such a degree that daily visits to and from fields are not sufficient for the amount of labor required in the fields, and (2) a highly formalized land tenure system based on bilateral inheritance that scatters the land holdings of *some* households. It is instructive that *not all* Rarámuri households practice seasonal residential mobility; in fact, Rarámuri households try to avoid or minimize this residential movement by consolidating land holdings if possible. Similarly, not all East Community households moved seasonally; some were occupied year round. If the reconstruction by Windes and others is correct, it appears that East Community households claimed an exceptionally productive agricultural patch, perpetuated these land use rights through time, and had access to land use rights somewhere else in the region as well. This reconstruction of the East Community settlement system is telling us that the cultural landscape of the Chacoan world is more complex than we had previously imagined. It is also telling us about agrarian ecology, land use, and land tenure in the local community and in the larger region. Expanding studies like this one to include detailed excavation data is crucial to fully understanding the Chacoan social landscape.

TIME AND HISTORY

Many chapters discuss changes in the form and composition of Chacoan communities through time. The transition from Chacoan to post-Chacoan communities is discussed by several authors, but is most explicitly addressed in the chapter on the Lowry community by Jim Kendrick and Jim Judge. They argue that Chacoan communities were characterized by household autonomy, with community interaction facilitated by ritual integration. In the subsequent period, households lost their autonomy as the formality of community economic control increased. I think this model has merit; for example, Gilpin and Purcell's analysis supports the notion of household autonomy during the Chaco era.

The Kendrick and Judge chapter also raises questions that deserve further research. First, how does the household autonomy model fit into current interpreta-

tions for a Chacoan regional system? To me, household autonomy is at odds with models that characterize the Chacoan regional system as having been based on powerful centralized political control, whether that control emanated from Chaco itself or from aggrandizing leaders of local communities. Of the Lowry community model, I believe the following questions deserve further clarification. First, how does ideology and ritual powerful enough to integrate a regional system also accommodate household independence? Second, what is the role of household production in financing this large-scale ritual integration? Finally, if household production does finance this ritual, how does this appropriation of surplus production compromise household autonomy? It may be entirely possible to reconcile these issues, but they will only be resolved with additional research as we continue to examine Chacoan communities.

The issue of whether households lose their autonomy to the larger community in the post-Chaco period also deserves further research. Elsewhere, I have argued that the system of land tenure was transformed during the Chaco to post-Chaco period from a usufruct system to one in which the rights to land were inherited (Varien 1999). I therefore agree that land tenure became more formal through time, but I question whether the loss of household autonomy was total. Comparing the architectural layout of Mesa Verde region communities of the mid-to-late A.D. 1200s with roughly contemporaneous communities in the Zuni, Upper Little Colorado, and Rio Grande regions leads me to argue that households in the Mesa Verde region, with their kiva-unit settlement organization, retained much more autonomy than households in those other areas. Additionally, computer simulations of food sharing among hypothetical Puebloan households indicate that a degree of autonomy, as measured by household control over agricultural production, was essential to their survival (Hegmon 1989).

The role of history in the development of these communities is first an empirical question of chronology: we need to refine our understanding of how long and how continuously these communities were occupied. A better understanding of the period immediately before the construction of a Chacoan great house is crucial to clarifying community origins and development, and the A.D. 1150 to 1180 period is particularly important for understanding the Chacoan to post-Chacoan transition. Several chapters in this volume reconstruct community histories that lasted for six centuries or more (for example, Gilpin and Purcell, Windes and others). Future research needs to document whether these are single communities with historical continuity, or whether the area was repeatedly occupied and abandoned by a series of short-lived, unrelated communities.

The question of community continuity also illustrates how a historical perspective is more than chronology. It includes a recognition that communities were situated in a particular historical context. Great houses, great kivas, and the larger cultural landscape had meaning for the people who lived in these Chacoan communities, meaning that was constituted as a part of their historical development. People drew on this historically derived meaning in the ongoing process of creating their communities and their cultural landscape. Fowler and Stein (1992) and Stein and Lekson (1992) have pioneered approaches that incorporate a historical perspective, and Bradley (1996) and Lekson (1999) have offered recent interpretations of Chacoan and post-Chacoan communities that acknowledge the importance of historic events in community development. We need more studies that develop the method and theory for reconstructing the historical development of communities and the Chacoan cultural landscape.

GREAT HOUSES AND GREAT KIVAS

Settlement clusters came and went through the entire Puebloan sequence. It's the great house that makes Chacoan communities distinctly Chacoan. Or is it? It is worth noting that architectural differentiation was present in communities before and after the Chaco era. McPhee Pueblo was the center of a dense community in the Dolores River Valley in the middle-to-late A.D. 800s. McPhee was one of the largest buildings in the community cluster, it was the only building with some full height masonry walls, and it had oversize pit structures with important ritual features. Post-Chaco great houses, which were extra-large buildings with blocked-in kivas, were widespread and numerous and continued to be a part of communities in and around Mesa Verde until the final migrations from the region.

So what makes a Chaco-era great house Chacoan? Ruth Van Dyke and Winston Hurst ask a similar question when they examine this problem: were great houses constructed under the supervision of Chacoans as a part of an expansionist political system, or were they constructed as a result of local emulation of a Chaco Canyon style? Van Dyke, through the examination of several data sets, concludes that great houses were the result of local emulation in a social context of competition among communities. Her reconstruction of

the chronology is most compelling. The Red Mesa Valley great houses were built in preexisting communities early in the Chaco era, earlier than any presumed Chacoan expansion.

Both Van Dyke and Hurst evaluate the "Chacoanness" of a great house by focusing on specific architectural attributes. As noted, Van Dyke makes a persuasive argument for local emulation. Hurst, who has the benefit of excavation data, makes an equally compelling point when he documents the presence of Chacoan architectural traits that would *not* have been visible to the casual observer, including intramural beams and foundation trenches. It is difficult to dismiss his contention that the builders of the structure at Edge of the Cedars had intimate knowledge of Chacoan construction. I do not think that Van Dyke's and Hurst's conclusions necessarily contradict each other. The Red Mesa great houses and the Edge of the Cedars structure were built in two different historical contexts: the former at a time when the main part of Chaco Canyon was not particularly differentiated from the remainder of the Puebloan world and the latter at a time when it was the most differentiated. This change emphasizes the importance of pulling the Chacoan system apart spatially and temporally in our future analyses.

Hurst describes Edge of the Cedars as "homespun" when compared to the more impressive great houses located to the southeast, but he argues it was a great house nonetheless because it clearly drew on Chacoan symbolism. Edge of the Cedars may have been small-scale when compared to great houses in Chaco Canyon and to buildings like those at Aztec and Salmon Ruin, but it fits very comfortably within the range of variation of great house size in the Mesa Verde region (Varien 1999). These great houses were simply not large buildings; almost every Mesa Verde region great house was *smaller than* the 1,172 square meter average for the small great house category created by Powers and others (1983, Table 41). Although these great houses were small when compared to other great houses, they were also clearly larger than the other residences in their local communities. Most of the great houses that dotted the landscape of the Chacoan regional system were fundamentally different from the larger great houses in Chaco Canyon, but they were also fundamentally different from the remainder of the structures in their own communities. We need to consider both points in our future analyses of Chacoan great house communities and the Chacoan regional system.

Van Dyke argues that great houses served as settings for ritual activities. Kendrick and Judge argue that the

Lowry great house was a residence for local leaders who wanted to attract community members and not a structure built by and maintained for the community as a whole. Considering Mahoney's reconstruction of the small population size of these communities, I think there is merit to the idea that communities needed to attract new members. But a better understanding of the activities that occurred at great houses is critical to our reconstruction of Chacoan communities. Although there is much variation among great houses, there are similarities that I believe provide a good starting point for examining how they were used. When compared to residences, virtually all great houses are characterized by the following: (1) high room-to-kiva ratios; (2) low hearth-to-room ratios; and (3) high energy investment in their construction. Regarding the artifact assemblages, I see two generalizations that might hold up to further scrutiny: (1) the assemblages include evidence of activities that did not occur at residences, such as fauna and pottery indicative of feasting; and (2) the assemblages cannot be entirely ascribed to specialized ritual activities and therefore indicate that some domestic activities occurred as well. Based on these observations, I offer the following generalizations: great houses were residences for small social groups (small relative to the total size of the building) and also a setting for ritual events.

As settings for ritual, we need to distinguish between great houses and great kivas. The small great houses that existed in most Chacoan communities seem to have been segmented for use by small social groups; they exhibited more restricted access and they were therefore more exclusive. Great kivas, on the other hand, were designed for use by large groups, had less restrictive access, and were generally more inclusive. Great kivas were a part of the Puebloan ritual landscape for centuries, but great houses were an innovation in the cultural landscape. In many communities, great houses appropriated the space in the landscape that was previously reserved for great kivas, resulting in community centers that provided a new setting for ceremonies that likely included two distinct, but perhaps complementary, forms of ritual activity. We need detailed comparisons of great house and great kiva refuse to help clarify the activities that occurred in these structures.

Returning to the importance of history, several chapters document that great houses were used for extended periods of time, almost certainly much longer than the associated residences in the community. Mahoney discusses how great houses and great kivas fixed the location of activities that occurred in these settings across space and for extended periods of time, formatting the social landscape in time and space at a scale unlike what had come before. Some models focus on ambitious leaders who sponsored the construction of these buildings in a setting of competitive social relations. Perhaps, but our understanding of how these buildings were used and the social groups that took advantage of them must take into account that they were used through many human generations. This duration suggests to me that the construction of these buildings was initiated not by individuals, but rather by larger factions within communities and that it was the social power that these factions could muster that resulted in the long-term use of these structures.

LOCAL COMMUNITIES AND THE CHACOAN REGIONAL SYSTEM

There is a tendency in some of the chapters to describe communities as entities, reifying the concept and implying that communities somehow act. It is important to remember that it is people, and not communities, who act. Community members *do* develop institutions through the extension of repeated practices during long periods of time and across vast areas of space. These institutions are an important aspect of the historically derived structure that was a part of ancient Puebloan society. Great kiva ceremonialism is an example of one such Puebloan institution; a system of community land tenure is another. But, again, it is the practices of individuals, often acting in concert with other individuals as part of a larger faction, that reproduce and transform these institutions. In our consideration of Chacoan communities, we could examine this interplay of structure and agency by reconstructing the following: the social landscape that was formatted in part by the relatively fixed location of great houses and great kivas; the historically rooted practices that occurred in these centers; the imperfectly shared historical awareness of these events; and the way that successive generations used these spaces and drew on this history in the ongoing constitution of their communities.

A fundamental question addressed by the studies in this book is the degree to which local Chacoan communities were directly influenced by communities located in Chaco Canyon itself. Several authors emphasize local concerns and do not document much evidence of direct contact between outlying communities and those in Chaco Canyon. Durand and Durand directly address this issue and make the strongest statement about it. They argue that Chacoan communities located throughout the northern Southwest exhibit a similarity to Chaco Canyon communities because they were all drawing on the same broad regional style; the communities located outside of Chaco Canyon are not viewed as having been connected to Chaco Canyon communities in any formal or organized sense.

The research presented here is an excellent step toward refining this debate, but clearly the issue requires further investigation. My guess is that Chaco Canyon communities were more influential than simply being an archetypal expression of a regional style. I think this is likely because of the scale of the canyon communities and their persistence through time. Most people would agree that the canyon communities grew to occupy a position in the regional social landscape that was unequaled by any other center, and their persistence through time would have likely resulted in Chaco Canyon having a unique position in the history of the Puebloan world. But my guesses are of little value and what is needed are more studies like these. Future research faces two important challenges, among others. First, we must ask how adequately our particular analyses measure the relationship between the Chacoan communities where we work and the communities in Chaco Canyon. For example, what does the presence or absence of pottery exchange with Chaco Canyon communities really tell us about the political and ideational relationship between communities? Second, we need to continue to remind ourselves that the Chaco regional system is not one thing. Instead, the relationship between Chaco Canyon communities and other Chacoan communities located elsewhere varied across space and through time. For example, the relationship between Red Mesa Valley great house communities and Chaco Canyon great house communities between A.D. 950 and 1050 was almost certainly different than the relationship between the Skunk Springs community on the Chuska slope and the Chaco Canyon communities during this same period. In the early 1100s, the relationship between great house communities in the Mesa Verde region and Chaco Canyon communities likely differed as well. We also need to unpack our understanding of the individual Chaco Canyon communities. A largely unexplored area of research is whether different great house communities in Chaco Canyon had distinct relationships with outlying areas.

This issue reminds me of a visit to a Mesa Verde region great house that I made with Steve Lekson. We fell into a debate, me arguing for the importance of understanding communities in local terms and Steve replying that this perspective was fine and good, but that it was ultimately impossible to understand outlying communities without reference to Chaco Canyon. I think both perspectives are correct and that research into Chacoan communities has to work at both scales. The chapters in this volume are a fine example of this kind of multifaceted approach. I learned a great deal from these authors, and from the conjoining of their views, and look forward to future studies inspired by their research.

CHAPTER TWELVE

GREAT!

Stephen H. Lekson

Think great thoughts: *Great* Houses, *Great* Kivas, and what the rest of us call roads, but Winston Hurst calls *Great* Trails. Ralph Waldo Emerson, that old Transcendentalist, once said that to be great is to be misunderstood (giving false hope to writers of convoluted prose). Are great houses, kivas and trails misunderstood? Do we share a common understanding of what "great" is? It all depends on what our definition is of what makes "great" great.

Casa Grande, with its magnificent tin roof, has historical precedence. Two centuries before excavations began at Chaco Canyon, Father Kino translated its Pima name, *hottai-ki*, as "casa grande." Archaeological English makes Kino's phrase "great house." Earl Morris, it seems, first used the term "great house" on the Colorado Plateau. In 1916 he excavated Site 39, a Chaco-looking ruin, about 25 m by 15 m in plan, which he later called a small Great House. His definition of "Great House" was admirably vague, but . . .

> Structures of the great-house style occur in all sizes from small to enormous. . . . And as the very largest stand Pueblo Bonito and Pueblo Chettro Kettle [Morris' orthography]. The relatively tiny representatives of the class could be enumerated by the hundred; the intermediate ones are far fewer, while in all the San Juan country there could probably not be found a score of towns comparable in size with Bonito and Chettro Kettle (Morris 1939: 41)

Morris considered Mesa Verde cliff dwellings too "thin and flimsy," too light-weight for great-house status, but he nominated Yucca House as a likely contender (Morris 1939: 37). Morris' definitions-by-example match more recent listings, which exclude Cliff Palace but retain Yucca House. Modern great house enthusiasts see the same things that Morris saw.

But what makes a "great house" great? We tried, long ago, to define the criteria of greatness: multiple stories, "blocked-in" kivas, core-and-veneer banded masonry, and other architectural details (for example, Powers and others 1983; see also Hurst, this volume). These were the features of the large buildings of Chaco Canyon, certified "great" by inclusion in the National Park system and UNESCO's World Heritage List.

We also spent a moderate amount of time and money excavating Pueblo Alto, a genuine, USDA Prime, Chaco Canyon great house. It turned out to be only one story tall, one very tall story, but one story nevertheless. Pueblo Alto had a couple of "blocked-in" kivas, but more and larger kivas in the plaza. At least Pueblo Alto had banded sandstone masonry; but at the same time we were working at Pueblo Alto, the Navajo Tribe was excavating Bis sa'ani, maybe 6 km (3.7 miles) from the park boundary, and finding a great house built of massive poured adobe. Our great house definitions were routed by data.

A few characteristics appeared at most or almost all excavated great houses (note well, *excavated*): peculiarities of construction, as Hurst has found at Edge of the Cedars; room furniture and kiva features; small tricks of construction, beginning at the very foundation and continuing to the very roof. We could see these details at the handful of *excavated* sites, and they were convincing, perhaps even conclusive. Emerson's old pal, Henry David Thoreau, noted that some circumstantial evidence is very strong, as when you find a trout in the milk. At excavated sites, we sometimes find trout in the milk.

Those excavated sites formed a tight class, defined by details. But, once they were laid bare and we knew their ground plans, it became clear that form was as important, *more* important, than technology. Technology was, after all, only *in the service* of form. The same form could be created with sandstone or poured adobe. Being Southwestern archaeologists trained in the 1970s, it took us some time to realize that great houses were architecture, designed *to be seen*. We had been looking for banded masonry, but we quickly moved to geometries, ratios, canons, and sitings (Fowler and Stein 1992; Sofaer 1997; Stein and Lekson 1992). So, perhaps, it was acceptable for Bis sa'ani to be adobe; it still *looked like* a great house. If it looks, walks, and talks like a duck, then, in the words of a great contemporary Transcendentalist, let's call it a duck.

Excavations, back in the mythic age when it was not only possible but desirable to dig a whole site, showed us that Morris was on to something. Something was *out there*: something bigger than a breadbox, bigger than a canyon, bigger than a resource area or a ranger district. But how to research those hundreds of "tiny representatives of the class"? Today, we do not dig; we survey. We cannot see those details that turned up every time someone of Morris' era stuck a shovel in a great house.

Indeed, we can only approximate form. It's one thing to map Wijiji or Peñasco Blanco or any of the Chaco Canyon sites, where the walls rise up to greet you. It's quite another thing to map Peach Springs or Hinkson or Bluff, where centuries of wind and water, cattle and sheep, gravity and depravity have razed the walls down to a rounded mound.

Rounded, mounded, enigmatic: too often our survey observations on great house mounds are compressed exasperations, like "big bump." We now have between 150 and 200 "big bumps" of which maybe 20 have been even partly excavated. It is highly unlikely that anyone will excavate, extensively, another great house in my lifetime, so I proposed a definition that de-emphasized excavated detail and checklist criteria and instead featured the site's form (Lekson 1991), insofar as we could know form from the surface. Absent a consistent set of observable excavated features, greatness is manifest by superficial, relative virtues, whose beauty is skin deep. Great houses, seen from survey, are bigger, more massive, taller than the surrounding sites of the country, the unit pueblos of their community. Great houses *are* big bumps, compared with the surrounding community of smaller bumps and rubble hummocks, the homes of the people, the community.

Communities are, of course, the principal focus of this volume. The authors almost all suggest, explicitly or implicitly, that communities were *local* units, with local histories and local economies. In the ancient Pueblo world, where the logistics of bulk transportation were problematic, food was a local matter, as were crafts, and maybe even mates (or maybe not: Mahoney's analysis is a strong hint that "community" may be complicated). The Red Mesa Valley, the Chaco East Community, Cottonwood Falls, Peach Springs, Guada-

lupe, and Bluff were, we would like to think, local communities.

Tip O'Neill, that old ward-healer, told us that all politics are local. Most pots and rocks were local, too. Kantner and Gilpin and others note that pots and rocks hang around fairly small little areas. The kind of entity that Chaco might-have-been did a certain amount of business in pots and rocks but, principally, it valued wonderful things: prestige economies of macaws, copper bells, turquoise, and other costly baubles. We must avoid equating bulk goods and baubles in tump-line economies.

Macaw feathers and copper bells were easy to move; they gained their value because they came from great distances and because their procurement and distribution were controlled (Lekson 1999). There has been a tendency to minimize rare things at Chaco and its region *because they are rare*: we have lots of pots and rocks, but only a few macaws; therefore, macaws are not important. That logic escapes me. Rare stuff is supposed to be rare. If we found a jade mask at Pueblo Bonito, would we belittle it because there was only one? Some of us, apparently, would. Macaws are the moral equivalent of jade masks. The highly specialized knowledge needed to transport and maintain macaws makes the 1,000–km (621–mile) trip (one way) to obtain those cantankerous birds a *very* big deal, fully comparable to jade-working. This was no "down-the-line" exchange; the idea of a macaw being passed up and over the Sierra Madres, from hill tribe to hill tribe, is absurd. Instead of minimizing the 30 macaws and two dozen copper bells recovered at Chaco, wishing them away, we should dance jigs of joy that the archaeology gods have given us these astonishing data.

But enough of high finance. At base, Chaco and its region were good, honest, local Anasazi stuff. Communities, the potential matrix of daily face-to-face encounters, *must* be local, at least before telecommunications. Our ideas about communities (summarized by Mahoney and Kantner) begin with at least a degree of stability, a bit of permanence. We picture happy, peaceful people, at harmony with their local environment; but that, too, is probably wrong. As a wide range of scholars have noted, village mobility was constant from the time of the earliest Anasazi villages (Powell 1983, one of the first among many others). Villages lasted only a generation or so before they were reassembled in a new valley. Families moved from one village to another. Windes and his colleagues (this volume) present a provocative recreation of the chaotic dynamics of the East Chaco community. "Community" must have been a bit more dynamic than our theoretical models might admit. But, within that framework of Brownian motion, communities and community subsistence economies may well have been "local," whatever that means.

Chacoan communities, however, are defined by an architectural superstructure, and that superstructure was (again, by definition) not local: the architectural *idea*, at least, of a great house was demonstrably regional, whatever it was that Morris saw. We will return to that architectural idea later, but meanwhile we can agree that the various great house maps are mapping *something*. We must consider what the reality of great houses, coupled with flagrantly exotic birds and baubles, implies. For modern democracies, politics are at least as local as the district or state. But for preindustrial elites, politics were remarkably nonlocal; chiefly or princely power consistently had a strong dimension of distance (Helms 1988, 1993). Power was manifest by knowledge, objects, or alliances that transcended the local and by symbolism, particularly architecture, that referenced temporally and spatially distant authority.

Chaco was a central place, but not the central place of bulk transport economies. (It may have been that, too, in its early days; Judge 1979 still works for me.) It controlled knowledge and prestige goods, and those move rather differently than pots and rocks. Pots and rocks are poor proxies for chiefly politics. We should not pin our hopes (or test our models) of Southwestern geopolitics on the quotidian: a jar, an ax, a peck of corn. Subsistence and craft economies were mostly local; political economies were regional, even continental. This is not to say that everyone made their own pottery (they did not); but the scale of ceramic exchange was necessarily smaller than the scale of political-prestige economies.

Great houses were architecture with a capital "A," buildings designed and built (we assume) to impress and even to awe. Great houses shared canons, geometries, and details that created a monument, changing the built environment of the community that surrounded them. Whoever designed great houses shared a set of ideas about form and, presumably, about meaning. And, we can assume, communities throughout the region of great houses understood that same set of supraregional canons and symbols: architecture carries meaning, and its intended audience must be able to decode and understand those meanings.

If great houses were Architecture, unit pueblos were machines for living. We know that machine by its several parts: a few storage rooms, a couple of generalized living rooms, a mealing room, activity areas, ramadas, middens, and, the core of the unit, the difficult, intractable "kiva."

The idea of pre-14th century "kivas" has long outlived its archaeological usefulness, but we see it here: Kendrick and Judge juke and jive to have a kiva become a pit house and then revert to its prior sanctity; Van Dyke thinks room:kiva ratios are, somehow, indices of ceremony. Pre-14th century "kivas" were houses: pit houses (Lekson 1988). We inherited the misconception that little round rooms were "kivas" from Fewkes and Kidder and Morris, and it resists correction. Gilpin and Purcell, in this volume, seem to be shaking it off. I urge everyone to shake off "kivas": they misdirect research, of course, but, more importantly, we lose our single best index of population when we mistake houses as churches.

There *was* a community structure that clearly filled the ceremonial pigeon hole. That, of course, was the great kiva. As Windes and others note, the archaeological career of great kivas intersects but does not necessarily parallel that of great houses. There is a respectable range of form and detail within excavated great kivas that exceeds the range of architectural variation in great houses. Great kivas may have belonged to the people, to the community. There were great kivas before, during, and after Chaco; there were, apparently, communities with great kivas but no great house; and in many cases, the earthen berm that surrounds the great house excludes the great kiva; that is, the great kiva is outside the berm and indeed sometimes far distant from the great house.

We are back, then, to the great house as the principal oddity, something weird and wonderful. We should follow the superficial, survey definition of great houses to its conclusion, its logical end. Its end, to the west, might well be Wupatki; to the east, we might reach the "big bump" in the middle of Ponsipa'a keri. The north we know, roughly defined by the arc that encompasses Bluff, Far View House, and Chimney Rock. To the south are Mimbres roads (most convincingly documented by Darrell Creel) and Mimbres (square) great kivas and, I think, at least one or two Mimbres great houses (Lekson 1999).

Mimbres great houses are not built of fine banded sandstone, they do not have little round "kivas," and they were lucky if they reached two stories. How can I possibly call them great houses? Is my definition of "great house" so encompassing, so elastic? That question brings us to the set of alternate models, current in great house research, that are addressed, at least in part, by every author in this book: were great houses the result of independent development or of local emulation of Chacoan forms or of Chaco-controlled design and construction?

Completely independent development, with each great house evolving, *sui generis*, from fundamentally local circumstances is an argument that I reject out-of-hand: 150 cases of simultaneous equifinality is simply beyond belief. No one in this volume advocates that extreme position. Durand and Durand come close, but they maintain a sensible distance from complete independence, and they acknowledge that "something special is going on in the central canyon." Van Dyke and Kantner and others lean that way, too. But given the undeniable fact of Chaco itself and the reality of great houses *as an empirical pattern* across a large landscape, none of our authors seem ready to treat each and every great house as an independently evolved form.

Thus, the issue reduces to a simpler dichotomy: *emulation* of a Chacoan model versus *export* of Chacoan control. "Emulation" can mean any scenario of local people copying the Big City, for whatever purpose; "export" means Chaco architects, Chaco bosses, Chaco control.

Opinion has swung, in recent years, from export to emulation. Morris identified a class of structures that he called great houses; he did not specify a specific cultural or historical dynamic to account for them. Nor did other archaeologists of the first half of the 20th century. With the emergence of Chaco, in the 1970s, as a central place in Southwestern prehistory, we began to think of great houses as exported "outliers": buildings built to Chacoan specifications, under Chacoan control. We looked for a laundry list of traits and attributes derived from Pueblo Bonito and Chetro Ketl and the other buildings of the Chacoan center. When we found those very rare buildings that had everything on the list, we talked about Chacoan colonies, or migrants, or export, or "outliers." Aztec Ruins and Salmon Ruins, for example, were called all of those things, with good reason. The only major differences between Aztec and Pueblo Bonito were petrology and timing.

Other "outliers" were less perfect copies of Chaco Canyon originals. Indeed, they lacked many Chacoan attributes and sported, instead, alarming architectural idiosyncrasies. With more research, we found that Morris' great houses admit a range of variation. Back then, we brushed aside those differences; today, they suggest (to authors in this book) *emulation*: local interpretations of a watered-down, vaguely Chacoan model. Van Dyke can speak for the rest: "substantial regional

diversity is contained under the rubric of the Chacoan system." Several authors in this volume exploit this diversity to question the Chaco-centric, Chaco-controlled, Chaco-export models of yesteryear.

Substantial diversity is contained under the rubric "Chaco Canyon," too. There is probably *almost* as much variation within Chaco Canyon great houses as within Chaco regional great houses. "Almost": we have yet to find great houses *in the canyon* built of poured adobe or of Mimbres river cobbles. How much variation is enough? And "enough" for what?

Simply demonstrating that great houses vary gets us nowhere; we would be astonished if they did not. Morris said as much, 60 years ago (his quote, above). How do we calibrate that variation, make those differences meaningful? If we focus on a single great house in its singular context, as Durand and Durand would like us to do at Guadalupe, we will almost certainly conclude that the singular contexts are singularly important. Multiple cases (as in Van Dyke's research) help. But I suspect that we will make more progress if we look at architectural diversity at a geographic range of great houses compared to the architectural diversity at their associated unit pueblos.

The reality of great houses can be illustrated, anecdotally, by contrasting Chimney Rock and the ugly unit-pueblos-by-courtesy of its community with Escalante Ruin and its tight little Prudden units. In this four-point comparison, Chimney Rock and Escalante look very much alike; the architecture of their respective communities looks remarkably *un*alike. There is far *less* diversity between these two (carefully chosen) great houses than there is between the architecture of their communities. This, of course, does not prove my case; it simply demonstrates a method by which to calibrate diversity.

We might also shift our point-of-view. I say great houses look alike; everyone else in this book says they look different. We both look from Chaco *out*, from the center out into its region. We could also work from the far distant fringe *in*. The far distant fringe, for me, is not Guadalupe or Bluff; it is Wupatki or Mimbres. I submit that a real "emulation" would look sort of like a great house, but on a local fabric with local forms: for example, my Mimbres river-cobble great houses are more massively built, geometrically regular, and larger than the family houses of their surrounding community (Lekson 1999). If these Mimbres sites are great houses, then they are better candidates for "emulations" than any Plateau great house. I am aware of the circularity in my proposal, but *somehow* we must get beyond simple demonstrations of architectural variation, followed by local arguments.

The arguments in this volume are framed locally, by sites, study areas, or districts: Peach Springs, Guadalupe, Chaco East, the Red Mesa Valley, the northern San Juan, the southern San Juan Basin periphery. Those small scales reflect the way field research is traditionally conducted in the Southwest and, of course, the editorial direction of the volume by Kantner and Mahoney.

In many fields, these would be called "case studies": discrete inquiries, limited by meaningful boundaries, which have an intrinsic interest but which also reflect on wider issues. When the wider issue is thematic, like Kantner and others' exchange and Mahoney's community demographics, then case studies can be well-suited for larger insights. When the wider issue is geographic, the Chacoan Region, whatever it might have been, then case studies become more problematic. How do we sample regions? Not by single cases, be they sites, study areas, districts. It is difficult to evaluate diversity from a sample of one, or two, or three, unless you handpick your "samples," like my use of Chimney Rock and Escalante. Case studies, as an interrogation of regional questions, will almost certainly favor local peculiarities over regional generalities.

Small scales are a symptom of a larger problem that, for want of a kinder expression, I will call Southwestern provincialism. Every archaeological region has its internal research dynamics: histories, personalities, institutions, conventions. In this regard, the Southwest is no more or less provincial than any other archaeological region. But the presence of contemporary tribal peoples, the enormous weight of the ethnographic and historical studies of those tribes, and the relatively short span of Puebloan prehistory all draw Southwestern interests extraordinarily inward.

In few other parts of the world are indigenous peoples so immediately connected to the archaeological record. In Europe, for example, it is difficult to determine who is indigenous and impossible to make meaningful connections, for example, between contemporary and Neolithic societies. Throughout most of the world, consequently, archaeology routinely appeals to anthropology, to data and theory from the widest range of societies, to interpret the past. In the Southwest, *we know how the story ends* (at least, we know how things stood at contact; the story is still going on). Our job, it seems, is to make the archaeological plot lead to its well-known denouement.

Amplifying that teleological tendency, the Southwestern story is very *short*, compared to the Eastern Woodlands, or Mexico, or Peru. Those regions saw a series of rise-and-fall archaeologies, stretching back into the far distant past. The storyline for the Pueblo Southwest was short and necessarily simple: only 12 or 13 centuries to get from early agricultural villages to modern Pueblos. There were subplots, of course: regional abandonments, aggregations, conquistadors. The compressed timeline does not allow those subplots to develop. The principal matter of Pueblo archaeology must be *Pueblo*; where did the Pueblos come from? Subplots are simply side issues. Happily, we are beginning to realize that the subplots are tremendously interesting, but we still look for insights and references *internally*, from within the Southwest. In that sense, the Southwest is indeed much more provincial than regions with more complex sequences and less happy histories.

How do we escape this provincialism? Mahoney and Varien make good use of cross-cultural data, bringing them to bear on local Southwestern issues. Global, cross-cultural compendia help them understand small-scale case studies. A good start; but I suggest that we must go even further: we must consciously use our unparalleled archaeological record to address global archaeological issues, a tough challenge in these days of particularizing historicity. We will write *better local history* if we allow the Southwest a place in the larger anthropological and human world. We should break out of our internal, provincial affairs, woes that seem more than sufficient for workaday research. (*Mea culpa*, by the way; I am no better than anyone else in this regard. I make many internally referenced arguments, reasoning about the Southwest based almost entirely on Southwestern data.)

There is actual resistance to using available anthropological insights for understanding the past when those insights suggest a plot incommensurate (or inconvenient) for the story's known ending. There are rules and conventions, approaching middle-range theory, for situations like Chaco; we use them everywhere else in the great wide world (they are summarized in textbooks; I will not review them here). Those rules apparently *do not apply* in the American Southwest. Southwestern prehistory, particularly for the later Puebloan horizons, is a litany of exceptions, anomalies, and special pleading: why things are *not* as they seem.

Try a "what if" exercise: what if, somehow, we dropped Chaco Canyon and its regional archaeology into a remote, agriculturally "iffy" corner of the Middle East or western Mexico or Ecuador, transmogrified its pottery and tweaked its architecture to make them fit regional fashions, and made the whole business truly prehistoric, unattached to any living peoples. If we did that, we would see a central city (yes; compare Chaco to any third-tier Mesoamerican or Mesopotamian city) with "roads" connecting 150 to 200 secondary centers, each constituting a small farming community. Toss in a fair number of exotics, suitably transformed into jade, bronze, or whatever, and add a few high status burials. I *cannot imagine* that we would suffer through the arguments that take up so much space in the Chacoan literature. The discourse, instead, would go something like this:

Regional system? *Obviously!*
Politically complex? *Of course!*
Something like a chiefdom? *Yes, certainly!*
State? *Don't be silly.*

End of conversation. And, now that we established, approximately, *what* this "what if" entity was, we could get on with the business of figuring out how it worked. If Chaco was *not* complex, it was a notable exception to global archaeological and ethnological patterns. Most things that look like Chaco came with a political price-tag. Perhaps the burden of proof should be on those who argue that Chaco was *not* hierarchical and complex.

Gwinn Vivian (1990) did just that, in reaction to a short-lived, 1980s fad for political complexity in the Chacoan Regional System (for example, Judge 1979 and Schelberg 1984, and surviving in Sebastian 1992 and various works of David Wilcox 1993, 1996). Then, Vivian's arguments were the minority view. But the pendulum swings. As several chapters in this book demonstrate, Chaco is rapidly being demoted from "something like a chiefdom" to merely "something special" (to pick on Durand and Durand, again). "Special" can mean "unusual" or even "aberrant." More complex political models of the Chacoan region necessarily reference archaeological conventions from beyond the Southwest, and, for that very reason, these imported insights met and meet unceasing resistance.

Our peculiar Southwestern ground rules play out in strange ways. Ben Nelson, in a thoughtful and useful article (Nelson 1995), compared Chaco and La Quemada; this is the kind of external comparison we need, so very badly, in the Southwest to break out of provincial frames-of-reference. Yet, in the end, Nelson politely honors Southwestern custom and lets local conventions overrule the evident implications of the comparison. Chaco outscored La Quemada in several measurable dimensions (labor, scale, region,), but La Quemada was hierarchical and Chaco was not (Nelson 1995: 614–615). Nelson's conclusion was based in part

on evidence (and its absence), but ultimately his evaluation of Chaco, specifically, conformed to the Southwestern ground rules.

First, evidence. La Quemada exhibited symptoms of hierarchy that were absent at Chaco: specifically, institutionalized violence and an architecture of repression (Nelson 1995: 615). At La Quemada, remains of mutilated victims were publicly displayed; at Chaco, Nelson says, violence was a private affair. Violence at Chaco was not "a mechanism of social control" (Nelson 1995: 613). More recent evaluations (LeBlanc 1999 and, with some reservations, Turner and Turner 1999) suggest that Chaco, indeed, had institutionalized violence of a grimly spectacular nature. (Of course, LeBlanc's and the Turners' arguments violate the ground rules, and are being summarily rejected by many Southwesterners.)

Architecture plays the decisive role in Nelson's comparison of La Quemada and Chaco. Whatever the truth about violence, Chaco's built environment, Nelson concludes, was not a setting for hierarchy. "The temple/ball court/pyramid complex at La Quemada is related to hierarchical structure and repression" whereas "the symbolism associated with Chacoan kivas, as known ethnographically, is linked to collaboration and consultation" (Nelson 1995: 615). The kiva is key. Nelson assumes that Chacoan kivas are formally equivalent to ethnographic kivas, and cites Zuni as a kiva-using society free of hierarchical government (Nelson 1995: 614). There is, of course, a sizable ethnohistoric literature questioning that elysian view of western Pueblo governance, but of more archaeological relevance is the uncritical acceptance that Chaco "kivas" represent the same social formations as Zuni kivas. They do not, indeed cannot, but habit and custom make the archaeological "kiva" an almost unavoidable error (Lekson 1988). Kivas are part of the ground rules. Chaco "kivas" were not Zuni kivas; their architectural message was as likely "palace" as "collaboration." More importantly, there *was*, in fact, a very conspicuous architecture of hierarchy at Chaco: great houses, defined by their striking grandeur *compared* to normal, contemporary, common housing. One-tenth of Chaco's architecture was great and the other nine-tenths were not. The implications for hierarchy are obvious; any arguments against hierarchy must explain that glaring architectural symbolism.

Turn Nelson's argument on its head: whatever the reality of Chacoan violence (and Nelson acknowledges the problem), Chaco looks pretty complex, as we conventionally measure these things: energy, region, roads. But Chaco has kivas and therefore is "Pueblo" and nonhierarchical. Because Chaco was *known to be nonhier-archical* (in the traditional, neoevolutionary sense of that term), Nelson concludes that our tools for measuring that type of complexity, energy, regions, and roads, must be flawed. They are: there was more than one way to organize complexity, as Nelson notes, but one common way was good old-fashioned hierarchy.

Chaco was larger and more expensive than La Quemada (and, I would add, had remarkable high-status burials, shocking institutional violence, and an extraordinary architecture), but La Quemada was hierarchical and Chaco was . . . something else. What an interesting conclusion: Chaco cannot be, is not allowed to be, hierarchically complex. The procrustean conventions of Southwestern archaeology forbid it, even when an impressive array of middle-range measures suggest that *it might have been*.

With those ground rules, what are we to do with great houses and Chacoan communities? How can we understand the "substantial regional diversity"? Should we divide the old "outlier" maps into 150 separate case studies or 150 normalizing local histories? We could, of course: the Bluff great house does not look exactly like Andrews, and neither looks exactly like Pueblo Bonito. Ralph Waldo Emerson said, memorably, if rudely, that a foolish consistency is the hobgoblin of little minds. If we take a Pueblo Bonito laundry list out to the edge, we should not be surprised if some linen goes missing. "In the long run, men hit only what they aim at," said Thoreau. There is no point looking for Pueblo Bonito at Bluff or Andrews, much less at Wupatki or in the Mimbres Valley. It's not there. But the great house *pattern* is. The best way to understand that pattern is *not* to fragment this great big problem into tiny analytical units, but rather to jump up a scale and put our big problem into even bigger contexts. Look at Chaco *and* Mimbres and Sinagua. Look at Chaco *and* Catal Huyuk and Cahokia and LBK. I began this essay by asking us to "think great thoughts." I end with this amended request: Don't just think "great," think *BIG*.

References

Adler, Michael A.

    1989   Ritual Facilities and Social Integration in Non-ranked Societies. In "The Architecture of Social Integration in Prehistoric Pueblos," edited by William D. Lipe and Michelle Hegmon. *Occasional Papers of the Crow Canyon Archaeological Center* 1: 35–52. Cortez, Colorado: Crow Canyon Archaeological Center.

    1990   *Communities of Soil and Stone: An Archaeological Investigation of Population Aggregation Among the Mesa Verde Region Anasazi, A.D. 900–1300.* Doctoral dissertation, University of Michigan, Ann Arbor. Ann Arbor: University Microfilms.

    1992   The Upland Survey. In "The Sand Canyon Archaeological Project: A Progress Report," edited by William D. Lipe. *Occasional Papers of the Crow Canyon Archaeological Center* 2: 11–23. Cortez, Colorado: Crow Canyon Archaeological Center.

    1994   Population Aggregation and the Anasazi Social Landscape: A View from the Four Corners. In *The Ancient Southwestern Community: Models and Methods for the Study of Prehistoric Social Organization*, edited by Wirt H. Wills and Robert D. Leonard, pp. 85–101. Albuquerque: University of New Mexico Press.

    1996a   Fathoming the Scale of Anasazi Communities. In "Interpreting Southwestern Diversity: Underlying Principles and Overarching Patterns," edited by Paul R. Fish and J. Jefferson Reid. *Anthropological Research Papers* 48: 97–106. Tempe: Arizona State University.

    1996b   [Editor] *The Prehistoric Pueblo World, A.D. 1150–1350.* Tucson: University of Arizona Press.

Adler, Michael A., and Mark D. Varien

    1994   The Changing Face of the Community in the Mesa Verde Region, A.D. 1000–1300. In *Proceedings of the Anasazi Symposium 1991*, compiled by Art Hutchinson and Jack E. Smith, pp. 83–97. Mesa Verde, Colorado: Mesa Verde National Park Association.

Adler, Michael A., and Richard H. Wilshusen

    1990   Large-Scale Integrative Facilities in Tribal Societies: Cross-Cultural and Southwestern US Examples. *World Archaeology* 22(2): 133–146.

Ahlstrom, Richard V. N., David A. Breternitz, and Richard L. Warren

    1985   Archival Excavation. New Tree-Ring Dates from Lowry Ruin. *The Kiva* 51(1): 39–42.

Akins, Nancy J.

    1985   Prehistoric Faunal Utilization in Chaco Canyon Basketmaker III through Pueblo III. In "Environment and Subsistence of Chaco Canyon, New Mexico," edited by Frances Joan Mathien. *Chaco Canyon Studies, Publications in Archeology* 18E: 305–445. Albuquerque: National Park Service.

    1986   A Biocultural Approach to Human Burials from Chaco Canyon, New Mexico. *Reports of the Chaco Center* 9. Santa Fe: Branch of Cultural Research, National Park Service.

Akins, Nancy J., and John D. Schelberg

    1984   Evidence for Organizational Complexity as seen from the Mortuary Practices at Chaco Canyon. In "Recent Research on Chaco Prehistory," edited by W. James Judge and John D. Schelberg. *Reports of the Chaco Center* 8: 89–102. Albuquerque: Division of Cultural Research, National Park Service.

Aldenderfer, Mark

    1993   Ritual, Hierarchy, and Change in Foraging Societies. *Journal of Anthropological Archaeology* 12(1): 1–40.

Allan, William C., and Rory P. Gauthier

    1976   Preservation and Conservation of Archaeological Resources. MS on file, Office of Contract Archeology, University of New Mexico, Albuquerque.

Arnold, Dean E.

    1985   *Ceramic Theory and Cultural Process.* Cambridge: Cambridge University Press.

Ashmore, Wendy, and Richard R. Wilk

    1988   Household and Community in the Mesoamerican Past. In *Household and Community in the Mesoamerican Past*, edited by Richard R. Wilk and Wendy Ashmore, pp. 1–27. Albuquerque: University of New Mexico Press.

Baker, Larry L.

    1991a   History of the Rio Puerco Valley Project. In *Anasazi Puebloan Adaptation in Response to Climatic Stress: Prehistory of the Middle Rio Puerco Valley*, edited by Cynthia Irwin-Williams and Larry

Baker, Larry L. (*continued*)
L. Baker, pp. 8–32. Albuquerque: Bureau of Land Management.

1991b   Anasazi Settlement Distribution and Relationship to the Environment. In *Anasazi Puebloan Adaptation in Response to Climatic Stress: Prehistory of the Middle Rio Puerco Valley,* edited by Cynthia Irwin-Williams and Larry L. Baker, pp. 290–324. Albuquerque: Bureau of Land Management.

Baker, Larry L., and Stephen R. Durand
1991   Regional Spatial Organization of Anasazi Settlement. In *Anasazi Puebloan Adaptation in Response to Climatic Stress: Prehistory of the Middle Rio Puerco Valley*, edited by Cynthia Irwin-Williams and Larry L. Baker, pp. 325–342. Albuquerque: Bureau of Land Management.

Bell, Catherine M.
1992   *Ritual Theory, Ritual Practice.* New York: Oxford University Press.
1997   *Ritual: Perspectives and Dimensions.* New York: Oxford University Press.

Bernardini, Wesley
1999   Reassessing the Scale of Social Action at Pueblo Bonito, Chaco Canyon, New Mexico. *Kiva* 64(4): 447-470.

Betzig, Laura L.
1988   Redistribution: Equity or Exploitation? In *Human Reproductive Behavior: A Darwinian Perspective,* edited by Laura L. Betzig, Monique Borgerhoff Mulder, and Paul W. Turke, pp. 49–63. Cambridge: Cambridge University Press.

Bishop, Ronald L., and Hector Neff
1989   Compositional Data Analysis in Archaeology. In "Archaeological Chemistry IV," edited by Ralph O. Allen. *Advances in Chemistry Series* 220: 57–86. Washington: American Chemical Society.

Blinman, Eric
1989   Potluck in the Protokiva: Ceramics and Ceremonialism in Pueblo I Villages. In "The Architecture of Social Integration in Prehistoric Pueblos," edited by William E. Lipe and Michelle Hegmon. *Occasional Papers of the Crow Canyon Archaeological Center* 1: 113–124. Cortez, Colorado: Crow Canyon Archaeological Center.
1997   Ceramic Analysis. In "Report on the 1996 Season at the Bluff Great House," by Catherine M. Cameron, William E. Davis, and Stephen H. Lekson. MS on file, Department of Anthropology, University of Colorado, Boulder.

Blinman, Eric, and C. Dean Wilson
1993   Ceramic Perspectives on Northern Anasazi Exchange. In *The American Southwest and Mesoamerica: Systems of Prehistoric Exchange*, edited

by Jonathon E. Ericson and Timothy G. Baugh, pp. 65–94. New York: Plenum Press.

Bloch, Maurice
1987   The Ritual of the Royal Bath in Madagascar. In *Rituals of Royalty: Power and Ceremonial in Traditional Societies*, edited by David Cannadine and Simon R. F. Price, pp. 271–297. Cambridge: Cambridge University Press.

Bower, N. W., C. M. Lewis, P. E. Neifert,
and E. S. Gladney
1992   Elemental Concentrations in Twenty NIST Standards of Geochemical Interest. *Geostandards Newsletter* 16: 27–40.

Bradfield, Richard Maitland
1971   The Changing Pattern of Hopi Agriculture. *Occasional Papers* 30. London: Royal Anthropological Institute of Great Britian and Ireland.
1995   *An Interpretation of Hopi Culture.* Derby, England: Richard Bradfield.

Bradley, Bruce A.
1974   Preliminary Report of Excavations at Wallace Ruin, 1969–1974. *Southwestern Lore* 40(3-4): 63–71.
1988   Wallace Ruin Interim Report. *Southwestern Lore* 54(2): 8–33.
1993   Wallace Ruin: Implications for Outlier Studies. In "The Chimney Rock Archaeological Symposium," edited by J. McKim Malville and Gary Matlock. *Forest Service General Technical Report* RM–227: 72–75. Fort Collins, Colorado: Rocky Mountain Forest and Range Experiment Station.
1996   Pitchers to Mugs: Chacoan Revival at Sand Canyon Pueblo. *Kiva* 61(3): 241–255.

Bradley, Richard
1993   Altering the Earth: The Origins of Monuments in Britain and Continental Europe, The Rhind Lectures 1991–92. *Society of Antiquaries of Scotland Monograph Series* 8. Stroud: Sutton Publishing.

Brand, Donald D., Florence M. Hawley,
and Frank C. Hibben
1937   Tseh So, A Small House Ruin, Chaco Canyon, New Mexico. *University of New Mexico Bulletin* 308, *Anthropological Series* 2(2). Albuquerque: University of New Mexico.

Brandi, James
1988   Lithic Analysis and Results. In *The Casamero and Pierre's Outliers Survey: An Archaeological Class III Inventory of the BLM Lands Surrounding the Outliers*, edited by Randy A. Harper, Marilyn K. Swift, Barbara J. Mills, James Brandi, and Joseph C. Winter, pp. 99–114. Albuquerque: Office of Contract Archaeology, University of New Mexico.

Braun, David P., and Stephen Plog
1982   Evolution of "Tribal" Social Networks: Theory

and Prehistoric North American Evidence. *American Antiquity* 47(3): 504–525.

Breternitz, Cory D., and David E. Doyel
1987　Methodological Issues for the Identification of Chacoan Community Structure: Lessons from the Bis sa'ani Community Study. *American Archeology* 6(3): 183–189.

Breternitz, Cory D., David E. Doyel,
and Michael P. Marshall, Editors
1982　Bis sa'ani: A Late Bonito Phase Community on Escavada Wash, Northwest New Mexico. *Navajo Nation Papers in Anthropology* 14. Window Rock, Arizona: Navajo Nation Cultural Resource Management Program.

Breternitz, David A.
1988　*Dolores Archaeological Program: Final Synthetic Report,* compiled by David A. Breternitz, C. K. Robinson, and G. T. Gross. Denver: Bureau of Reclamation, U.S. Department of the Interior.

Brunson, J. L.
1979　Corrugated Ceramics as Indicators of Interaction Spheres. MS, Master's thesis, Department of Anthropology, Arizona State University, Tempe.

Cameron, Catherine M.
1984　A Regional View of Chipped Stone Raw Material Use in Chaco Canyon. In "Recent Research on Chaco Prehistory," edited by W. James Judge and John D. Schelberg. *Reports of the Chaco Center* 8: 137–152. Albuquerque: Division of Cultural Research, National Park Service.
1995　Migration and the Movement of Southwestern Peoples. *Journal of Anthropological Archaeology* 14(2): 104–124.
1996　Archaeological Testing at the Bluff Great House, Southeastern Utah, October 1995. MS on file, Southwest Heritage Foundation, Bluff, Utah, and the Department of Anthropology, University of Colorado, Boulder.
1997a　The Chipped Stone of Chaco Canyon, New Mexico. In "Ceramics, Lithics, and Ornaments of Chaco Canyon: Analyses of Artifacts from the Chaco Project 1971–1978, Volume II. Lithics," edited by Frances Joan Mathien, pp. 531–659. *Publications in Archeology* 18G. Santa Fe: Chaco Canyon Studies, National Park Service.
1997b　The Chacoan Era in the Northern Southwest: 1996 Excavations at the Bluff Great House. MS on file, Southwest Heritage Foundation, Bluff, Utah, and the Department of Anthropology, University of Colorado, Boulder.
1997c　The Bluff Great House and the Chacoan Regional System. Paper presented at the 62nd Annual Meeting of the Society for American Archaeology, Nashville.
1997d　A Preliminary Report on the 1997 Excavations at the Bluff Great House. MS on file, Southwest Heritage Foundation, Bluff, Utah, and the Department of Anthropology, University of Colorado, Boulder.
1998　On the Northern Frontier: Chacoan and Post-Chacoan Archaeology in the Northern San Juan Region. Paper presented at the 63rd Annual Meeting of the Society for American Archaeology, Seattle.

Cameron, Catherine M., William E. Davis,
and Stephen H. Lekson
1996　The Chacoan Era in the Northern Southwest: The Bluff Great House Project Research Design. MS on file, Department of Anthropology, University of Colorado, Boulder.
1997　Report on the 1996 Excavations at the Bluff Great House. MS on file, University of Colorado, Southwest Heritage Foundation, Abajo Archaeology.

Cannadine, David
1987　Introduction: Divine Right of Kings. In *Rituals of Royalty: Power and Ceremonial in Traditional Societies,* edited by David Cannadine and Simon R. F. Price, pp. 1–19. Cambridge: Cambridge University Press.

Carneiro, Robert L.
1981　The Chiefdom: Precursor of the State. In *Transition to Statehood in the New World,* edited by Grant D. Jones and Robert R. Kautz, pp. 37–79. Cambridge: Cambridge University Press.

Chapman, Richard C., and Jan V. Biella
1980　*An Archaeological Survey on Four Sections of Land near Black Lake, San Juan County, New Mexico.* Santa Fe: Contract Archaeology Program, School of American Research.

Christenson, Andrew L.
1991　The Microenvironment of Cliffdwellings in Tsegi Canyon, Arizona. *The Kiva* 57(1): 39–54.
1994　A Test of Mean Ceramic Dating Using Well-dated Kayenta Anasazi Sites. *Kiva* 59(3): 297–317.

Cohen, Abner
1979　Political Symbolism. *Annual Review of Anthropology* 8: 87–113.

Cooper, Laura M.
1995　*Space Syntax Analysis of Chacoan Great Houses.* Doctoral dissertation, University of Arizona, Tucson. Ann Arbor: University Microfilms.

Cordell, Linda S.
1984　*Prehistory of the Southwest.* Orlando: Academic Press.
1997　*Archaeology of the Southwest.* Second edition. San Diego: Academic Press.

Crown, Patricia L.
1994　*Ceramics and Ideology: Salado Polychrome Pot-*

Crown, Patricia L. (*continued*)
  tery. Albuquerque: University of New Mexico Press.

Crown, Patricia L., and W. James Judge, Editors
  1991 *Chaco & Hohokam: Prehistoric Regional Systems in the American Southwest*. Santa Fe: School of American Research Press.

Cully, Anne C., Marcia L. Donaldson, Mollie S. Toll, and Klara B. Kelley
  1982 Agriculture in the Bis sa'ani Community. In "Bis sa'ani: A Late Bonito Phase Community on Escavada Wash, Northwest New Mexico," edited by Cory D. Breternitz, David E. Doyel, and Michael P. Marshall. *Navajo Nation Papers in Anthropology* 14(1): 115–166. Window Rock, Arizona: Navajo Nation Cultural Resource Management Program.

Cummings, Linda Scott, Kathryn Puseman, Thomas E. Moutoux, and Laura L. Ruggiero
  1998 Pollen and Macrofloral Analysis. In "Archaeological Investigations in the Peach Springs Chacoan Community: Data Recovery on Navajo Route 9, Segment 5-1, McKinley County, New Mexico," by Dennis Gilpin. *SWCA Report* 98-15: 237–290. Flagstaff: SWCA Environmental Consultants.

Cushing, Frank Hamilton
  1966 *Zuni Fetiches*. Flagstaff: K. C. Publications. Reprinted from *Second Annual Report of the Bureau of American Ethnology for the Years 1880–1881*, pp. 3–45, Washington, 1883.

Damp, Jonathan E., and James W. Kendrick
  1998 Agricultural Production and Household Economic Autonomy on the Zuni Landscape. Paper presented at the 98th Annual Meeting of the American Anthropological Association, Philadelphia.

Dean, Jeffrey S.
  1969 Chronological Analysis of Tsegi Phase Sites in Northeastern Arizona. *Papers of the Laboratory of Tree-Ring Research* 3. Tucson: University of Arizona.

Dean, Jeffrey S., Robert C. Euler, George J. Gumerman, Fred Plog, Richard H. Hevly, and Thor N. V. Karlstrom
  1985 Human Behavior, Demography, and Paleoenvironment on the Colorado Plateaus. *American Antiquity* 50(3): 537–554.

Deutchman, Haree L.
  1980 Chemical Evidence of Ceramic Exchange on Black Mesa. In "Models and Methods in Regional Exchange," edited by Robert E. Fry. *Society for American Archaeology Papers* 1: 119–133.

Doebley, John F., and Vorsila L. Bohrer
  1980 Maize. In "The Analysis of Ethnobotanical Remains," Part 7 in *Investigations at the Salmon Site: The Structure of Chacoan Society in the*

Northern Southwest, Vol. 3, edited by Cynthia Irwin-Williams and Phillip H. Shelley, pp. 175–220. Portales: Eastern New Mexico University.

Doyel, David E.
  1992a [Editor] Anasazi Regional Organization and the Chaco System. *Maxwell Museum of Anthropology Anthropological Papers* 5. Albuquerque: University of New Mexico.
  1992b Exploring Chaco. In "Anasazi Regional Organization and the Chaco System," edited by David E. Doyel. *Maxwell Museum of Anthropology Anthropological Papers* 5: 3–14. Albuquerque: University of New Mexico.

Doyel, David E., and Stephen H. Lekson
  1992 Regional Organization in the American Southwest. In "Anasazi Regional Organization and the Chaco System," edited by David E. Doyel. *Maxwell Museum of Anthropology Anthropological Papers* 5: 15–22. Albuquerque: University of New Mexico.

Doyel, David E., Cory D. Breternitz, and Michael P. Marshall
  1984 Chacoan Community Structure: Bis sa'ani Pueblo and the Chaco Halo. In "Recent Research on Chaco Prehistory," edited by W. James Judge and John D. Schelberg. *Reports of the Chaco Center* 8: 37–54. Albuquerque: Division of Cultural Research, National Park Service.

Duff, Andrew I.
  1994a Post-Chacoan Community Dynamics as Revealed by Household Interaction. Paper presented at the 59th Annual Meeting of the Society for American Archaeology, Anaheim.
  1994b The Scope of Post-Chacoan Community Organization in the Lower Zuni River Region. In "Exploring Social, Political, and Economic Organization in the Zuni Region," edited by Todd L. Howell and Tammy Stone. *Arizona State University Anthropological Research Papers* 46: 25–45. Tempe: Arizona State University.

Durand, Stephen R.
  1992 *Architectural Change and Chaco Prehistory*. Doctoral dissertation, University of Washington, Seattle. Ann Arbor: University Microfilms.

Durand, Stephen R., and Winston B. Hurst
  1991 A Refinement of Anasazi Cultural Chronology in the Middle Rio Puerco Valley Using Multidimensional Scaling. In *Anasazi Puebloan Adaptation in Response to Climatic Stress: Prehistory of the Middle Rio Puerco Valley*, edited by Cynthia Irwin-Williams and Larry L. Baker, pp. 233–255. Albuquerque: Bureau of Land Management.

Durkheim, Emile
  1965 *The Elementary Forms of the Religious Life*.

Translated by Joseph Ward Swain. Originally published in 1915 by George Allen and Unwin, Ltd., New York. New York: Free Press.

Dutton, Bertha P.
1938   Leyit Kin, A Small House Ruin, Chaco Canyon, New Mexico. *School of American Research Monograph* 7. Santa Fe.

Dykeman, Douglas D.
1982   Architecture of the Bis sa'ani Community. In "Bis sa'ani: A Late Bonito Phase Community on Escavada Wash, Northwest New Mexico," edited by Cory D. Breternitz, David E. Doyel, and Michael P. Marshall. *Navajo Nation Papers in Anthropology* 14(2, Part 2): 835–870. Window Rock, Arizona: Navajo Nation Cultural Resource Management Program.

Dykeman, Douglas D., and Kristin Langenfeld
1987   Prehistory and History of the La Plata Valley, New Mexico. *Contributions to Anthropology Series* 891. Farmington, New Mexico: San Juan County Archaeological Research Center and Library.

Earle, Timothy K.
1978   Economic and Social Organization of a Complex Chiefdom: The Halelea District, Kaua'i, Hawaii. *Anthropological Papers* 63. Ann Arbor: Museum of Anthropology, University of Michigan.
1991   The Evolution of Chiefdoms. In *Chiefdoms: Power, Economy, and Ideology,* edited by Timothy Earle, pp. 1–15. Cambridge: Cambridge University Press.

Ebert, James I., and Robert K. Hitchcock
1980   Locational Modeling in the Analysis of the Pre-historic Roadway System at and around Chaco Canyon, New Mexico. In *Cultural Resources Remote Sensing*, edited by Thomas R. Lyons and Frances Joan Mathien, pp. 169–207. Washington: National Park Service.

Eddy, Frank W.
1966   Prehistory in the Navajo Reservoir District, Northwestern New Mexico. *Museum of New Mexico Papers in Anthropology* 15. Santa Fe: Museum of New Mexico.
1972   Culture Ecology and the Prehistory of the Navajo Reservoir District. *Southwestern Lore* 38(1–2): 1–75.
1977   Archaeological Investigations at Chimney Rock Mesa: 1970–1972. *Memoirs of the Colorado Archaeological Society* 1. Boulder: Colorado Archaeological Society.

Farwell, Robin E.
1980   The Peach Springs Survey: A Cultural Resource Survey and Inventory along New Mexico State Road 566, McKinley County, for the New Mexico State Highway Department. *Laboratory of*

Anthropology Notes 162. Santa Fe: Museum of New Mexico.

Ferguson, William M., and Arthur H. Rohn
1987   *Anasazi Ruins of the Southwest in Color.* Albuquerque: University of New Mexico Press.

Fetterman, Jerry, and Linda Honeycutt
1987   The Mockingbird Mesa Survey, Southwestern Colorado. *Cultural Resource Management Series* 22. Denver: Bureau of Land Management.

Fewkes, J. Walter
1917   A Prehistoric Mesa Verde Pueblo and Its People. *Annual Report of the Smithsonian Institution, 1916*: 461–488. Washington.

Fish Suzanne K., and Paul R. Fish
1992   The Marana Community in Comparative Context. In "The Marana Community in the Hohokam World," edited by Suzanne K. Fish, Paul R. Fish and John H. Madsen. *Anthropological Papers of the University of Arizona* 56: 97–105. Tucson: University of Arizona Press.

Flam, Louis
1974   Excavations at the Eleanor Site, ENM883: A Brief Interim Report. MS on file, Agency for Conservation Archaeology, Eastern New Mexico University, Portales.

Fletcher, Thomas F., Editor
1994   Archaeological Data Recovery Excavations at the Sanders Great House and Six Other Sites along U.S. Highway 191, South of Sanders, Apache County, Arizona. *Zuni Archaeological Program Research Series* 9. Zuni Pueblo, New Mexico: Zuni Archaeology Program.

Ford, Richard I.
1972   An Ecological Perspective on the Eastern Pueblos. In *New Perspectives on the Pueblos,* edited by Alfonso Ortiz, pp. 1–17. Albuquerque: University of New Mexico Press.

Foucault, Michel
1977   *Discipline and Punish: The Birth of the Prison.* New York: Vintage Books.
1980   *Power/Knowledge: Selected Interviews and Other Writings 1972–1977,* edited by Colin Gordon. New York: Pantheon.
1982   The Subject and Power. In *Michel Foucault: Beyond Structuralism and Hermeneutics*, edited by Hubert L. Dreyfus and Paul Rabinow, pp. 208–226. Chicago: University of Chicago Press.

Fowler, Andrew P., and John R. Stein
1992   The Anasazi Great House in Space, Time, and Paradigm. In "Anasazi Regional Organization and the Chaco System," edited by David E. Doyel. *Maxwell Museum of Anthropology Anthropological Papers* 5: 101–122. Albuquerque: University of New Mexico.

Fowler, Andrew P., John R. Stein, and Roger Anyon
1987   An Archaeological Reconnaissance of West-Central New Mexico: The Anasazi Monuments Project. MS on file, report submitted to the Office of Cultural Affairs, Historic Preservation Division, State of New Mexico, Santa Fe.

Franklin, Hayward H.
1982   Ceramic Analysis of Nineteen Sites in the Bis sa'ani Community. In "Bis sa'ani: A Late Bonito Phase Community on Escavada Wash, Northwest New Mexico," edited by Cory D. Breternitz, David E. Doyel, and Michael P. Marshall. *Navajo Nation Papers in Anthropology* 14(3): 873–934. Window Rock, Arizona: Navajo Nation Cultural Research Management Program.

Gaines, Sylvia W., and W. M. Gaines
1997   Simulating Success or Failure: Another Look at Small-Population Dynamics. *American Antiquity* 62(4): 683–697.

Giddens, Anthony
1984   *The Constitution of Society: Outline of the Theory of Structuration.* Berkeley and Los Angeles: University of California Press.

Gillespie, William B.
1993   Vertebrate Remains from 29SJ 629. In "Investigations at 29SJ 629, Chaco Canyon, New Mexico: Artifactual and Biological Analyses," Vol. 2, edited by Thomas C. Windes. *Reports of the Chaco Center* 12: 343–395. Santa Fe: National Park Service.

Gilman, Patricia A., Veletta Canouts, and Ronald L. Bishop
1994   The Production and Distribution of Classic Mimbres Black-on-white Pottery. *American Antiquity* 59(4): 695–709.

Gilpin, Dennis
1998   Environmental Setting. In "Archaeological Investigations in the Peach Springs Chacoan Community: Data Recovery on Navajo Route 9, Segment 5-1, McKinley County, New Mexico," by Dennis Gilpin. *SWCA Report* 98-15: 11–26. Flagstaff: SWCA Environmental Consultants.

Gladwin, Harold S.
1945   The Chaco Branch: Excavations at White Mound and in the Red Mesa Valley. *Medallion Papers* 33. Globe, Arizona: Gila Pueblo.

Glowacki, D. M., Hector Neff, Michelle Hegmon, James W. Kendrick, and W. James Judge
1997   Chemical Variation, Resource Use, and Vessel Movement in the Northern San Juan Region. Paper presented at the 62nd Annual Meeting, Society for American Archaeology, Nashville.

Godelier, Maurice
1978   Economy and Religion: An Evolutionary Optical Illusion. In *The Evolution of Social Systems*, edited by J. Friedman and M. J. Rowlands,

pp. 3–11. Pittsburgh: University of Pittsburgh Press.

Goetze, Christine E., and Barbara J. Mills
1993   Classification Criteria for Wares and Types. In *Across the Colorado Plateau: Anthropological Studies for the Transwestern Pipeline Expansion Project*, Vol. 16, *Interpretation of Ceramic Artifacts*, edited by Barbara J. Mills, Christine E. Goetze, and María Nieves Zedeño, pp. 21–86. Albuquerque: Office of Contract Archeology and Maxwell Museum of Anthropology, University of New Mexico.

Graham, Martha
1993   Settlement Organization and Residential Variability among the Rarámuri. In *Abandonment of Settlements and Regions: Ethnoarchaeological and Archaeological Approaches*, edited by Catherine M. Cameron and Steve A. Tomka, pp. 25–42. Cambridge: Cambridge University Press.
1994   Mobile Farmers: An Ethnoarchaeological Approach to Settlement Organization among the Rarámuri of Northwestern Mexico. *International Monographs in Prehistory, Ethnoarchaeological Series* 3. Ann Arbor, Michigan.

Grebinger, Paul F.
1973   Prehistoric Social Organization in Chaco Canyon, New Mexico: An Alternative Reconstruction. *The Kiva* 39(1): 3–23.

Green, Dee F.
1971   First Season's Excavations at Edge of the Cedars Pueblo, Blanding, Utah. *Newsletter of the Utah Statewide Archaeological Society*.

Greenwald, Dawn M.
1998   Flaked Stone and Ground Stone Assemblages. In "Archaeological Investigations in the Peach Springs Chacoan Community: Data Recovery on Navajo Route 9, Segment 5-1, McKinley County, New Mexico," by Dennis Gilpin. *SWCA Report* 98-15: 303–340. Flagstaff: SWCA Environmental Consultants.

Gregory, Herbert E.
1938   The San Juan Country; A Geographic and Geologic Reconnaissance of Southeastern Utah. *Geological Survey Professional Paper* 188. Washington: U.S. Department of the Interior.

Greubel, R. A.
1991   Hovenweep Resource Protection Zone Class III Cultural Resource Inventory, Montezuma County, Colorado, and San Juan County, Utah. MS, Alpine Archaeological Consultants 17, submitted to Bureau of Land Management, Colorado and Utah.

Grissino-Mayer, Henri D., Thomas W. Swetnam, and Rex K. Adams
1997   The Rare, Old-aged Conifers of El Malpais:

Their Role in Understanding Climatic Change in the American Southwest. *New Mexico Bureau of Mines and Mineral Resources Bulletin* 156.

Hantman, Jeffrey L.
1983   *Social Networks and Stylistic Distributions in the Prehistoric Plateau Southwest.* Doctoral dissertation, Arizona State University, Tempe. Ann Arbor: University Microfilms.

Hard, Robert J., and William L. Merrill
1992   Mobile Agriculturalists and the Emergence of Sedentism: Perspectives from Northern Mexico. *American Anthropologist* 94(3): 601–620.

Hargrave, Lyndon L.
1931   Excavations at Kin Tiel and Kokopnyama. In "Recently Dated Pueblo Ruins in Arizona," by Emil W. Haury and Lyndon L. Hargrave. *Smithsonian Miscellaneous Collections* 82(11): 80–120. Washington: Smithsonian Institution.

Harper, Christopher L.
1993   Seasons and Settlement Patterns at Walnut Canyon National Monument, Arizona. MS, Master's thesis, Department of Anthropology, Northern Arizona University, Flagstaff.

Harper, Randy A., Marilyn K. Swift, Barbara J. Mills, James Brandi, and Joseph C. Winter
1988   *The Casamero and Pierre's Outliers Survey: An Archaeological Class III Inventory of the BLM Lands Surrounding the Outliers.* Albuquerque: Office of Contract Archeology, University of New Mexico.

Hasbargen, Jim, Dennis Gilpin, and James M. Potter
1998   Ceramic Analysis. In "Archaeological Investigations in the Peach Springs Chacoan Community: Data Recovery on Navajo Route 9, Segment 5-1, McKinley County, New Mexico," by Dennis Gilpin. *SWCA Report* 98-15: 341–439. Flagstaff: SWCA Environmental Consultants.

Hayes, Alden C.
1964   The Archeological Survey of Wetherill Mesa, Mesa Verde National Park, Colorado. *Archeological Research Series* 7A. Washington: National Park Service.

Hayes, Alden C., and Thomas C. Windes
1975   An Anasazi Shrine in Chaco Canyon. In "Collected Papers in Honor of Florence Hawley Ellis," edited by Theodore R. Frisbie. *Papers of the Archaeological Society of New Mexico* 2: 143–156. Santa Fe: Archaeological Society of New Mexico.

Hayes, Alden C., David M. Brugge, and W. James Judge
1981   Archeological Surveys of Chaco Canyon, New Mexico. *Chaco Canyon Studies, Publications in Archeology* 18A. Washington: National Park Service.

Hegmon, Michelle
1989   Risk Reduction and Variation in Agricultural Economies: A Computer Simulation of Hopi Agriculture. *Research in Economic Anthropology* 11: 89–121.
1991   Risks of Sharing and Sharing as Risk Reduction: Interhousehold Food Sharing in Egalitarian Societies. In "Between Bands and States," edited by S. A. Gregg. *Center for Archaeological Investigations Occasional Paper* 9: 309–329. Carbondale: Southern Illinois University.

Hegmon, Michelle, Winston Hurst, and James R. Allison
1995   Production for Local Consumption and Exchange: Comparisons of Early Red and White Ware Ceramics in the San Juan Region. In *Ceramic Production in the American Southwest*, edited by Barbara J. Mills and Patricia L. Crown, pp. 30–62. Tucson: University of Arizona Press.

Helms, Mary W.
1988   *Ulysses' Sail: An Ethnographic Odyssey of Power, Knowledge, and Geographical Distance.* Princeton: Princeton University Press.
1993   *Craft and the Kingly Ideal: Art, Trade, and Power.* Austin: University of Texas Press.

Huckleberry, Gary A., and Brian R. Billman
1998   Floodwater Farming, Discontinuous Ephemeral Streams, and Puebloan Abandonment in Southwestern Colorado. *American Antiquity* 63(4): 595–616.

Huntley, Deborah, Nancy Mahoney, and Keith Kintigh
1998   Modeling Cibolan Community Interaction through Ceramic Compositional Analysis. Paper presented at the 63rd Annual Meeting of the Society for American Archaeology, Seattle.

Hurst, Winston B.
1985   Chapter 7–42SA8887–Bullpup Shelter. In "Final, Recapture Wash Archaeological Project, 1981–1983," edited by Asa S. Nielson, Joel C. Janetski, and James D. Wilde. *Technical Series* 85-7: 7-1 through 7-56. Provo: Brighan Young University Museum of Peoples and Cultures.
1991   Typological Analysis of Ceramics from the Middle Rio Puerco of the East. In *Anasazi Puebloan Adaptation in Response to Climatic Stress: Prehistory of the Middle Rio Puerco Valley*, edited by Cynthia Irwin-Williams and Larry L. Baker, pp. 103–232. Albuquerque: Bureau of Land Management.

Irwin-Williams, Cynthia
1972   [Editor] The Structure of Chacoan Society in the Northern Southwest: Investigations at the Salmon Site, Eastern New Mexico, 1972. *Contributions in Anthropology* 4(3). Portales: Eastern New Mexico University.
1977   A Network Model for the Analysis of Prehistoric Trade. In *Exchange Systems in Prehistory*, edited by Timothy K. Earle and Jonathon E. Ericson,

Irwin-Williams, Cynthia (*continued*)
        pp. 141–151. New York: Academic Press.
  1980 The San Juan Valley Archaeological Program Investigations at Salmon Ruin. In *Investigations at the Salmon Site: The Structure of Chacoan Society in the Northern Southwest*, Vol. 1, edited by Cynthia Irwin-Williams and Phillip H. Shelley, pp. 3–104. Portales: Eastern New Mexico University.
  1991 Introduction: Overview and Theoretical Framework. In *Anasazi Puebloan Adaptation in Response to Climatic Stress: Prehistory of the Middle Rio Puerco Valley*, edited by Cynthia Irwin-Williams and Larry L. Baker, pp. 1–7. Albuquerque: Bureau of Land Management.

Irwin-Williams, Cynthia, and Larry L. Baker, Editors
  1991 *Anasazi Puebloan Adaptation in Response to Climatic Stress, Prehistory of the Middle Rio Puerco Valley*. Albuquerque: Bureau of Land Management.

Irwin-Williams, Cynthia, and Phillip H. Shelley, Editors
  1980 *Investigations at the Salmon Site: The Structure of Chacoan Society in the Northern Southwest.* 4 Vols. Portales: Eastern New Mexico University.

Jacobson, LouAnn
  1984 Chipped Stone in the San Juan Basin: A Distributional Analysis. MS, Master's thesis, Department of Anthropology, University of New Mexico, Albuquerque.

Johnson, A. W., and Timothy K. Earle
  1987 *The Evolution of Human Societies.* Palo Alto, California: Stanford University Press.

Johnson, Brian K.
  1987 Space Heating Performance of the Ghost Ranch Sundwellings. MS, Civil Engineering Master's thesis, Department of Civil, Architectural, and Environmental Engineering, University of Colorado, Boulder.

Johnson, Gregory A.
  1980 Rank-size Convexity and System Integration: A View from Archaeology. *Economic Geography* 56(3): 234–247.

Judd, Neil M.
  1954 Material Culture of Pueblo Bonito. *Smithsonian Miscellaneous Collections* 124(1). Washington: Smithsonian Institution.
  1964 The Architecture of Pueblo Bonito. *Smithsonian Miscellaneous Collections* 147(1). Washington: Smithsonian Institution.

Judge, W. James
  1979 The Development of a Complex Cultural Ecosystem in the Chaco Basin, New Mexico. In "Proceedings of the First Conference on Scientific Research in the National Parks 3," edited by Robert M. Linn. *National Park Service*

Transactions and Proceedings Series 5: 901–906. Santa Fe: National Park Service.
  1984 New Light on Chaco Canyon. In *New Light on Chaco Canyon*, edited by David Grant Noble, pp. 1–12. Santa Fe: School of American Research Press.
  1989 Chaco Canyon-San Juan Basin. In *Dynamics of Southwest Prehistory*, edited by Linda S. Cordell and George J. Gumerman, pp. 209–261. Washington: Smithsonian Institution Press.
  1991 Chaco: Current Views of Prehistory and the Regional System. In *Chaco & Hohokam: Prehistoric Regional Systems in the American Southwest*, edited by Patricia L. Crown and W. James Judge, pp. 11–30. Santa Fe: School of American Research Press.
  1993 Resource Distribution and the Chaco Phenomenon. In "The Chimney Rock Archaeological Symposium," edited by J. McKim Malville and Gary Matlock. *Forest Service General Technical Report* RM-227: 35–36. Fort Collins, Colorado: Rocky Mountain Forest and Range Experiment Station.
  1998 Report on Archaeological Investigations at Puzzle House. MS submitted to the Colorado Historical Society, Denver.

Judge, W. James, and John D. Schelberg, Editors
  1984 Recent Research on Chaco Prehistory. *Reports of the Chaco Center* 8. Albuquerque: Division of Cultural Research, National Park Service.

Judge, W. James, H. Wolcott Toll, William B. Gillespie, and Stephen H. Lekson
  1981 Tenth Century Developments in Chaco Canyon. In "Collected Papers in Honor of Erik Kellerman Reed," edited by Albert H. Schroeder. *Papers of the Archaeological Society of New Mexico* 6: 65–98. Albuquerque.

Kane, Allen E.
  1993 Settlement Analogues for Chimney Rock: Models of 11th & 12th Century Northern Anasazi Society. In "The Chimney Rock Archaeological Symposium," edited by J. McKim Malville and Gary Matlock. *Forest Service General Technical Report* RM-227: 43–60. Fort Collins, Colorado: Rocky Mountain Forest and Range Experiment Station.

Kantner, John
  1995 Actor-Based Modeling of Political Behavior among the Chacoan Anasazi of the American Southwest. MS, extended version of a paper presented at the 60th Annual Meeting of the Society for American Archaeology, Minneapolis.
  1996a Political Competition among the Chaco Anasazi of the American Southwest. *Journal of Anthropological Archaeology* 15(1): 41–105.
  1996b Archaeological Inventory and Limited Testing of

LA 68896 and LA 12574, Two Sites in the Upper San Jose Valley near Grants, New Mexico. Report submitted to the New Mexico Historic Preservation Division, Santa Fe.

1997 Ancient Roads, Modern Mapping: Evaluating Chaco Anasazi Roadways Using GIS Technology. *Expedition* 39(3): 49–62.

1999 *The Influence of Self-Interested Behavior on Sociopolitical Change: The Evolution of the Chaco Anasazi in the Prehistoric American Southwest.* Doctoral dissertation, University of California, Santa Barbara. Ann Arbor: University Microfilms.

Kendrick, James W.
1996 Archaeological Survey in the Lowry Area of Southwestern Colorado. MS, Report submitted to the Wenner-Gren Foundation for Anthropological Research, New York.

1998 Results of the Lowry Community Pattern Survey: A Report Submitted to the Colorado Historical Society. In "Appendix A, Report on Archaeological Investigations at Puzzle House," by W. James Judge. MS submitted to the Colorado Historical Society, Denver.

Kendrick, James W., and W. James Judge
1996 The Lowry Community: Testing Great House Models on the Chaco Frontier. Paper presented at the 61st Annual Meeting of the Society for American Archaeology, New Orleans.

Kincaid, Chris, Editor
1983 *Chaco Roads Project, Phase 1: A Reappraisal of Prehistoric Roads in the San Juan Basin.* Albuquerque: Bureau of Land Management.

Kintigh, Keith W.
1994 Chaco, Communal Architecture, and Cibolan Aggregation. In *The Ancient Southwestern Community: Models and Methods for the Study of Prehistoric Social Organization*, edited by Wirt H. Wills and Robert D. Leonard, pp. 131–140. Albuquerque: University of New Mexico Press.

Kintigh, Keith W., Todd L. Howell, and Andrew I. Duff
1996 Post-Chacoan Social Integration at the Hinkson Site, New Mexico. *Kiva* 61(3): 257–274.

Knowles, Ralph L.
1974 *Energy and Form: An Ecological Approach to Urban Growth.* Cambridge: MIT Press.

Kojo, Yasushi
1996 Production of Prehistoric Southwestern Ceramics: A Low-Technology Approach. *American Antiquity* 61(2): 325–339.

Kolb, Michael J., and James E. Snead
1997 It's a Small World after All: Comparative Analyses of Community Organization in Archaeology. *American Antiquity* 62(4): 609–628.

Kosse, Krisztina
1993 Middle Range Societies from a Scalar Perspective. Paper presented at the Third Southwest Symposium, Tucson, Arizona. [Published, 1996, in "Interpreting Southwestern Diversity: Underlying Principles and Overarching Patterns," edited by Paul R. Fish and J. Jefferson Reid. *Anthropological Research Papers* 48: 87–96. Tempe: Arizona State University.]

LaPere, L.
1979 Factors Influencing the Distribution of Lithic Material on Archaeological Sites, Apache-Sitgreaves National Forests. MS on file, Department of Sociology and Anthropology, New Mexico State University, Las Cruces.

LeBlanc, Steven A.
1999 *Prehistoric Warfare in the American Southwest.* Salt Lake City: University of Utah Press.

Lekson, Stephen H.
1984 Great Pueblo Architecture of Chaco Canyon, New Mexico. *Chaco Canyon Studies, Publications in Archeology* 18B. Albuquerque: National Park Service. [Published in 1986, Albuquerque: University of New Mexico Press.]

1988 The Idea of the Kiva in Anasazi Archaeology. *The Kiva* 53(3): 213–234.

1989 *Sociopolitical Complexity at Chaco Canyon, New Mexico.* Doctoral dissertation, University of New Mexico, Albuquerque. Ann Arbor: University Microfilms.

1990 Cross-Cultural Perspectives on the Community. In "Vernacular Architecture: Paradigms of Environmental Response," edited by Mete Turan. *Ethnoscapes* 4: 122–145. Avebury, England: Aldershot.

1991 Settlement Patterns and the Chaco Region. In *Chaco & Hohokam: Prehistoric Regional Systems in the American Southwest,* edited by Patricia L. Crown and W. James Judge, pp. 31–55. Santa Fe: School of American Research Press.

1995 Introduction. In "Migration and the Movement of Southwestern Peoples," edited by Catherine M. Cameron. *Journal of Anthropological Archaeology* 14(2): 99–103.

1996a Scale and Process in the Southwest. In "Interpreting Southwestern Diversity: Underlying Principles and Overarching Patterns," edited by Paul F. Fish and J. Jefferson Reid. *Anthropological Research Papers* 48: 81–86. Tempe: Arizona State University.

1996b The Pueblo Southwest after A.D. 1150. In "Interpreting Southwestern Diversity: Underlying Principles and Overarching Patterns," edited by Paul F. Fish and J. Jefferson Reid. *Anthropological Research Papers* 48: 41–44. Tempe: Arizona State University.

Lekson, Stephen H. (*continued*)

1997   Anasazi Communities in Context. In *Anasazi Architecture and American Design*, edited by B. H. Morrow and V. B. Price, pp. 27–35. Albuquerque: University of New Mexico Press.

1999   *The Chaco Meridian: Centers of Political Power in the Ancient Southwest*. Walnut Creek, California: AltaMira Press.

Lekson, Stephen H., and Catherine M. Cameron

1995   Abandonment of Chaco Canyon, the Mesa Verde Migrations, and the Reorganization of the Pueblo World. *Journal of Anthropological Archaeology* 14(2): 184–202.

Lekson, Stephen H., Thomas C. Windes,

John R. Stein, and W. James Judge

1988   The Chaco Canyon Community. *Scientific American* 256(7): 100–109.

LeTourneau, Philippe D.

1997   Sources and Prehistoric Use of Yellowish Brown Spotted Chert in Northwest-Central New Mexico. Paper presented at the 62nd Annual Meeting of the Society for American Archaeology, Nashville, Tennessee.

Lightfoot, Ricky R.

1994   The Duckfoot Site, Vol. 2, Archaeology of the House and Household. *Occasional Papers of the Crow Canyon Archaeological Center* 3–4. Cortez, Colorado: Crow Canyon Archaeological Center.

Lipe, William D.

1970   Anasazi Communities in the Red Rock Plateau, Southeastern Utah. In *Reconstructing Prehistoric Pueblo Societies,* edited by William A. Longacre, pp. 84–139. Albuquerque: University of New Mexico Press.

1989   Social Scale of Mesa Verde Anasazi Kivas. In "The Architecture of Social Integration in Prehistoric Pueblos," edited by William D. Lipe and Michelle Hegmon. *Occasional Papers of the Crow Canyon Archaeological Center* 1: 53–71. Cortez, Colorado: Crow Canyon Archaeological Center.

1994   Material Expression of Social Power in the Northern San Juan, A.D. 1150–1300. Extended version of a paper presented at the 59th Annual Meeting of the Society for American Archaeology, Anaheim. MS on file, Crow Canyon Archaeological Center, Cortez, Colorado.

1995   Depopulation of the Northern San Juan: Conditions in the Turbulent 1200s. *Journal of Anthropological Archaeology* 14(2): 143–169.

Lister, Robert H.

1964   Contributions to Mesa Verde Archaeology: I, Site 499, Mesa Verde National Park, Colorado. *University of Colorado Studies, Series in Anthropology* 9. Boulder: University of Colorado.

1965   Contributions to Mesa Verde Archaeology: II, Site 875, Mesa Verde National Park Colorado. *University of Colorado Studies, Series in Anthropology* 11. Boulder: University of Colorado.

1966   *Contributions to Mesa Verde Archaeology: III, Site 866, and the Cultural Sequence at Four Villages in the Far View Group, Mesa Verde National Park, Colorado*. Boulder: University of Colorado Press.

Loose, Richard W.

1979   Research Design. In *Anasazi Communities of the San Juan Basin*, edited by Michael P. Marshall, John R. Stein, Richard W. Loose, and Judith E. Novotny, pp. 355–363. Albuquerque: Public Service Company of New Mexico and Santa Fe: New Mexico Historic Preservation Bureau.

Lyman, Albert R.

1972   *The Trail of the Ancients*. Blanding, Utah: Trail of the Ancients Association.

Mahoney, Nancy M.

1998a   1996 Cottonwood Wash Survey Project Report, San Juan County, Utah. MS, report on file, Bureau of Land Management, Monticello, Utah.

1998b   1997 Cottonwood Wash Survey Project Report, San Juan County, Utah. MS, report on file, Bureau of Land Management, Monticello, Utah.

1998c   Beyond Bis sa'ani: Rethinking the Scale and Organization of Great House Communities. Paper presented at the 63rd Annual Meeting of the Society for American Archaeology, Seattle.

Mahoney, Nancy M., Andrew I. Duff, and Keith W. Kintigh

1995   The Role of Chacoan Outliers in Local Organization. Paper presented at the 60th Annual Meeting of the Society for American Archaeology, Minneapolis.

Marshall, Michael P.

1982   Bis sa'ani Pueblo: An Example of Late Bonito Phase Great-House Architecture. In "Bis sa'ani: A Late Bonito Phase Community on Escavada Wash, Northwest New Mexico," edited by Cory D. Breternitz, David E. Doyel, and Michael P. Marshall. *Navajo Nation Papers in Anthropology* 14(2, Part 1): 169–358. Window Rock, Arizona: Navajo Nation Cultural Resource Management Program.

Marshall, Michael P., and David E. Doyel

1981   An Interim Report on Bis sa'ani Pueblo, With Notes on the Chacoan Regional System. MS on file, Navajo Nation Cultural Resource Management Program, Window Rock, Arizona.

Marshall, Michael P., David E. Doyel,

and Cory D. Breternitz

1982   A Regional Perspective on the Late Bonito Phase. In "Bis sa'ani: A Late Bonito Phase Community on Escavada Wash, Northwest New Mexico," edited by Cory D. Breternitz, David E. Doyel, and Michael P. Marshall. *Navajo Nation Papers in Anthropology* 14(3): 1227–1240. Window Rock, Arizona: Navajo Nation Cultural Resource Management Program.

Marshall, Michael P., John R. Stein, Richard W. Loose, and Judith E. Novotny, Editors

1979   *Anasazi Communities of the San Juan Basin.* Albuquerque: Public Service Company of New Mexico and Santa Fe: New Mexico Historic Preservation Bureau.

Martin, Paul S.

1929   The 1928 Archaeological Expedition of the State Historical Society of Colorado. *Colorado Magazine* 6(1): 1–35.

1930   The 1929 Archaeological Expedition of the State Historical Society of Colorado. *Colorado Magazine* 7(1).

1936   Lowry Ruin in Southwestern Colorado. *Anthropological Series* 23(1). Chicago: Field Museum of Natural History.

1938   Archaeological Work in the Ackmen-Lowry Area, Southwestern Colorado, 1937. *Anthropological Series* 23(2). Chicago: Field Museum of Natural History.

Mathien, Frances Joan

1985   Ornaments and Minerals from Chaco Canyon: National Park Service Project, 1971–1978. MS on file, Division of Cultural Research, National Park Service, Santa Fe.

1986   External Contact and the Chaco Anasazi. In *Ripples in the Chichimec Sea: New Considerations of Southwestern-Mesoamerican Interactions*, edited by Frances Joan Mathien and Randall H. McGuire, pp. 220–242. Carbondale: Southern Illinois University Press.

1993   Exchange Systems and Social Stratification among the Chaco Anasazi. In *The American Southwest and Mesoamerica: Systems of Prehistoric Exchange*, edited by Jonathon E. Ericson and Timothy G. Baugh, pp. 27–63. New York: Plenum Press.

1997a   [Editor] Ceramics, Lithics, and Ornaments of Chaco Canyon: Analyses of Artifacts from the Chaco Project, 1971–1978. *Chaco Canyon Studies, Publications in Archeology* 18G. Santa Fe: National Park Service.

1997b   Ornaments of the Chaco Anasazi. In "Ceramics, Lithics, and Ornaments of Chaco Canyon: Analyses of Artifacts from the Chaco Project, 1971–1978," edited by Frances Joan Mathien. *Chaco Canyon Studies, Publications in Archeology* 18G: 1119–1219. Santa Fe: National Park Service.

Mathien, Frances Joan, and Thomas C. Windes

1989   Greathouse Revisited: Kin Nahasbas, Chaco Cul-

ture National Historical Park. In "From Chaco to Chaco: Papers in Honor of Robert H. Lister and Florence C. Lister," edited by M. S. Duran and D. T. Kirkpatrick. *Archaeological Society of New Mexico* 15: 11–34. Albuquerque: Archaeological Society of New Mexico.

McAlister, J.

1978   A Synagraphic Distribution of Black-on-white Ceramics in the Apache-Sitgreaves Forests. MS on file, Department of Sociology and Anthropology, New Mexico State University, Las Cruces.

McGuire, Randall H., and Dean J. Saitta

1996   Although They Have Petty Captains, They Obey Them Badly: The Dialectics of Prehispanic Western Pueblo Social Organization. *American Antiquity* 61(2): 197–213.

McKenna, Peter J.

1991   Chaco Canyon's Mesa Verde Phase. In "Excavations at 29SJ 633: The Eleventh Hour Site, Chaco Canyon, New Mexico," edited by Frances Joan Mathien. *Reports of the Chaco Center* 10: 127–137. Santa Fe: Branch of Cultural Research, National Park Service.

McKenna, Peter J., and H. Wolcott Toll

1991   Ceramics from 29SJ 633, the Eleventh Hour Site. In "Excavations at 29SJ 633: The Eleventh Hour Site, Chaco Canyon, New Mexico," edited by Francis Joan Mathien. *Reports of the Chaco Center* 10: 139–205. Santa Fe: Branch of Cultural Research, National Park Service.

1992   Regional Patterns of Great House Development among the Totah Anasazi, New Mexico. In "Anasazi Regional Organization and the Chaco System," edited by David E. Doyel. *Maxwell Museum of Anthropology Anthropological Papers* 5: 133–143. Albuquerque: Maxwell Museum of Anthropology.

Mills, Barbara J.

1988   Chronological, Distributional and Functional Analyses of the Ceramic Assemblages from the Casamero and Pierre's Outliers. In *The Casamero and Pierre's Outliers Survey: An Archaeological Class III Inventory of the BLM Lands Surrounding the Outliers*, edited by Randy A. Harper, Marilyn K. Swift, Barbara J. Mills, James Brandi, and Joseph C. Winter, pp. 59–98. Albuquerque: Office of Contract Archeology, University of New Mexico.

1994   Community Dynamics and Archaeological Dynamics: Some Considerations of Middle-Range Theory. In *The Ancient Southwestern Community: Models and Methods for the Study of Prehistoric Social Organization*, edited by Wirt H. Wills and Robert D. Leonard, pp. 55–65. Albuquerque: University of New Mexico Press.

Mobley-Tanaka, Jeannette L.
1990   Prehistoric Community and Community Interaction at Chimney Rock, Colorado. MS, Master's
thesis, Department of Anthropology, University
of Colorado, Boulder.
1993   Intracommunity Interactions at Chimney Rock:
The Inside View of the Outlier Problem. In "The
Chimney Rock Archaeological Symposium,"
edited by J. McKim Malville and Gary Matlock.
Forest Service General Technical Report RM-
227: 37–42. Fort Collins, Colorado: Rocky
Mountain Forest and Range Experiment Station.
1997   Gender and Ritual Space during the Pithouse to
Pueblo Transition: Subterranean Mealing Rooms
in the North American Southwest. *American
Antiquity* 62(3): 437–448.

Monks, Gregory G.
1981   Seasonality Studies. In *Advances in Archaeological Method and Theory*, Vol. 4, edited by
Michael B. Schiffer, pp. 177–240. New York:
Academic Press.

Morris, Earl H.
1919   The Aztec Ruin. *Anthropological Papers of the
American Museum of Natural History* 26(1). New
York.
1939   Archaeological Studies in the La Plata District:
Southwestern Colorado and Northwestern New
Mexico. *Carnegie Institution of Washington Pub-
lication* 519. Washington.

Munro, Natalie D.
1994   An Investigation of Anasazi Turkey Production in
Southwestern Colorado. MS, Master's thesis, Department of Archaeology, Simon Frasier University, Burnaby, Canada.

Murdock, George P.
1949   *Social Structure.* New York: Macmillan.

Murdock George P., and Suzanne R. Wilson
1972   Settlement Patterns and Community Organization:
Cross Cultural Codes. *Ethnology* 11(3): 254–295.

Naranjo, Tessie
1995   Thoughts on Migration by Santa Clara Pueblo. In
"Migration and the Movement of Southwestern
Peoples," edited by Catherine M. Cameron. *Journal of Anthropological Archaeology* 14(2): 247–250.

Neff, Hector, Editor
1992   *Chemical Characterization of Ceramic Pastes in
Archaeology.* Madison: Prehistory Press.

Neff, Hector, Michael D. Glascock, Ronald L. Bishop,
and M. James Blackman
1996   An Assessment of the Acid-Extraction Approach
to Compositional Characterization of Archaeological Ceramics. *American Antiquity* 61(2):
389–404.

Neily, Robert B.
1983   *The Prehistoric Community on the Colorado
Plateau: An Approach to the Study of Change and
Survival in the Northern San Juan Area of the
American Southwest.* Doctoral dissertation, South-
ern Illinois University. Ann Arbor: University
Microfilms.

Neitzel, Jill E.
1989   The Chacoan Regional System: Interpreting the
Evidence for Sociopolitical Complexity. In *The
Sociopolitical Structure of Prehistoric South-
western Societies*, edited by Steadman Upham,
Kent G. Lightfoot, and Roberta A. Jewett, pp.
509–556. Boulder, Colorado: Westview Press.
1994   Boundary Dynamics in the Chacoan Regional
System. In *The Ancient Southwestern Community:
Models and Methods for the Study of Prehistoric
Social Organization*, edited by Wirt H. Wills and
Robert D. Leonard, pp. 209–240. Albuquerque:
University of New Mexico Press.

Neitzel, Jill E., and Ronald L. Bishop
1990   Neutron Activation of Dogoszhi Style Ceramics:
Production and Exchange in the Chacoan Regional System. *Kiva* 56(1): 67–85.

Nelson, Ben A.
1994   Introduction: Approaches to Analyzing Prehistoric Community Dynamics. In *The Ancient
Southwestern Community: Models and Methods
for the Study of Prehistoric Social Organization*,
edited by Wirt H. Wills and Robert D. Leonard,
pp. 3–7. Albuquerque: University of New Mexico Press.
1995   Complexity, Hierarchy, and Scale: A Controlled
Comparison Between Chaco Canyon, New Mexico and La Quemada, Zacatecas. *American Antiquity* 60(4): 597–618.

Nelson, Ben A., D. L. Martin, A. C. Swedlund,
Paul R. Fish, and G. J. Armelagos
1994   Studies in Disruption: Demography and Health in
the Prehistoric Southwest. In "Understanding
Complexity in the Prehistoric Southwest," edited
by George J. Gumerman and Murray Gell-Mann,
pp. 38–58. *Santa Fe Institute Studies in the
Sciences of Complexity Proceedings* 24. Reading:
Addison-Wesley.

Netting, Robert McCormick
1990   Population, Permanent Agriculture, and Polities:
Unpacking the Evolutionary Portmanteau. In *The
Evolution of Political Systems: Sociopolitics in
Small-Scale Sedentary Societies,* edited by Stead-
man Upham, pp. 21–91. Cambridge: Cambridge
University Press.

Nials, Fred L.
1991   Geology and Geomorphology of the Middle Rio
Puerco Valley. In *Anasazi Puebloan Adaptation
in Response to Climatic Stress: Prehistory of the
Middle Rio Puerco Valley*, edited by Cynthia

Irwin-Williams and Larry L. Baker, pp. 33–57. Albuquerque: Bureau of Land Management.

Nials, Fred L., John R. Stein,
and John R. Roney
  1987   Chacoan Roads in the Southern Periphery: Results of Phase II of the BLM Chaco Roads Project. *Cultural Resources Series* 1. Albuquerque: Bureau of Land Management.

Obenauf, Margaret Senter
  1980   A History of Research on the Chacoan Roadway System. In *Cultural Resources Remote Sensing*, edited by Thomas R. Lyons and Frances Joan Mathien, pp. 123–167. Washington: National Park Service, Cultural Resources Management Division.

Olgyay, Victor
  1963   *Design with Climate: Bioclimatic Approach to Architectural Regionalism*. Princeton: Princeton University Press.

Ortiz, Alfonso, Editor
  1979   *Handbook of North American Indians 9: Southwest*. Washington: Smithsonian Institution Press.

Palkovich, Ann M.
  1984   Disease and Mortality Patterns in the Burial Rooms of Pueblo Bonito: Preliminary Considerations. In "Recent Research on Chaco Prehistory," edited by W. James Judge and John D. Schelberg. *Reports of the Chaco Center* 8: 103–113. Albuquerque: Division of Cultural Research, National Park Service.

Palmer, Jay W.
  1994   Copper Bells from Anasazi Sites. *Blue Mountain Shadows* 13: 44–45. Monticello, Utah: San Juan County Historical Commission.

Parsons, Elsie Clewes
  1939   *Pueblo Indian Religion*. Chicago: University of Chicago Press.

Peckham, Stewart L.
  1958   Salvage Archaeology in New Mexico 1957–58: A Partial Report. *El Palacio* 65(5): 161–168.

Pepper, George H.
  1920   Pueblo Bonito. *Anthropological Papers of the American Museum of Natural History* 27. New York.
  1976   The Exploration of a Burial Room in Pueblo Bonito, New Mexico. *Putnam Anniversary Volume*, pp. 196–252. New York: G. E. Strechert. First published 1909.

Phillips, David A., Jr., Dennis Gilpin,
and Richard A. Anduze
  1997   Report on Archaeological Testing and Proposal for Data Recovery along Navajo Route 9(5-1), McKinley County, New Mexico. *SWCA Report* 97-50. Flagstaff: SWCA Environmental Consultants.

Pippin, Lonnie C.
  1987   Prehistory and Paleoecology of Guadalupe Ruin, New Mexico. *University of Utah Anthropological Papers* 107. Salt Lake City: University of Utah Press.

Plog, Fred T.
  1974   *The Study of Prehistoric Change*. New York: Academic Press.
  1978   The Keresan Bridge: An Ecological and Archaeological Account. In *Social Archaeology: Beyond Subsistence and Dating*, edited by Charles L. Redman, Mary Jane Berman, Edward V. Curtin, William T. Langhorne, Jr., Nina M. Versaggi, and Jeffery C. Wanser, pp. 349–372. New York: Academic Press.
  1983   Political and Economic Alliances on the Colorado Plateaus, A.D. 400–1450. In *Advances in World Archaeology*, Vol. 2, edited by Fred Wendorf and Angela E. Close, pp. 289–330. New York: Academic Press.

Plog, Stephen
  1989   Ritual, Exchange, and the Development of Regional Systems. In "The Architecture of Social Integration in Prehistoric Pueblos," edited by William D. Lipe and Michelle Hegmon. *Occasional Papers of the Crow Canyon Archaeological Center* 1: 143–154. Cortez, Colorado: Crow Canyon Archaeological Center.
  1990   Agriculture, Sedentism, and Environment in the Evolution of Political Systems. In *The Evolution of Political Systems: Sociopolitics in Small-Scale Sedentary Societies*, edited by Steadman Upham, pp. 177–199. Cambridge: Cambridge University Press.
  1995   Paradigms and Pottery: The Analysis of Production and Exchange in the American Southwest. In *Ceramic Production in the American Southwest*, edited by Barbara J. Mills and Patricia L. Crown, pp. 268–280. Tucson: University of Arizona Press.

Pollard, A. Mark, and Carl Heron
  1996   *Archaeological Chemistry*. Cambridge: The Royal Society of Chemistry Information Services.

Potter, James M.
  1998   Faunal Remains. In "Archaeological Investigations in the Peach Springs Chacoan Community: Data Recovery on Navajo Route 9, Segment 5-1, McKinley County, New Mexico," by Dennis Gilpin. *SWCA Report* 98-15: 291–301. Flagstaff: SWCA Environmental Consultants.

Powell, Shirley
  1983   *Mobility and Adaptation: The Anasazi of Black Mesa, Arizona*. Carbondale: Southern Illinois University Press.
  1988   Anasazi Demographic Patterns and Organizational

Powell, Shirley (*continued*)
    Responses: Assumptions and Interpretive Difficulties. In *The Anasazi in a Changing Environment,* edited by George J. Gumerman, pp. 168–191. Cambridge: Cambridge University Press.

Powers, Robert P.
    1984   Regional Interaction in the San Juan Basin: The Chacoan Outlier System. In "Recent Research on Chaco Prehistory," edited by W. James Judge and John D. Schelberg. *Reports of the Chaco Center* 8: 23–36. Albuquerque: Division of Cultural Research, National Park Service.

Powers, Robert P., William B. Gillespie,
and Stephen H. Lekson
    1983   The Outlier Survey: A Regional View of Settlement in the San Juan Basin. *Reports of the Chaco Center* 3. Albuquerque: Division of Cultural Research, National Park Service.

Proper, Michael J.
    1997   Standing at the Foot of Guadalupe Ruin: Eleanor Site (ENM 883). MS, Anthropology Program, Eastern New Mexico University, Portales.

Prudden, T. Mitchell
    1903   Prehistoric Ruins of the San Juan Watershed of Utah, Arizona, Colorado, and New Mexico. *American Anthropologist* n.s. 5(2): 224–288.

Reed, Lori Stephens
    1998   Basketmaker III to Pueblo III Ceramic Trends in the Southern Chuska Valley. In *Exploring Ceramic Production, Distribution, and Exchange in the Southern Chuska Valley: Analytical Results from the El Paso Natural Gas North System Expansion Project,* edited by L. S. Reed, J. Goff, and K. N. Hensler, pp. 7-1-7-40. Farmington, New Mexico: Western Cultural Resource Management.

Renfrew, Colin
    1999   Production and Consumption in a Sacred Economy: The Material Correlates of High Devotional Expression at Chaco Canyon. Paper presented at the Chaco Organization of Production Conference, organized by Catherine M. Cameron and H. Wolcott Toll, Boulder.

Renfrew, Colin, and John F. Cherry, Editors
    1986   *Peer Polity Interaction and Socio-Political Change.* Cambridge: Cambridge University Press.

Rice, Prudence M.
    1987   *Pottery Analysis: A Sourcebook.* Chicago: University of Chicago Press.

Roberts, Frank H. H., Jr.
    1929   Shabik'eshchee Village: A Late Basket Maker Site in the Chaco Canyon, New Mexico. *Bureau of American Ethnology Bulletin* 92. Washington.
    1932   The Village of the Great Kivas on the Zuni Reservation, New Mexico. *Bureau of American Ethnology Bulletin* 111. Washington.

    1935   A Survey of Southwestern Archeology. *American Anthropologist* 37(1): 1–35.
    1991   *The Ceramic Sequence in the Chaco Canyon, New Mexico, and its Relation to the Cultures of the San Juan Basin.* New York: Garland Publishers. Originally presented as a doctoral dissertation, Harvard University, 1927.

Robertson, Ian G.
    1997   Sharing, Debt and Incipient Inequality in Small Scale Agricultural Economies: A Computer Simulation. Paper presented at the 62nd Annual Meeting of the Society for American Archaeology, Nashville.

Rohn, Arthur H.
    1977   *Cultural Change and Continuity on Chapin Mesa.* Lawrence: Regents Press of Kansas.

Roler, Kathy Lynne
    1999   The Chaco Phenomenon: A Faunal Perspective from the Peripheries. Doctoral dissertation, Arizona State University, Tempe. Ann Arbor: University Microfilms.

Roney, John R.
    1992   Prehistoric Roads and Regional Integration in the Chacoan System. In "Anasazi Regional Organization and the Chaco System," edited by David E. Doyel. *Maxwell Museum of Anthropology Anthropological Papers* 5: 123–132. Albuquerque: University of New Mexico.
    1996   The Pueblo III Period in the Eastern San Juan Basin and Acoma-Laguna Areas. In *The Prehistoric Pueblo World, A.D. 1150–1350,* edited by Michael A. Adler, pp. 145–169. Tucson: University of Arizona Press.

Roscoe, Paul B.
    1993   Practice and Political Centralisation. *Current Anthropology* 34(2): 111–140.

Roys, Lawrence
    1936   Lowry Ruin as an Introduction to the Study of Southwestern Masonry. In "Lowry Ruin in Southwestern Colorado," by Paul S. Martin. *Anthropological Series* 23(1): 115–142. Chicago: Field Museum of Natural History.

Saitta, Dean J.
    1994   Class and Community in the Prehistoric Southwest. In *The Ancient Southwestern Community: Models and Methods for the Study of Prehistoric Social Organization,* edited by Wirt H. Wills and Robert D. Leonard, pp. 25–43. Albuquerque: University of New Mexico Press.
    1997   Power, Labor, and the Dynamics of Change in Chacoan Political Economy. *American Antiquity* 62(1): 7–26.

Schelberg, John D.
    1984   Analogy, Complexity and Regionally-Based Perspectives. In "Recent Research on Chaco Pre-

history," edited by W. James Judge and John E. Schelberg. *Reports of the Chaco Center* 8: 5–21. Albuquerque: Division of Cultural Research, National Park Service.

1992   Hierarchical Organization as a Short-term Buffering Strategy in Chaco Canyon. In "Anasazi Regional Organization and the Chaco System," edited by David E. Doyel. *Maxwell Museum of Anthropology Anthropological Papers* 5: 59–74. Albuquerque: University of New Mexico.

Schepp, Brad, and Stephen M. Hastie
1985   *The Complete Passive Solar Home Book.* Blue Ridge Summit, Pennsylvania: TAB Books.

Schlanger, Sarah H.
1987   Population Measurement, Size, and Change, A.D. 600–1175. In *Dolores Archaeological Program: Supporting Studies: Settlement and Environment,* compiled by K. L. Petersen and J. D. Orcutt, pp. 568–613. Denver: Bureau of Reclamation, Engineering and Research Center.

Schlegel, Alice
1992   African Political Models in the American Southwest: Hopi as an Internal Frontier Society. *American Anthropologist* 94(2): 376–397.

Sebastian, Lynne
1991   Sociopolitical Complexity and the Chaco System. In *Chaco & Hohokam: Prehistoric Regional Systems in the American Southwest*, edited by Patricia L. Crown and W. James Judge, pp. 109–134. Santa Fe: School of American Research.

1992   *The Chaco Anasazi: Sociopolitical Evolution in the Prehistoric Southwest.* Cambridge: Cambridge University Press.

Shelley, Phillip H.
1983   *Lithic Specialization at Salmon Ruin, San Juan County, New Mexico.* Doctoral dissertation, Washington State University, Pullman. Ann Arbor: University Microfilms.

Sigleo, Anne C.
1981   Casamero: A Chacoan Site in the Red Mesa Valley, New Mexico. MS on file, Chaco Center, National Park Service, Albuquerque.

Skinner, Elizabeth, and Dennis Gilpin
1997   Cultural Resources Investigations along Navajo Route 9, U.S. Highway 666 to Standing Rock, McKinley County, New Mexico. *SWCA Report* 96-144. Flagstaff, Arizona: SWCA Environmental Consultants.

Smith, Duane A.
1988   *Mesa Verde National Park: Shadows of the Centuries.* Lawrence: University Press of Kansas.

Smith, Jack E.
1987   *Mesas, Cliffs, and Canyons: The University of Colorado Survey of Mesa Verde National Park,* *1971–1977.* Mesa Verde, Colorado: Mesa Verde Museum Association.

Sofaer, Anna
1997   The Primary Architecture of the Chacoan Culture: A Cosmological Expression. In *Anasazi Architecture and American Design,* edited by Baker H. Morrow and Vincent B. Price, pp. 88–132. Albuquerque: University of New Mexico Press.

South, Stanley A.
1972   Evolution and Horizon as Revealed in Ceramic Analysis in Historical Archaeology. *The Conference on Historic Sites Archaeology Papers* 6(2): 71–116. (Reprinted in *Method and Theory in Historical Archeology*, by Stanley South, pp. 201–235, Academic Press, New York, 1976.)

Stein, John R., and Stephen H. Lekson
1992   Anasazi Ritual Landscapes. In "Anasazi Regional Organization and the Chaco System," edited by David E. Doyel. *Maxwell Museum of Anthropology Anthropological Papers* 5: 87–100. Albuquerque: University of New Mexico.

Steponaitis, Vincas P.
1981   Settlement Hierarchies and Political Complexity in Nonmarket Societies: The Formative Period of the Valley of Mexico. *American Anthropologist* 83(2): 320–363.

Steward, Julian H.
1937   Ecological Aspects of Southwestern Society. *Anthropos* 32: 87–104.

Stone, Glenn D.
1991a   Agricultural Territories in a Dispersed Settlement System. *Current Anthropology* 32(3): 343–353.

1991b   Settlement Ethnoarchaeolgy: Changing Patterns among the Kofyar of Nigeria. *Expedition* 33(1): 16–23.

Strahler, Arthur N.
1952   Hypsometric (Area-Altitude) Analysis of Erosional Topography. *Geological Society of America Bulletin* 63: 1117–1142.

Stubbs, Stanley A.
1950   *Bird's-Eye View of the Pueblos.* Norman: University of Oklahoma Press.

Tainter, Joseph A., and David "A" Gillio
1980   *Cultural Resources Overview: Mt. Taylor Area, New Mexico.* Albuquerque: USDA Forest Service, Southwestern Region and Santa Fe: Bureau of Land Management.

Terrell, James A., and Stephen R. Durand
1979   Architectural Analysis at Guadalupe Ruin, Sandoval County, New Mexico. Final report submitted to the National Endowment for the Humanities, Grant AY-31274-78-466. MS on file, Department of Anthropology, Eastern New Mexico University, Portales.

Thomas, William J., Nathan W. Bower, John W. Kantner, Marianne L. Stoller, and David H. Snow
  1992   X-Ray Fluorescence Pattern Recognition Analysis of Pottery from an Early Historic Hispanic Settlement near Santa Fe, New Mexico. *Historical Archaeology* 26(2): 24–36.
Toll, H. Wolcott
  1984   Trends in Ceramic Import and Distribution in Chaco Canyon. In "Recent Research on Chaco Prehistory," edited by W. James Judge and John D. Schelberg. *Reports of the Chaco Center* 8: 115–135. Albuquerque: Division of Cultural Research, National Park Service.
  1985   *Pottery, Production, Public Architecture, and the Chaco Anasazi System.* Doctoral dissertation, University of Colorado, Boulder. Ann Arbor: University Microfilms.
  1990   A Reassessment of Chaco Cylinder Jars. In "Clues to the Past: Papers in Honor of William M. Sundt," edited by Meliha S. Duran and David T. Kirkpatrick. *Papers of the Archaeological Society of New Mexico* 16: 273–305. Albuquerque: Archaeological Society of New Mexico.
  1991   Material Distributions and Exchange in the Chaco System. In *Chaco & Hohokam: Prehistoric Regional Systems in the American Southwest*, edited by Patricia L. Crown and W. James Judge, pp. 77–107. Santa Fe: School of American Research Press.
Toll, H. Wolcott, and Peter J. McKenna
  1997   Chaco Ceramics. In "Ceramics, Lithics, and Ornaments of Chaco Canyon: Analyses of Artifacts from the Chaco Project 1971–1978," edited by Frances Joan Mathien, pp. 17–530. *Chaco Canyon Studies, Publications in Archeology* 18G: 17–530. Santa Fe: National Park Service.
Toll, H. Wolcott, Dean C. Wilson, and Eric Blinman
  1992   Chaco in the Context of Ceramic Regional Systems. In "Anasazi Regional Organization and the Chaco System," edited by David E. Doyel. *Maxwell Museum of Anthropology Anthropological Papers* 5: 147–157. Albuquerque: University of New Mexico.
Toll, H. Wolcott, Thomas C. Windes, and Peter J. McKenna
  1980   Late Ceramic Patterns in Chaco Canyon: The Pragmatics of Modeling Ceramic Exchange. In "Models and Methods in Regional Exchange," edited by Robert E. Fry. *Society for American Archaeology Papers* 1: 95–117.
Total Environmental Action and Los Alamos National Laboratory
  1984   *Passive Solar Design Handbook.* New York: Van Nostrand Reinhold.
Truell, Marcia L.
  1975   Archaeological Explorations at the Ravine Site, Chimney Rock, Colorado. MS, Master's thesis, Department of Anthropology, University of Colorado, Boulder.
  1986   A Summary of Small Site Architecture in Chaco Canyon, New Mexico. In "Small Site Architecture of Chaco Canyon, New Mexico," by Peter J. McKenna and Marcia L. Truell, pp. 115–508. *Chaco Canyon Studies, Publications in Archeology* 18D. Santa Fe: Division of Cultural Research, National Park Service.
Tucker, Gordon C., Jr.
  1993   Chimney Rock and Chaco Canyon: A Critical Re-examination of the Outlier Concept. In "The Chimney Rock Archaeological Symposium," edited by J. McKim Malville and Gary Matlock, pp. 65–71. *Forest Service General Technical Report* RM–227. Fort Collins, Colorado: Rocky Mountain Forest and Range Experiment Station.
Turner, Christy G., II, and Jacqueline A. Turner
  1999   *Man Corn: Cannibalism and Violence in the Prehistoric American Southwest.* Salt Lake City: University of Utah Press.
Van Dyke, Ruth M.
  1997a Tracking the Trachyte Boundary: A Southern Perspective on Exchange and Interaction among Chacoan Communities. Paper presented at the 62nd Annual Meeting of the Society for American Archaeology, Nashville.
  1997b The Andrews Great House Community: A Ceramic Chronometric Perspective. *Kiva* 63(2): 137–154.
  1998   *The Chaco Connection: Bonito Style Architecture in Outlier Communities.* Doctoral dissertation, University of Arizona, Tucson. Ann Arbor: University Microfilms.
  1999a The Andrews Community: A Chacoan Outlier in the Red Mesa Valley, New Mexico. *Journal of Field Archaeology* 26(1): 55–67.
  1999b The Chaco Connection: Evaluating Bonito Style Architecture in Outlier Communities. *Journal of Anthropological Archaeology* 18(4): 471–506.
  1999c Space Syntax Analysis at the Chacoan Outlier of Guadalupe. *American Antiquity* 64(3): 461–473.
Van West, Carla
  1990   *Modeling Prehistoric Climatic Variability and Agricultural Production in Southwestern Colorado.* Doctoral dissertation, Washington State University. Ann Arbor: University Microfilms.
Vargas, Victoria D.
  1995   Copper Bell Trade Patterns in the Prehispanic U.S. Southwest and Northwest Mexico. *Arizona State Museum Archaeological Series* 187. Tucson: University of Arizona.
Varien, Mark D.
  1997   *New Perspectives on Settlement Patterns: Sed-*

entism and Mobility as a Social Process. Doctoral dissertation, Arizona State University, Tempe. Ann Arbor: University Microfilms.

1999 *Sedentism and Mobility in a Social Landscape: Mesa Verde and Beyond.* Tucson: University of Arizona Press.

Varien, Mark D., and Barbara J. Mills
1997 Accumulations Research: Problems and Prospects for Estimating Site Occupation Span. *Journal of Archaeological Method and Theory* 4(2): 141–191.

Varien, Mark D., William D. Lipe,
Michael A. Adler, Ian M. Thompson,
and Bruce A. Bradley
1996 Southwestern Colorado and Southeastern Utah Settlement Patterns, A.D. 1100 to 1300. In *The Prehistoric Pueblo World, A.D. 1150–1350,* edited by Michael A. Adler, pp. 86–113. Tucson: University of Arizona Press.

Vivian, R. Gordon, and Paul Reiter
1960 The Great Kivas of Chaco Canyon and Their Relationships. *Monographs of the School of American Research* 22. Santa Fe: School of American Research.

Vivian, R. Gwinn
1989 Kluckhohn Reappraised: The Chacoan System as an Egalitarian Enterprise. *Journal of Anthropological Research* 45(1): 101–113.

1990 *The Chacoan Prehistory of the San Juan Basin.* San Diego: Academic Press.

1991 Chacoan Subsistence. In *Chaco & Hohokam: Prehistoric Regional Systems in the American Southwest,* edited by Patricia L. Crown and W. James Judge, pp. 57–75. Santa Fe: School of American Research Press.

1996 "Chaco" as a Regional System. In "Interpreting Southwestern Diversity: Underlying Principles and Overarching Patterns," edited by Paul F. Fish and J. Jefferson Reid. *Arizona State University Anthropological Research Papers* 48: 45–53. Tempe.

1997a Chacoan Roads: Morphology. *Kiva* 63(1): 7–34.
1997b Chacoan Roads: Function. *Kiva* 63(1): 35–67.

Warburton, Miranda, and Donna K. Graves
1992 Navajo Springs, Arizona: Frontier Outlier or Autonomous Great House? *Journal of Field Archaeology* 19(1): 51–69.

Warren, A. Helene
1979 *Lithics Identification and Quarry Source Workshop.* Las Cruces: Cultural Resources Management Division, New Mexico State University.

Washburn, Dorothy Koster
1974 Nearest Neighbor Analysis of Pueblo I–III Settlement Patterns Along the Rio Puerco of the East, New Mexico. *American Antiquity* 39(2, Part 1): 315–335.

Whiteley, Peter M.
1986 Unpacking Hopi "Clans," II: Further Questions about Hopi Descent Groups. *Journal of Anthropological Research* 42(1): 69–79.

Wilcox, David R.
1979 The Hohokam Regional System. In "An Archaeological Test of Sites in the Gila Butte-Santan Region, South-Central Arizona," edited by Glen E. Rice, David R. Wilcox, K. Rafferty, and James Schoenwetter. *Arizona State University Anthropological Research Papers* 18: 77–116. Tempe.

1980 The Current Status of the Hohokam Concept. In "Current Issues in Hohokam Prehistory: Proceedings of a Symposium," edited by David E. Doyel and Fred Plog. *Arizona State University Anthropological Research Papers* 23: 236–242. Tempe.

1993 The Evolution of the Chacoan Polity. In "The Chimney Rock Archaeological Symposium," edited by J. McKim Malville and Gary Matlock, pp. 76–90. *Forest Service General Technical Report* RM-227. Fort Collins, Colorado: Rocky Mountain Forest and Range Experiment Station.

1996 Pueblo III People and Polity in Relational Context. In *The Prehistoric Pueblo World, A.D. 1150–1350,* edited by Michael A. Adler, pp. 241–254. Tucson: University of Arizona Press.

Wills, Wirt H., and Robert D. Leonard
1994 Preface. In *The Ancient Southwestern Community: Models and Methods for the Study of Prehistoric Social Organization,* edited by Wirt H. Wills and Robert D. Leonard, pp. xiii–xvi. Albuquerque: University of New Mexico Press.

Wills, Wirt H., and Thomas C. Windes
1989 Evidence for Population Aggregation and Dispersal during the Basketmaker III Period in Chaco Canyon, New Mexico. *American Antiquity* 54(2): 347–369.

Wilshusen, Richard H.
1988 Sipapus, Ceremonial Vaults, and Foot Drums (Or, A Resounding Argument for Protokivas). In *Dolores Archaeological Program: Supporting Studies: Additive and Reductive Technologies,* compiled by Eric Blinman, Carl T. Phagan, and Richard H. Wilshusen, pp. 649–671. Denver: Bureau of Reclamation.

Wilshusen, Richard H., and Scott G. Ortman
1999 Rethinking the Pueblo I Period in the San Juan Drainage: Aggregation, Migration, and Cultural Diversity. *Kiva* 64(3): 369–399.

Wilshusen, Richard H., Melissa J. Churchill,
and James M. Potter
1997 Prehistoric Reservoirs and Water Basins in the Mesa Verde Region: Intensification of Water Collection Strategies during the Great Pueblo Period. *American Antiquity* 62(4): 664–681.

Wilson, C. Dean, and Eric Blinman
1995   Changing Specialization of White Ware Manufacture in the Northern San Juan Region. In *Ceramic Production in the American Southwest*, edited by Barbara J. Mills and Patricia L. Crown, pp. 63–87. Tucson: University of Arizona Press.

Windes, Thomas C.
1978   Stone Circles of Chaco Canyon, Northwestern New Mexico. *Reports of the Chaco Center* 5. Albuquerque: Division of Cultural Research, National Park Service.
1982   Lessons from the Chacoan Survey: The Pattern of Chacoan Trash Disposal. *New Mexico Archaeological Council Newsletter* 4(5–6): 5–14.
1987   Investigations at the Pueblo Alto Complex, Chaco Canyon, New Mexico, 1975–1979. *Chaco Canyon Studies, Publications in Archeology* 18F. Santa Fe: National Park Service.
1991   The Prehistoric Road Network at Pueblo Alto, Chaco Canyon, New Mexico. In *Ancient Road Networks and Settlement Hierarchies in the New World*, edited by Charles D. Trombold, pp. 111–131. Cambridge: Cambridge University Press.
1992   Blue Notes: The Chacoan Turquoise Industry in the San Juan Basin. In "Anasazi Regional Organization and the Chaco System," edited by David E. Doyel. *Maxwell Museum of Anthropology Anthropological Papers* 5: 159–168. Albuquerque: University of New Mexico.
1993a   The Spadefoot Toad Site: Investigations at 29SJ 629 in Marcia's Rincon and the Fajada Gap Pueblo II Community, Chaco Canyon, New Mexico. *Reports of the Chaco Center* 12(1). Santa Fe: Branch of Cultural Research, National Park Service.
1993b   Appendix F: The East Community. In "The Spadefoot Toad Site: Investigations at 29SJ 629 in Marcia's Rincon and the Fajada Gap Pueblo II Community, Chaco Canyon, New Mexico," by Thomas C. Windes. *Reports of the Chaco Center* 12(1): 459–464. Santa Fe: Branch of Cultural Research, National Park Service.
1993c   The Human Remains at 29SJ 629. In "Investigations at 29SJ 629, Chaco Canyon, New Mexico: Artifactual and Biological Analyses," edited by Thomas C. Windes. *Reports of the Chaco Center* 12(2): 397–401. Santa Fe: Branch of Cultural Research, National Park Service.
1997   This Old House: Construction and Abandonment at Pueblo Bonito. Manuscript submitted for *Pueblo Bonito's Centennial: New Approaches to Big Site Archaeology in Chaco Canyon, NM*, edited by Jill E. Neitzel. Washington: Smithsonian Institution Press, in preparation.

Windes, Thomas C., and Dabney Ford
1992   The Nature of the Early Bonito Phase. In "Anasazi Regional Organization and the Chaco System," edited by David E. Doyel. *Maxwell Museum of Anthropology Anthropological Papers* 5: 75–85. Albuquerque: University of New Mexico.
1996   The Chaco Wood Project: The Chronometric Reappraisal of Pueblo Bonito. *American Antiquity* 61(2): 295–310.

Windes, Thomas C., and Peter J. McKenna
1989   Cibola Whiteware and Cibola Grayware; The Chaco Series. New Mexico Archaeological Council Ceramics Workshop, Red Rock State Park. MS on file, National Park Service Chaco Collections, University of New Mexico, Albuquerque.

Wobst, H. Martin
1974   Boundary Conditions for Paleolithic Social Systems: A Simulation Approach. *American Antiquity* 39(2, Part 1): 147–178.

Wright, Henry T.
1994   Prestate Political Formations. In "Chiefdoms and Early States in the Near East: The Organizational Dynamics of Complexity," edited by G. Stein and M. Rothman. *Monographs in World Archaeology* 18: 67–84. Madison: Prehistory Press.

Index

Abstract

Beginning in the 10th century, Chaco Canyon emerged as an important cultural center whose influence shaped subsequent developments throughout the American Southwest. Archaeologists investigating this cultural tradition have long been impressed by the massive architecture, extensive trading activities, and ancient roadways that extended across the Four Corners area. Attention now focuses on what these remains indicate about the social, political, and ideological organization of the Chacoan people. Communities located some distance from Chaco Canyon are of particular interest, for determining how and why these peripheral areas associated themselves with the central canyon provide insight into the evolution of the Chacoan tradition. These 12 chapters consider how we can define "Chacoan" communities, the relationship of these communities with Chaco Canyon, and their interactions with one another.

The authors emphasize that the concept of community has many possible dimensions along geographic, temporal, and demographic scales and that although the community core, its great house, did tend to persevere through many generations, the small house habitations were rarely occupied for that long. A high degree of residential mobility was a common quality that created a fluid and ever-changing landscape. Similarly, community boundaries were flexible and permeable, especially since most communities during the Chaco era were demographically too small to be reproductively or economically self-sustaining without frequent interaction with neighbors.

The community great houses shared many architectural details with the massive great houses found in Chaco Canyon, leading archaeologists to propose that the occupants of the Canyon were socially, politically, and culturally tied to communities throughout the Four Corners region. The notion of the outlying communities serving in a subservient role to Chaco Canyon great houses, however, obscures the considerable variability that exists in these communities. New research herein indicates that distant groups may have simply appropriated Chacoan symbolism for shaping local social and political relationships. At the same time, it is possible that people living in the less distant communities interacted more regularly with the central canyon and perhaps even lived there on a seasonal basis.

Analyses of artifact distributions and spatial patterning emphasize that, like the communities of which they were members, households during the Chaco era enjoyed a degree of autonomy that was later lost during the post-Chaco era. The early households engaged in independent exchange partnerships and may have had usufruct rights over arable lands, while negotiating their own social and political relationships both within and outside of communities. Great house architecture may have served to attract new members

Resumen

A partir del siglo X, el Cañón de Chaco emergió como un importante centro cultural cuya influencia definió desarrollos subsiguientes a través del suroeste norteamericano. Por largo tiempo, esta tradición cultural, con su masiva arquitectura, extensas actividades de intercambio, y sistema de caminos que cruzaron el área de Four Corners, ha impresionado a los arqueólogos que la investigan. La atención hoy se enfoca en lo que estos restos indican sobre la organización social, política, e ideológica de la población de Chaco. Las comunidades localizadas a cierta distancia del Cañón de Chaco son particularmente interesantes para determinar de qué manera estas áreas periféricas asociadas con el cañón central pueden iluminar la evolución de la tradición Chaco. Estos 12 capítulos consideran los factores que definen a las comunidades "Chaco", la relación de estas comunidades con el Cañón de Chaco, y sus interacciones mutuas.

Los autores enfatizan que el concepto de comunidad tiene muchas posibles dimensiones a lo largo de escalas geográficas, temporales, y demográficas y que, aunque la comunidad núcleo o gran casa, tendió a perseverar por muchas generaciones, las habitaciones pequeñas raramente fueron ocupadas por largo tiempo. Un alto grado de mobilidad residencial fue una cualidad común que creó un paisaje fluido y cambiante. Similarmente, los límites de la comunidad fueron flexibles y permeables, especialmente desde que la población de muchas comunidades durante la era de Chaco fue demasiado pequeña como para sostenerse economicamente y reproducirse sin la frecuente interacción con sus vecinos.

Las comunidades de grandes casas compartieron muchos detalles arquitectónicos con aquéllas construídas en el Cañón de Chaco, lo que ha llevado a arqueólogos a proponer que los ocupantes del cañón mantuvieron lazos sociales, políticos, y culturales con otras comunidades en la región de Four Corners. Sin embargo, la noción de que las comunidades periféricas mantuvieron una posición servil en relación con las grandes casas de Chaco obscurece la considerable variabilidad que existió en estas comunidades. Las nuevas investigaciones presentadas aquí indican que grupos distantes simplemente hubieron apropiado el simbolismo Chaco para dar forma a sus relaciones sociales y políticas locales. Al mismo tiempo, es posible que los habitantes de comunidades menos distantes interactuaron más regularmente con el Cañón central y que tal vez vivieron allí periodicamente.

Los análisis de distribuciones artefactuales y patrones espaciales enfatizan que, así como las comunidades de las que fueron miembros, las unidades domésticas durante la era de Chaco gozaron de un grado de autonomía que más tarde perdieron durante la era pos-Chaco. Las unidades do-

to kin-based factions and to generate labor to assist in agricultural pursuits. As such, the variability in the intensity of interaction with Chaco Canyon and in the appearance of Chacoan features such as great houses was most closely related to local contextual factors. Today, the permanency exhibited by the archaeology of Chaco Canyon, with its imposing architecture and wide roadways, belies the evolving and shifting cultural landscape that characterized the puebloan occupation of the Four Corners region some 900 years ago.

mésticas tempranas se envolvieron en relaciones de intercambio independientes, pudieron haber tenido derechos de usufructo sobre tierras arables y al mismo tiempo nego-ciaron sus propias relaciones sociales y políticas tanto dentro como fuera de las comunidades. La arquitectura de la gran casa pudo haber servido para atraer nuevos miem-bros a las faciones basadas en relaciones de parentesco así como trabajadores que asistieron en actividades agrícolas. Por lo tanto, la variabilidad en la intensidad de la inter-acción con el Cañón de Chaco y en la apariencia de los rasgos Chaco, tales como las grandes casas, se relacionó más cercanamente con factores contextuales locales. Hoy en día, la permanencia exhibida por la arqueología del Cañón de Chaco, con su imponente arquitectura y amplios cami-nos, contradice el cambiante paisaje cultural que caracte-rizó la ocupación Pueblo de la región de Four Corners 900 años atrás.

ANTHROPOLOGICAL PAPERS OF THE UNIVERSITY OF ARIZONA